The Waters Run Deep

by J. Wesley Gunther

When thou passest through the waters, I will be with thee;
And through the rivers, they shall not overflow thee. Isaiah 43:2

Chalfont House
Dumfries, VA

The Waters Run Deep. By J. Wesley Gunther.

Published by: Chalfont House, PO Box 84, Dumfries, VA 22026 USA
Info@ChalfontHouse.com   http://www.ChalfontHouse.com

Scripture quotations marked NLT are taken from the Holy Bible, New Living Translation, copyright 1996. Used by permission of Tyndale House Publishers, Inc., Wheaton, Illinois 60189. All rights reserved.

Scripture marked KJV is from the King James Version, which is in the public domain.

ISBN 0-9720111-7-X
ISBN-13 978-0-9720111-7-4

First Printing 2009
Printed in the United States of America

Dedication

To Beverly Friesen Gunther who
married me in 1948
and has been my
faithful companion and
constant source of encouragement.

J. WESLEY GUNTHER

Table of Contents

Acknowledgments

Several years ago I was rummaging through a file cabinet that had been relegated to a dark corner of a bedroom closet. To my surprise, I discovered page upon page of stories written in broken English on a typewriter. Upon closer examination I realized these were stories my mother had written over a period of time. Several told about my grandparents emigrating from Russia to America in the late eighteen-hundreds. Others described pioneer life on the prairies of the mid-west. The problem with my mother's stories was that she had written and re-written many of them over a period of time, and each version changed with the re-writing.

I got my first computer in 1999, a new toy that was beckoning me to be used. So one day I decided to get out Mother's stories, try to sort them out and put them into some logical sequence. Whether for good or bad, this book is my attempt at retelling my mother's stories.

Without the repeated encouragement of my wife, Beverly, and that of family and friends who learned about what I had set out to do, my manuscript would never have come to the place of being printed in book form. So I want to thank all those who have contributed in making this project a reality.

First and foremost, my deepest thank you to Beverly for putting up with me as I spent hundreds of frustrating hours in front of this computer when I should have been helping with her work as she continues to teach piano to this very day. How I value the time she has taken to read and reread my work, making corrections and suggesting editorial changes.

My thanks to Tessa Willianson for designing a cover that, I believe, beautifully illustrates my story. It was a joy to work with her. How truely grateful I am to Lynellen Perry for doing such a great job on the layout of the book and getting it to the printers.

Next, I want to thank those who have read and made extensive editorial comments. Wayland Jackson got me started in what I consider the right direction as I began writing this story. My son Jeffery, who edits many of the papers published by the Federal Reserve Bank of Dallas, did the first major edit. I have so much appreciated my friends Hans and Frieda Kasdorf and Roland and Eleanor Bergthold who gave necessary editorial pointers and encouragement, and Linda and Dennis Perry (Dennis is my cousin to the second generation) for writing the foreword. Finally, my deepest gratitude to Pauline Kliewer who spent endless hours doing the final edit of the manuscript.

Others who have had a part in typing, reading and making helpful comments are my daughter, Cindy Wiens, a very talented typist who has her own typing business, my grand daughter-in-law, Christa Wiens, and my sister Rubena Ewell. Roland Bergthold provided me with several pictures, as did Dennis and Linda Perry. European maps are courtesy of William Schroeder and Helmut R. Huebert as published in their *Mennonite Historical Atlas*.

Much credit must be given to the California Mennonite Historical Society for producing the Grandma series of genealogical records. My thanks to those who had a part in tracing the ancestry of both the Guenther/Gunther and Jantz/Johnson sides of my family.

Sincerely,
J. Wesley Gunther

J. WESLEY GUNTHER

Foreword

When my husband and I began our genealogical search in the 1960s, Great Aunt Lena Johnson Gunther's huge family tree on a four by six feet piece of paper was a starting point. We loved reading the scrapbook history she wrote, illustrated by items taken from an old Sears catalog and from magazines. These were windows into another era and we were grateful for the thoughtful glimpse. Lena had a collection of wonderful portraits and photos of the family and even the prayer hat and shawl of an ancestress. We thanked God for Lena's gift of connecting us with the history and faith of our fathers.

Uncle John Gunther is remembered for his love of scripture and habit, long into old age, of committing the Word of God to memory. He would recite poems and verses learned in his youth in Plautdietsch and yesterday's verse in English. We were charmed by these dear saints who were known throughout the extended family for their children and for the service of these children for the kingdom of God.

Music, songs of praise, hard work, commitment to Christ and the worth of family are highly valued by our family throughout the generations. Wes Gunther has captured the story and spirit of the family as he shares with us the history of his family.

"Children are a reward from Him," Psalm 127:3b

–Linda Ellen Jones Perry and Dennis Gordon Perry

J. WESLEY GUNTHER

Preface

When I began seriously to consider writing a story about my family, I was primarily thinking of telling about growing up on a farm during the Great Depression of the 1930s and World War II of the 1940s. We were a family of twelve children, who together with our father and mother, faced the grim reality of eeking out an existence on a small acreage.

After I started working on the project, it occurred to me that my story needed an ancestral and historical backdrop. Thus I decided to go back into our family's distant past. In doing so I discovered that their faith in God determined the kind of people they became and in some way shaped the kind of person I became.

My family comes out of a people who were intense in what they believed and passionate in how they lived out their faith. For hundreds of years, each successive generation passed this heritage on to the next one. Our ancestral chart indicates no total break from the faith of our forefathers. Known as Mennonites, they impacted the centuries-old environment from which neither I, nor my siblings, could escape.

The story I am about to tell is true. The names of the people are real people. They lived and died at the times and places mentioned. The events recorded in my story are factual, although they are written in the form of a historical novel. I used a conversational style to surround factual events with created dialogue. For example, in Chapter One, the formation of the Anabaptist movement is historically accurate. The Cornelius Jantz family, an ancestor on my mother's side, actually lived during the period indicated. However, the way he gathered his family to pass on to them the facts about the early Anabaptists, is fictional.

I am aware that in using this form of storytelling I am running the risk of my readers not always being able to differentiate between fact and fiction. I believe that confusing the two is worth the risk. In using this style I have attempted to bring the events in the story into a cohesive, logical, and sequential whole, while preserving what is true.

The book is divided into three parts. I will begin by going back six generations and telling how Cornelius Jantz shared with his children the reason for migrating from western Europe to Prussia (modern-day Poland) and from there to Russia and then to America. In Part II, I shall tell how my parents met and married, and will trace their wanderings from Oklahoma, to Kansas, Michigan and California. In Part III, I will recall my boyhood years, growing up on a farm south of Dinuba, California.

I have also tried to tell the story in the perspective of other historical events so my readers can identify the impact of times and places surrounding the lives of the people I tell about. From my point of view, what was happening in history had a decisive bearing on the choices my ancestors and immediate family made on their journey through life.

My hope is that I have been successful in my endeavor to tell an accurate and interesting story. Keeping in mind that the story is based on facts and that all the persons mentioned were real people who actually lived at the times indicated should help distinguish the true from the imagined.

    Happy reading.
    --J. Wesley Gunther

J. WESLEY GUNTHER

Part I

Incredible Journey

"O Lord. . .I am your guest. . .
A traveler passing through,
As my ancestors were before me."
Psalm 39:12

Chapter 1
Tell Your Children

Young Cornelius Jantz was up before dawn. It was a cold, damp winter morning. He stoked the fire in the kitchen stove, then went out to milk the cow and feed the livestock while his wife put breakfast on the table. Within an hour he was back inside, seated at the table with his family. He read a passage from the Bible and prayed an earnest prayer before eating the very ample meal. It would be another long day clearing additional swamp land along the Vistula River in Prussia – land he needed for his growing family – land the government had grudgingly sold him at too high a price.

As Cornelius worked the land day after day he often thought about what had brought his family to Prussia. This was not his native country. His forefathers had migrated from Holland. Stories of their migration had been handed down from generation to generation. It was now his responsibility to pass these stories on to his children so they would gain a deeper appreciation for their priceless heritage. Cornelius was convinced that his children needed to understand that many within their faith community had become martyrs for what they believed about the Scriptures and the way they lived out their faith. Unless they knew this story they might:

take their heritage for granted,

deny their faith,

think it unnecessary to pass their faith on to future generations.

So after working the land by day he spent many long winter evenings recalling these stories to his wife, Trudcke, and sons, Peter and Cornels, as they sat around the table in the kitchen.

The earliest of these stories, dating back to 1525 A.D., was about a small group of men and women who met to study the Scriptures. For the next few years, they referred to themselves simply as "the brothers and sisters." (For the purposes of our story I will refer to this initial group as *The Brethren* who usually gathered for their meetings in secret places for reasons that will become evident as the story unfolds.)

Cornelius began by explaining that the movable metal printing press was invented by Johannes Gutenberg in 1450, making it possible for the first time in history to print books inexpensively. The first books to be printed were copies of the Bible that had been translated into the German language (the mother tongue of The Brethren). The Brethren had been able to secure a copy of one of these Bibles.

As they read and reread its pages they began to discover that the actual teachings of the Bible were not always in agreement with that of the Roman Catholic Church (hereafter referred to as the Church). In the matter of the sacraments, for instance, the Brethren became convinced that infant baptism and holy communion, as the Church practiced them, could not be supported by the Scriptures.

"What did the Church teach and practice in regard to baptism?" Peter asked.

"The Church taught that baptism was the only means of gaining salvation. It alone could wash away sin. Persons, including infants and children, not baptized by the Church were lost. It became the law of the land in European states and countries under the control of the Church that infants be baptized at the earliest possible moment after birth. As it turned out, the law requiring baptism conveniently became the means by which the entire population of a city or state could be put under the control of the Church."[1]

"And what understanding did The Brethren come to in this matter?" asked Trudcke as she got up to put another piece of wood into the kitchen stove.

"As The Brethren searched the Scriptures, they agreed with Martin Luther and other reformers that salvation is grounded in faith. Luther, you may remember, discovered the verses in the Bible (Romans 3:24 and 28) where Paul declares that we are *justified by faith.*"

"The Brethren agreed with that. They insisted, however, that the Scripture was very clear. Each individual must make a personal confession of faith in Jesus Christ as Savior, a confession only adults could make. Only after that did baptism mean anything at all. This new understanding of the Scriptures was not just adding another interpretation to the practice of baptism. It had nothing to do with mode or method. To them it was a whole new concept of what it meant to be baptized. They called it 'believer's baptism.' It became the watchword of The Brethren. They were so convinced of this truth that they totally rejected the Church's sacrament of baptism and refused to acknowledge that it had any scriptural validity at all."

A few evenings later Cornelius, tired as he was from a long day's work, continued the story of The Brethren. "There were other teachings of the Catholic Church, as well as Protestant churches such as Lutheran and Reformed, that The Brethren could not accept. Contrary to the teachings of the Church, The Brethren maintained that the Bible was their absolute and sole authority in matters of faith and daily living. And so, in continuing to search the Scriptures, they came to the conclusion that newness of life in Jesus Christ, discipleship as a way of life, suffering for Christ, holiness and separation from the sinful practices of the world, and the practice of love and nonresistance were truths they needed to live by on a daily basis."

"In the meantime, the Church kept an eye on The Brethren and warned them that their new teachings were heresy. The Brethren, however, became more and more convinced that the truths they had discovered had been directed by the Holy Spirit. Therefore, they needed to make them the foundation of their faith and to live out what they believed."

By this time, young Peter had really become interested in the stories his father was telling and wanted to know more. So he asked, "What were some of the things they felt they needed to act on?"

"The Brethren believed that the matter of baptism was such a basic issue that they first of all needed to take the step of baptizing those who had come to faith in Christ as adults. Their baptism as infants by the Church was, to them, a meaningless ritual. So in Zollikona, near Zurich, Switzerland, on a fateful day in January, 1525, Conrad Grebel performed the first adult baptism of The Brethren when he baptized George Blaurock in the home of Felix Manz. Several others joined them in their strong belief and were baptized."

"Those who were baptized that day as well as many who, in years to come, followed in their steps, became known as *Anabaptists* (meaning to be re-baptized). It was a name that did not really fit since they held that infant baptism was no baptism at all. Adult believer's baptism, they contended, was the only baptism taught in the Scriptures. As the movement grew, the Anabaptist label ultimately replaced the name of The Brethren. (The Brethren were now referred to as Anabaptists until the name changed again several years later.)

"So why did the Church become alarmed by what the Anabaptists came to believe? What harm were they doing?" Cornels asked.

"Salvation by means of the sacraments of baptism and holy communion were the foundation stones upon which the whole structure of the Church rested," Cornelius said. "The Anabaptists, taking the position they did, were in direct conflict with what the Church had taught and practiced for centuries."

"In spite of warnings as to the dire consequences of continuing to hold to these new teachings, the leaders of the Anabaptist movement went from village to village and city to city, teaching and preaching the good news of salvation by faith and the baptism of adults upon the confession of their faith. Their preaching found an immediate response in the hearts of both peasants and the educated. It spread like wild fire! Dozens, then hundreds and even thousands came to faith in Jesus Christ and were baptized."

On yet another evening Cornelius called his family together to continue his story. The rapid spread of the teachings of the Anabaptists was exactly what the Church feared would happen. The Church insisted that the Anabaptist teachings were synonymous with treason. Its response was immediate and severe. A battle cry was sounded. Edicts were passed making the act of baptism, as believed and practiced by the Anabaptists, a crime punishable by pain of the highest penalty of death. Believers were apprehended and placed in prisons and dungeons. They were again warned to stop spreading their teachings.

The Church's warnings went unheeded. The dynamic message of what was now referred to as the Free Church (a Church not under the control of the State) found lodging in the hearts of people prepared by the Spirit of God. The Church realized that if it was going to stem the tide of this new movement it would have to be more vigorous in seeking out those who were being re-baptized. They began vigorously to pursue the Anabaptists with an unrelenting zeal. "Death to the heretics," they cried. Thousands of Anabaptists became martyrs for their faith.

Felix Manz, the man in whose house the first Anabaptist believers were baptized, became the first leader of the movement to be put to death for what he believed and preached. He was drowned in the Limmat River in Switzerland.

Cornelius had borrowed a copy of the story, as told by a witness to the drowning of Felix Manz. He read,

> *They led him from the city hall to the fish market on the river. But on the way he sang. He actually sang the Te Deum (an ancient Christian hymn, We Praise Thee, O God) on the way to his death! By the bank of the river in those last moments while they tied his hands, he saw his mother and brother and, perhaps for their sake, asserted again his joy in Christ. His mother, with tears running down her face, called out as a parting word, 'Felix, my son just don't deny your Jesus.' Having bound his hands, they pulled his knees up between his arms and put a stick through under his knees. He couldn't even struggle. Then they took him into the river in a boat, and held him under the water until he was dead.*
>
> *–Pilgrim Aflame*, M. Augsburger

This kind of persecution continued for more than a hundred years. However, instead of putting a damper on the preaching and evangelistic zeal of the early Anabaptists, the persecution inspired in them a burning passion to spread the good news of their new-found faith farther and farther afield – always aware that they were being hunted down by those who would hurt them. They secretly spread the word that meetings were being held at night, deep in the forested areas. During these meetings they shared with seekers the Gospel of salvation by faith. Prayer, Bible study, words of encouragement, and singing became regular parts of these meetings. Their singing became especially helpful in encouraging one another in the faith and in witnessing to their neighbors. Some of these songs had from ten to twenty verses, telling the stories of the faith lessons they had learned. So they sang!" Cornelius said as he began to sing a hymn which dated as far back as 1530:

As God His Son was sending
Into this world of sin,
His Son is now commanding
That we this world should win.
He sends us and commissions
To preach the Gospel clear,
To call upon all nations
To listen and to hear.

To thee, O God, we're praying,
We're bent to do Thy will;
Thy Word we are obeying,
Thy glory we fulfill,
All peoples we are telling
To mend their sinful way,
That they might cease rebelling,
Lest judgment be their pay.

And if Thou, Lord, desire,
And should it be Thy will
That we taste sword and fire
By those who thus would kill;
Then comfort, pray, our loved ones,
And tell them, we've endured.
And we shall see them yonder–
Eternally secured.

Thy Word, O Lord, does teach us,
And we do understand;
Thy promises are with us
Until the very end.
Thou hast prepared a haven–
Praised be Thy holy name.
We laud Thee, God of heaven,
Through Christ, our Lord. Amen

As persecution became more and more intense, the Anabaptists had no choice but to flee their native lands – Switzerland, southern Germany, Austria and Moravia. They sought refuge in other parts of Europe, including Holland. "It was this persecution that caused our forefathers to migrate from Holland to where we now live, here in Prussia," Cornelius concluded.

Even though the family had spent a number of evenings rehearsing the stories of the early Anabaptists, Cornelius realized there were more stories to tell. And, although he often felt too tired to continue these long evenings, Cornelius insisted that his family must know why the Jantz family was now living in Prussia. So some weeks later, he gathered his family around the kitchen table to continue the story.

The government of Prussia promised people of Germanic and Dutch origin free land plus full religious freedom and other rights if they could drain the swamps in the Vistula River delta and turn them into farm land. The Dutch farmers who came to the delta were experienced in transforming marshes and bogs into rich arable land.

"So here we are today, descendants of one of the early Jantz families, clearing additional swamp land so you boys, Peter and Cornels, will have enough land to farm and make a living when you get married and have your own families," Peter said.

There were other stories Cornelius recounted during the long winter nights. One of these was about a Catholic priest, Menno Simons, who had been ordained into the priesthood of the Dutch Church in 1524. After eleven years of intense study of the Scriptures, he began having misgivings about some of the practices of the Church. This led to a great inner struggle. His search for biblical truth ultimately led him into the circle of the Anabaptists. After several more years of searching, he reluctantly renounced his priesthood in the Catholic church, confessed Jesus Christ as Savior, threw his lot in with the Anabaptists and was baptized. Soon thereafter he had to flee from his persecutors in Holland and find asylum in Prussia. It was his preaching and writing that ultimately defined many of the Anabaptist beliefs and practices. Through his strong leadership, his followers chose to become known as Menists and eventually, *Mennonites*.

Cornelius concluded, "Our family followed the teachings of Menno Simons and is the reason we are known as Mennonites today."

Menno Simons.
Courtesy: Schroeder and Huebert

Chapter 2
Vohlynia

In their diligent search of the New Testament, especially the Sermon on the Mount as found in Matthew chapters five through seven of the Bible, the Jantz family adopted many of the distinctive teachings of the early Anabaptists. These teachings had transformed the lifestyle of the followers of Menno Simons, now known as Mennonites. The Bible, the hymn book, and the fellowship of believers had become the focus of their family life. As one generation of Mennonites after another migrated to Prussia they became immersed in the daily life of the people of the land. Some remained farmers. Others pursued occupations such as craftsmen and bankers. They adhered tenaciously to the Low German language which they had brought with them from northern Holland. It was a part of what distinguished them from many of their neighbors and held them together as families, and as a community of Mennonites who shared

their sorrows and their joys,

their hardships and their blessings,

their poverty and their wealth.

As the years passed, the Prussian Mennonites began to realize that those freedoms that had enticed them to Prussia were beginning to erode. They were not being threatened with the kind of persecution that often led to death in other parts of Europe. However, various religious restrictions and prohibitions were imposed upon them. They were required to pay taxes to support the State Church. They could be exempt from military service, but only by paying a heavy annual tax. They were ordered to pay taxes from which they had previously been exempt because they had been classified as German colonists and Mennonites. It was also increasingly difficult to obtain land needed for their expanding families.

One night, near the end of the eighteenth century, Peter Jantz, the oldest son of Cornelius, gathered his own family around the kitchen table. "We have come to a crossroad in our journey," he said. He described the issues that he and all his Mennonite neighbors faced. "We can stay where we are or we can seek freedom in another country. If we stay, we may be able to keep our farm and home. We will also have our church and our relatives to surround and support us. As long as we pay our taxes and obey the orders of the government, we might be able to live in peace for years to come. But in doing so, we may have to give up many of those freedoms for which we and our forefathers have paid such a high price. If we refuse to go to war when called on by the Government, or disobey any other orders which we feel are contrary to our faith, the pain of persecution may well be our lot."

"On the other hand, if we can find another country that promises freedom to live out our faith, and decide to migrate, we will have to start all over again. Our lot will be to deal with the hardships of pioneer life as peasants. It will not be an easy life. But perhaps we will be able to keep those freedoms which we hold as a sacred trust."

> Note: The first Peter Jantz to appear on our genealogy charts was born in 1650. Four generations later, his great, great grandson (also named Peter) immigrated with his family to Vohlynia.

Many of the Mennonites who lived in Prussia at the time decided to stay in the land. Others decided that the price of freedom was worth the challenge of a new beginning. The Peter Jantz family was one of them.

One day news filtered from the plains of southeast Prussia that a certain official, Polish Count Potocki, was offering free land to ethnically Dutch Mennonites living in the Vistula Delta of Prussia. The land being offered to them was in the territory of Volhynia, near the city of Ostrog, in west-central Russia. In exchange for taming the rough, barren prairie plains of Volhynia they would be guaranteed complete religious freedom.

In 1791 the Peter Jantz family, together with 37 other Mennonite families, accepted the Count's offer and emigrated from Prussia to Dorf (German for village) Grünthal, in the colony of Karolswalde, Ostrog, about 200 miles west of the Russian city of Kiev. It was a trek of some 500 miles, traveling by oxen and carts, taking minimal earthly belongings with them.

In coming to this new land, these immigrant families gained their religious independence as promised by Polish Count Potocki. Ironically, however, the area came under Russian control two years after they had settled in the land. The sudden change in governmental control was a traumatic disappointment for them. The Russian government almost immediately began to heavily tax the Mennonite landowners. The new taxes caused concern about how the new government might affect the religious freedoms they had been promised. It seemed like the ground had been cut underneath them and their hopes for a lasting period of freedom had been dashed.

Map of Western Soviet Union, *Courtesy of Schroeder and Huebert*

Also, as time passed, it became questionable as to whether the Mennonites in the Volhynia colonies would be able to survive economically. Some became blacksmiths, carpenters, wagon makers, cabinet makers, weavers, millers and stone masons. Most remained farmers. Their farms were small, the soil poor. Whether tradesmen or farmers, their plight steadily deteriorated economically. Living conditions were primitive. The winters were

Helena Thomas Jantz

harsh. Many farmers had to supplement their income with work as day-laborers simply to survive. Pioneer life was not for the weak or indolent. It required determination, fortitude and resolve. Only time would tell whether they would endure.

In the meantime, the Peter Jantz clan continued to increase in numbers. One day Heinrich Jantz, a grandson of Peter, began to notice a neighbor girl by the name of Helena Thomas. They were married in 1862. The importance of this marriage will, hopefully, become clear as I proceed with my story. (See Appendix A, at the end of Part I.)

Heinrich Jantz had the habit of keeping a journal, written in Gothic German script, in which he recorded significant events in his life. He wrote descriptively about his marriage:

> In the year of Christ, 1862, on the seventh day of November, have I, Heinrich Jantzt [note change in spelling of the name], taken vows of marriage with a virtuous young woman, Helena Thomas. The wedding took place at my dear brother-in-law and neighbor's house. ...here in Karolswalde. ... I was 23 years, two months and fifteen days old and she was eighteen years, five months and five days old. The sign of the almanac or moon was the waterman (Aquarius) and she was in the sign of the zodiac, Gemini, the twin.

It is recorded that Helena was tall and slender and had black hair, a beautiful young lady. Besides that, she was a hard worker and a neat housekeeper. Heinrich and Helena soon had a son whom they named Jacob Jantz. Heinrich recorded Jacob's birth in his journal:

> In the year of 1865, on the eleventh of February, on Saturday at three o'clock in the morning, was born a son with the name of Jacob. The sign of the planet Uranus was Pisces the fish. He was born in Petagin Grüntha [in Karolswalde].

One other note from Heinrich Jantz's journal is especially significant. He wrote:

> In the year of Christ, 1857, on the 5th of April, I was baptized on Palm Sunday, when Elder Tobias Unruh was leader in the house of worship and prayer at Karolswalde. I was old enough, as I was 17 years, 7 months and 12 days.

The Koehn family also lived in the colony of Karolswalde. Jacob Koehn was just five years old at the time the group of Mennonites made the trek from Prussia. Young Jacob learned quickly that hard work was the key to existing on the hostile, untamed steppe of western Russia. The years passed slowly for Jacob. He spent long hours, day after day, help-ing with chores, gathering fire wood, and meeting many other demands of everyday life. The Heinrich Jantz family, grandson of Peter Jantz, and the Jacob Koehn family now take the spotlight in our drama as it unfolds.

> Note: Another family that be-comes important to my story is the Jacob Koehn family. Jacob Koehn eventually married Eliza-beth Wedel. Their second child was Peter Koehn who, one day, married Eva Ratzlaff. Their fifth child was Karolina Koehn. On May 23, 1886, Jacob Jantz, son of Heinrich and Helena Thomas Jantz married Karolina Koehn, the daughter of Peter and Eva Ratzlaff Koehn. Continue read-ing to get the rest of the story.

For seventy-two years the Volhynia Mennonites tried to improve their lot from a subsistence level to something better. Conditions, however, only be-came worse. Church life among them also became stagnant and tradition-bound. They were profound-ly influenced by a humanist and spiritualist culture in ways that were detrimental to them. Perhaps this explains why Heinrich Jantz used the signs of the Zodiac, as noted above, in recording his birth, and those of his children. Historian C. Henry Smith in his *Story of the Mennonites* writes, "They were influ-enced more than any other Mennonite group by their unwholesome environment."

Perhaps it was time for the Volhynia Mennonites to consider emigrating to the new world. But would they succeed there? Would they succumb to the defeat they had experi-enced in their past, or would they rise up to become self-sufficient and prosperous? Would they continue to live in ignorance and poverty, or would they find a better life through more favorable living conditions, hard work and education? Would they remain in a state of spiri-tual lethargy or would they find renewal through the help of churches in the new world? Would future generations seek occupations other than farming, and become doctors, law-yers, professors, pastors, missionaries or business people? Only time would tell.

The time came when the Mennonites who lived in Karolswalde finally admitted that Volhynia had nearly destroyed them. It was time to move on. So in 1874, the whole village of Karolswalde immigrated to America.

To sail across the Atlantic as emigrants in those days posed a threatening hardship. Beside the possibility of shipwreck because of stormy weather, these trips were aggravated by overcrowding, poor food and deplorable sanitation. Many, especially children, would die on the way. The people of the Karolswalde colony had already been warned about the conditions they might encounter, including the story of an English ship whose passengers became so hungry they began scouring the ship for ver-min. The value of a rat was eighteen pence; a mouse sold for six pence. It would be an incredible journey. They fully understood that after they departed their Russian homes there was no turning back.

> (Note: Heinrich was the grandson of the Peter Jantz that migrated from Prus-sia to Volhynia. In coming to America, Heinrich Jantz changed his name to Hein-rich Janzen. I will use Jan-zen in referring to the fam-ily until another change is made later in the story. See Appendix A.)

It is now important for my readers to understand that among those who joined the ranks of the emigrants from Karolswalde to America were Heinrich Janzen and his family and the Peter Koehn family. Both families now become principle characters in my story. They found their way to America on different ships. The Janzen family came across Europe to England where they boarded the ship *S.S. City of London*, departing from Liverpool. It was a steamship, but could also be powered by three masts of sail. It ultimately docked in the New York harbor.

The Koehn family came on a Belgian ship, the *S.S. Vaderland*, which departed from Antwerp, Belgium, in late November, 1874. It was a three-masted, one-smokestack steamship, about the same size as the *City of London*, and on this trip carried 710 passengers, 682 of which were Mennonites. Rather than docking in New York, it steamed up the Delaware River to Philadelphia, where it docked in the dead of winter, December 25, 1874. Although both of the above ships set sail at approximately the same time, the *S.S. Vaderland* reached

Engraving of the S.S. City of London

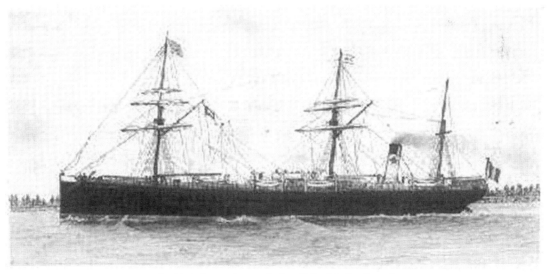

Artist drawing of the S.S. Vaderland

Details about the S.S. Vaderland (or Vaterland) are from an Unruh Family History online at
http://freepages.genealogy.rootsweb.ancestry.com/~troy/unruh/unruh_family_history.html
The drawing of the S.S. Vaderland is courtesy of Van Moorleghem Ludo at
http://users.telenet.be/ludo.van.moorleghem/dbboten3.htm
The engraving of the S.S. City of London appeared in The Graphic in 1872, and is courtesy of
http://www.norwayheritage.com

America after the *City of London* had docked in New York because the *Vaderland* was badly damaged on its voyage due to violent storms. The seas were heavy and the ship had an unusually rough journey. Barrels of cargo broke loose and rolled back and forth in the steerage area. The ship lost all three of its propeller blades coming across to America. The first one was lost in the English Channel and the second was lost halfway across the ocean. Still, the ship kept limping onward to its destination, until nearing the United States harbor, the last propeller blade was lost.

Would the Janzens and the Koehns, two families who had lived in the same village in Volhynia for so many years, ever find each other in the vast new world? The possibilities were remote, but not impossible.

Chapter 3
South Russia

About the time the Peter Jantz family migrated to Volhynia, two other Mennonite families were considering pulling up stakes in Prussia: the Guenthers and the Goertzens.

It appears to have been by divine providence that in 1763, Catherine II, Empress of Russia, issued a manifesto inviting German Mennonites, together with other Germanic people, to leave Prussia and settle in the vast uninhabited areas of the Ukraine in South Russia. They were guaranteed the freedom to govern their own communities and educate their children in their own schools. Each family was promised 165 acres of free land. Above all, they were promised that their young men would be permanently exempt from military service – an issue that was at the core of their faith.

Since our forefathers had put down such deep roots in the Prussian soil, they accepted the invitation of the Empress rather reluctantly. It was not until about the time the Peter Jantz family emigrated to Volhynia in 1791 (twenty-five years after the invitation had been given by Empress Catherine II) that 228 Mennonite families moved to South Russia. Thus began a mass migration of Mennonites to this new land.

The Chortitza (1780s and 1790s) and Molotschna (1804) colonies were the first settlements to be established in the former Ukrainian provinces in South Russia. In spite of the glowing promises that the Russian government would provide free transportation from the Russian border to the place of settlement, plus free land, and loans for building houses, the immigrants soon realized that life on the untamed prairie was less than what they thought had been promised. Living conditions were primitive, land and housing were hard to come by, and the winters were extremely cold. Initially, there were no schools or medical services. But once the immigrants arrived in this inhospitable wilderness, there was no turning back.

Among those who made the pilgrimage from Prussia to South Russia were the Guenthers and the Goertzens. Both families ultimately settled in the village of Ladekopp, in the Molotschna colony of the Taurida province. On January 11, 1811, Peter Goertzen married Sara Brandt. The Goertzen family was blessed with eight children, all girls.

In the meantime, the Guenther family (given name unknown) had at least one son whom they named Johann. Records indicate that, tragically, Johann's mother and father died while he was still a boy. Now an orphan, he was sent to live with the Goertzen family. From young Johann's perspective, this was the worst thing that could have happened to him. Being the only boy among the eight Goertzen girls was like being thrown into an all-girl Sunday School class and having every one of them stare at him as if he were a circus curiosity. However, as time went by and he became a young man, he decided that maybe it was not so bad being surrounded by these girls who had now become young ladies. As a matter of fact, he rather liked Helena. Even though she was four years older than he, she was the prettiest. He found himself paying more and more attention to her and in 1841 he married her. (See Appendix B, at the end of Part I.)

Little Maria was born just a year after Johann and Helena were married. They had anticipated the birth of their first child with high hopes and expectations. But their joy quickly turned to grief when Maria died the next day. "How could God give us such a beautiful child, then immediately take her away?" they asked. They thought they would never re-cover from the heartbreaking sadness of their loss.

The loss of many of their children continued from the years of 1842 to 1866. All but three died in infancy or were still-born. One after the other had to be laid to rest in the bar-rens of the prairies of South Russia. Living conditions were so primitive, the climate so se-vere and medical help so limited, the pain of losing family members through death was not uncommon among the early immigrants now living in Russia. But it seemed that the Johann Guenther family suffered more than its share of such grief.

First, Johann lost his parents at an early age. Now, he and his wife, Helena, had to deal with losses that were unbearable – finally leaving an indelible spiritual and emotional mark on them. They could not understand or accept God's ways with them. They had no answers to their misfortune, only anguish and bitterness of spirit. It seemed they had no-where to turn for help, not even the Mennonite church they attended.

During the first half of the nineteenth century, the Mennonite church in South Russia experienced a decline in spiritual vitality. Most of the early settlers were poor and un-educated, including most church leaders. Ministers read their sermons monotonously. Con-gregations were not challenged to lead moral and ethical lives. Without strong leadership, the church lost its ability to reach out to those in need, the Guenthers among them.

Beginning in 1845, however, a spiritual awakening spread across the villages of South Russia, especially in the Molotschna colony where the Guenthers lived. While there were other factors contributing to the awakening, perhaps the strongest was the coming of Ed-ward Wüst from Germany to be the pastor of a Lutheran Pietist congregation in a neigh-boring settlement. His preaching and teaching had a strong influence on several groups of Mennonites who began to meet for prayer and Bible study. These groups called themselves *Brethren* and ultimately gave birth to the *Mennonite Brethren* church in 1860. It should be noted that most churches in the various colonies were known simply as Mennonite churches. The newly formed Mennonite Brethren church stressed (as had their Anabaptist forebears) repentance from sin, conversion as a personal experience of faith in Christ, a life of prayer, and conduct consistent with the teachings of the Bible. The teachings of Menno Simons were once again taken seriously. Upon confession of faith in Jesus Christ, the immersion form of baptism became a prerequisite for church membership. The Mennonite Brethren church was spiritually alive and prepared to minister to individuals and families who were seeking a renewal of their own spiritual lives.

For instance, one Sunday morning, while attending the worship service of the church, the story of Job chapter one, was read from the Old Testament. While still seeking healing for the deep wounds left by of the loss of so many of their children, Johann and Helena listened intently as they compared the story of Job to their own experience. With God's permission, Satan was allowed to destroy Job's oxen, donkeys, sheep and camels. His farmhands, shep-herds and servants were killed. Last of all, while his sons and daughters were feasting in the home of his oldest son, a tornado hit the house and left all Job's children dead. The Bible records Job's response:

[He] Stood up and tore his robe in grief. Then he shaved his head and fell to the ground before God. He said, 'I came naked from my mother's womb, and I will be stripped of everything when

I die. The Lord gave me everything I had, and the Lord has taken it away. Praise the name of the Lord!,' (Job 1:21, 22, NLT).

Johann and Helena concluded that the point of Job's story was that in spite of all Job lost he could still praise the name of the Lord. The reading of the story of Job was like the *Balm of Gilead* to Johann and Helena. They soon discovered that they also could find release from their hurts by turning them over to God. Like Job, they also could praise God as they walked with Him in a fellowship of love.

Johann Guenther, 1826-1900

Helena Guenther, 1822-?

It was these life-changing encounters with God that enabled Johann and Helena to come to the place where they were finally ready to be baptized by immersion, according to Mennonite Brethren faith and practice and commit themselves to the renewal movement of the church. They slowly became deeply involved in the life of the church. As they did, they found that in the womb of the Church they could better deal with those things that had taken so much from them – their family losses as well as the hardships of pioneer life. The renewal of the spiritual life of the church was the key to finding healing and release from their hurts of the past.

Here they cried out to God in prayer.

Here they sang those songs that expressed the deep feelings of their souls.

Here they read from the Scriptures such passages as the story of Job.

While living in Ladekopp, God had given Johann and Helena thirteen children. Sadly, only three lived to adulthood – one son and two daughters (See Appendix B). Having experienced so much grief while in the Ladekopp village, they finally considered it expedient that they seek to leave the sorrows of their past behind and relocate to a new village. After much prayer and deliberation they decided to make their new home in the Prangenau village on the Molotschna colony's southern border. Perhaps one reason for choosing Prangenau was that it was closer to the heart of the church's renewal movement.

It was in Prangenau that their three surviving children were raised and ultimately found their life's helpmates. In 1872 their only son Peter married Margaretha Peters. Twelve years later he, together with his family, made a move that would lead Johann and Helena through some of the deepest waters they had ever been plunged into, waters they would be able to survive only with God's help. They would never see their only son, his wife, and their grandchildren again. The Johann Guenthers continued to live in the Molotschna colony in South Russia until they were finally laid to rest in their village. Johann was 74 years old when the Lord called him home. The date of Helena's death is unknown.

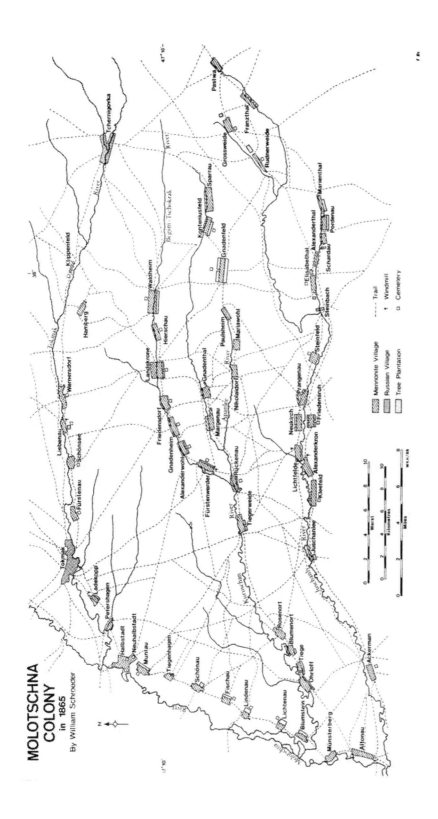

Map of the Molotschna Colony, *Courtesy of Schroeder and Huebert,*
available online (as of October 2009) at

http://www.mennonitechurch.ca/programs/archives/holdings/Schroeder_maps/058.pdf

Chapter 4
A Marriage Made In Heaven

Peter was one of the three children of Johann and Helena Guenther who grew to adulthood. He was born September 5, 1847 in Ladekopp, South Russia. Soon after his birth the Guenther family moved to the village of Prangenau, also in the Molotschna Colony. While living in this village Peter met young Margaretha Peters, the twelfth child of Johann Aron and Margaretha Peters' seventeen children.

Peter began courting Margaretha while in his early twenties. The record indicates that they did not become members of the Mennonite Brethren church until Peter and Margaretha were baptized on July 11, 1882, ten years after they had been married. Although they probably did not become deeply involved in the life of the church before they were married, the church was such a central part of village life that it dictated the mores and conventions of these close knit colonies. Peter and Margaretha were, no doubt, bound by the traditions of their village, including those related to courtship and marriage. It was believed that marriages were made in heaven. Once the solemn vows were spoken, there was little possibility of backing out. So Peter approached his courtship of Margaretha slowly and cautiously. Being a shy man, he had to devise ways of letting her know of his interest in her.

Some of the Mennonite churches of that day had a custom called *bundling*. Courtship, according to this custom, was a time for a couple to learn to know each other. Would the spouse be a good worker, parent and partner? Qualities of character were weighed carefully. Were family characteristics complementary? And, above all, did the couple agree on matters of faith? According to the bundling custom, no physical contact between the two persons was permissible during the courting period. Ideally, the couple might take a ride in the moonlight with horse and sleigh in the middle of winter, but the blankets used to keep warm were separate blankets. The couple was expected to learn the disciplines of spiritual, social, and reflective intimacy and love, rather than depend upon mere physical attraction. In the long run, successful marriage depended upon character, competence, and the ability to work together and raise a family in unity and with grace. (*Patterns of Amish Courtship*, By Gertrude Lindener-Stawski).

I do not know if Peter and Margaretha were bound by the strict customs described above. But apparently the rules they were expected to conform to were very similar. Neither of them could come to the marriage altar as a divorced person. Everyone knew that since it was a sign of worldliness, the wearing of wedding bands, or any other kind of jewelry, was strictly prohibited. Margaretha and Peter were very familiar with the church's long list of rules and were prepared to follow them. The fact that they had little money or other earthly possessions was not a concern to them. Nothing could spoil the joy they anticipated in their life together. On a cold day in February, 1872, Peter, age 24, took Margaretha Peters, age 22, daughter of Johann and Margaretha Peters, as his bride.

Note: I assume it was a cold day because they were married in the village of Prangenau on the prairies of South Russia. International Falls, Minnesota, often the coldest spot in the United States, is on almost identically the same parallel of latitude as Prangenau. So when it is 40 degrees below zero in February in International Falls, with a chill factor of 60 below, it could have been about the same in the village of Prangenau on the day Peter and Margaretha were married.

The wedding ceremony was considered one of the most sacred rites of the church. Whether they were members or not, weddings could not be held in places other than in the meeting house. So the ceremony was performed on a Sunday morning as part of the worship service. Peter came from where he was seated on the men's side to the front of the meeting house and Margaretha came from her place on the women's side. (It was a custom of theological significance that men and women never sat together in the meeting house. Most places of worship even had two entrances. The men came in through one door, the women through the other.) The couple stood facing the congregation, and before pronouncing them husband and wife, the pastor admonished them in a sermon that lasted an hour or more, to be faithful to each other until death. Two other couples were married that same morning. The wedding was followed with a sumptuous feast of a great variety of foods such as the traditional Zwieback, ham, sausage, and a kind of a plum pudding all brought together by the family and members of the church. Many of these foods were adapted from recipes borrowed from Russian housewives.

As time passed, the Russian government adopted new policies regarding the Mennonites who occupied the land. They could no longer govern their own communities. Their schools were taken over by the Russian government. Their children were required to learn the Russian language and customs. Above all, their young men were no longer exempt from military service. The Mennonite colonists were once again stripped of those precious freedoms they held to so tenaciously – those freedoms that had brought them to this land in the first place. They could foresee the day that persecution would be their fate if they persisted in practicing their faith according to their deeply held convictions based on biblical truths as they understood them.

So in the year 1884, numerous Mennonite families immigrated to America. Among them were Peter and Margaretha Guenther. This was the day Papa and Mama Johann Guenther had feared would come and had dreaded even to think about. For them, it was the saddest day they could imagine – like the loss of another child. Their only son was migrating to a new land while they were left behind. They knew they would never see him and his family again.

Peter and Margaretha set out on their long journey over land and sea with five children. Their eldest child, Margaret, was ten years old, their youngest, Anne, was a newborn baby. They traveled by train to Bremen, Germany, and from there to New York aboard the *S.S. Werra*, a miserable trip on the high seas of the Atlantic.

The Guenthers took whatever they could, not only for the long journey, but for making a fresh start on the raw prairies of America. The amount of goods they could take was limited by what the shipping line permitted. Blankets, heavy clothing, cooking utensils, and a myriad of household items they would need were packed in large wooden crates they had built for the purpose.

Peter Guenther had not been able to sleep well one night aboard ship. He was too deep in thought about the significance of the journey upon which he and Margaretha had embarked. They had left the old, familiar world in which they had grown up and to which they would very likely never return. A new world came to view in his mind. He had heard much about America with its freedoms and opportunities. But he wondered: was what he

```
S.S. WERRA, Br
New York Arr.

GÜNTHER, Peter
    Margth (33)
    Anna (13) r
    Cornelius (
    Margth (7)
    Peter (6) r
    Agneca (4)
    Daniel (3)
    Johann (11m
    Anna (11m)
EPP, Claus (52)
    (Not readab
FUNK, Johann (3
    Maria (33)
    Maria (7) n
    Helene (6)

    (Not readabl
    Anna (3m) no
```

S.S. Werra. Note Peter Günther on ship's passenger list.

Peter and Margaretha Guenther with baby Margaret (1847-1927)

Peter Guenther with children borne by Margaretha, his first spouse. Left to Right: Agenatha, Peter B., Father Peter Guenther, Anna (on lap), John P., Daniel, and Margaret.

had heard reality, or only myth? Would life be better and easier, or so cruel they would not be able to survive? Would the generations to follow be destined to a life of ignorance and poverty, or would they be able to get a proper education and rise to a higher station in life? Would his children and grandchildren be able to practice their faith as their conscience dictated, or would the government of the new world tighten its noose of intolerance as it had begun to do in the old country? Above all, would he and his family find a church that would foster and uphold the tenets of faith he cherished so dearly?

Still thinking about what lay ahead for him and his family, he suddenly realized that dawn was beginning to break over the eastern horizon. He got up quickly and made his way to the main deck of the ship. As he glanced westward he thought he saw land in the distance. He said to himself: this must be America – and those buildings – that must be New York City! He quickly ran down to the lower decks and called to Margaretha, "Get up! Help me wake the children! I see land! We must be arriving in America." It wasn't long before the whole family, together with hundreds of other immigrants, stood on the main deck of the ship as it neared the harbor. The date of their long anticipated arrival, Peter noted, was June 7, 1884. Since it was not erected until 1886, there was no Statue of Liberty to welcome them to America. Peter and Margaretha had come to a crossroad in their journey that would set the direction they and future generations would travel.

Welcome to America, Peter thought.

Chapter 5
The New World

Peter and Margaretha Guenther, with five children in tow and baby Anna in her mother's arms, were almost crowded over the edge of the deck as they waited in line with hundreds of other immigrants to walk down the gangplank of the *S.S. Werra*. Peter warned, "Hold each other's hands tightly, children, so no one gets lost. And Margaret (the oldest), make sure you keep holding my hand." Anxiety and suspense, more than excitement and elation were written all over their faces. Their sea legs almost gave way as they finally set foot on dry land. Before them was a panoramic view of the famous but confusing place called New York City.

The most urgent matter the Guenthers needed to attend to was to find the Immigration Office and register their arrival in America. To their surprise, they discovered that a number of harbor hands spoke German. History records that during the mid-nineteenth century more than forty thousand German immigrants had come to New York (*New York, An Illustrated History*, Burns and Sanders). A part of lower Manhattan became known as *Kliendeutschland* (Little Germany) because so many of them settled here and worked at menial harbor jobs. The migration of Germans to New York continued and by the end of the Nineteenth century their numbers reached more than 75,000. Fortunately, getting directions to the Immigration Office was not a problem.

Burns and Sanders also record that during this time even more immigrants came to New York from Ireland than from Germany. In 1854 alone, 319,000 emigrants from Europe landed at New York harbor. To handle the flood of newcomers, the city's governing council converted a circular structure, Castle Garden, into an immigrant processing center. This building, that had originally been built as a fort and then converted into a concert hall, became the first immigrant processing center ever established in the United States. The famous Ellis Island Immigration Center did not open its doors until 1892, eight years after the Guenthers arrived in America.

Since the Guenthers had arrived along with thousands of other immigrants who all needed to register their arrival in this new land, they really did not need directions. All they needed to do was follow the crowd to the distinctively designed Castle Garden and wait in line until their names were called. These were tense moments for Peter and Margaretha because they knew they would have to pass health tests, and although they were not aware of any health problems, no one knew what kind of disease they might have contracted while on board ship. They also knew that if the test suggested a problem, they could be turned away and would have to return to their homeland.

There were many people of German descent in the harbor area who, like the Guenther family, did not know a word of English. They soon realized that their ingenuity as immigrants would be taxed to the limit in this strange new city. They needed to find shelter for the night and buy food to replenish their depleted supply. The next day they found a drayman to transport them and their goods to the train that could carry them half way across the continent to the endless American prairie and, in the middle of that prairie, to a hamlet called Petersburg, Nebraska.

Train travel had become the leading means of transportation, not only within the city of New York and its environs, but across the continent. It was efficient, fast and inexpensive, but the downside was that its locomotives violently sputtered smoke and steam from the bellies of their monstrous engines, diffusing a blue haze into the air wherever they went. That, of course, did not stop the expansion of railroad lines that eventually crisscrossed America. The pioneer in this new venture was Cornelius "The Commodore" Vanderbilt who, after the Civil War, built the New York Central Railroad which connected New York City, on Manhattan Island, to Chicago. In the process he became America's richest man with a fortune estimated to exceed $100 million.

The hub of all train travel within New York City and beyond was Grand Central Depot built in 1871 by The Commodore at 42nd Street and 4th Avenue. The iron and glass depot stood 100 feet above ground level, was 200 feet wide and stretched four city blocks long. It was the largest interior space on the North American continent, spacious enough to hold 15,000 people and nearly 100 trains at one time. The trains, and the tracks upon which they ran, were below the ground level of the depot itself. Even though an exhaust system had been built to funnel the deadly fumes out of the terminal, the smoke and steam belching from their giant engines became stifling.

As huge as it was, the depot was too small to carry the heavy train and passenger traffic even before it was completed. It was not until the early twentieth century that Penn Station (1910) and a new Grand Central Terminal (1913) replaced Grand Central Depot in another part of the city.

The morning after the Guenther family arrived in New York harbor they loaded their cargo on to a dray-man's wagon. It was not long before they approached the entrance to Grand Central Depot. The whole family stared in disbelief at the monstrous structure. When they stepped inside, they gazed in utter amazement at the incomprehensible enormity of the building and its contents. Never in their wildest dreams had they imagined what their eyes were telling them when they later descended to the lower level. There were rows of trains as far as they could see, with people skittering about like ants whose nest has been disturbed.

The depot was actually three buildings under one roof, one depot for each of the main railroad lines it served. Before buying a ticket and boarding a train, Peter realized that he had to find the right depot and train that would take his family to Chicago and points west. How, he asked himself out loud, would he ever find that one train that would take them to an unheard of village 2,000 miles to the west? How would he manage to keep his family together with 15,000 people milling about, in and out of these doors and up and down these endless corridors?

The depot had three ticketing counters, each with a luggage area and waiting room. In desperation Peter began asking one person after the other, "*Sprechen sie Deutch* (Do you speak German)?" To his great surprise, he soon found someone who could point him in the right direction.

The train Peter needed to find was one that would take them to Chicago, where the family would board the Transcontinental Railroad. The Transcontinental was built immediately following the Civil War (1860s). Two railroad companies became involved in its construction. The Central Pacific began building from the west, the Union Pacific from the east. The two met at Promontory Point, Idaho. On May 10, 1869, with great fanfare, silver and gold spikes were driven into the last railroad tie that connected the two lines. Passengers and freight could now cross the continent by rail for the first time in American history.

All this was immaterial to Peter, as he and his family boarded a train that would take them to Chicago, St. Louis, and their final destination. At some point they would board the Union and Central train that would travel the steel rails of the Transcontinental route to a point west of Omaha, Nebraska, near the town which is now Grand Island. From there they would have to travel north to a desolate spot on the landscape, a place called Petersburg, in Boone County. Almost no one had heard of Petersburg, Nebraska.

The train trip from New York to Nebraska seemed endless for Peter and Margaretha. While trying to keep the children quiet and from getting into mischief, they could not help but think about what lay ahead for them in this strange new world. Life on the prairies of South Russia had been difficult. Living conditions had been primitive. Their farming implements were crude. They had lost two children in infancy. On the other hand, they had lived in an established village in Russia, with family, relatives, neighbors, and a church to surround them in times of need.

As their train slowly made its way west, Peter confided in Margaretha, "I get nervous when I think about what lies ahead – a new country, a farm we have never seen, living among neighbors *who are not our people*, making a new start on land that does not even have a house on it." Margaretha said, "I worry about the same things. It will not be easy." She thought about their parents and families they had left behind, and the deep wounds created in their souls by the fact that they had left them for this new land.

Both Peter and Margaretha had so many unanswered questions. They often wondered if they had made the right decision in coming to America. But after praying about it again, they felt sure that God had opened the door for them to make the move. And although the challenge of a new beginning was daunting, it held a certain fascination. The nearer they got to their new home, the more restless they became, and the more ready they were for the new adventure.

When Peter and his family finally reached the town and the train depot nearest Petersburg, they began searching the few stores in town for what they would need for their new beginning. Not being able to speak English was a distinct disadvantage. They were unfamiliar with the American currency they had exchanged for their Russian money. Being strangers in a small western town, they were not sure they could trust anyone.

Peter soon located the livery stable where he would have to buy a team of horses. He had heard some wild stories about western horse traders. Fortunately, he knew the difference between an old nag and a good work horse. He carefully checked out several, and struck a deal. He found a used flat-bed wagon that could be loaded with a sod-breaking plow, an assortment of farm implements, their furniture and household items. He also purchased a horse and buggy, food, mats for sleeping, and a tent in which they would camp until their new sod house was ready to move into.

Peter and Margaretha checked over the list they had made of things they would need to get started. Satisfied that they had most of them, they loaded everything onto their wagon and buggy, and were soon on their way across the open prairie. They stopped often to ask directions to the township of Petersburg. The incredible journey by land and sea, halfway around the world, from South Russia to Nebraska, was about to come to an end. But as they would discover, their journey's end was merely the beginning of another one that would prove to be more difficult, by far, than the one they were just ending.

Peter discovered that the town clerk in Petersburg knew a little German. The clerk got out a map, drew a circle around the acreage Peter had bought, and gave directions on how to get there.

"How will I know for sure that it's the farm I actually bought?" Peter asked with grave concern.

With his limited knowledge of the German language the clerk said, "It will be the only farm with weeds growing up to your knees. It has an old, broken down fence around it. A homesteader tried farming it for a couple of years, but then abandoned it. He dug a cistern, but that's about all you will find there. Good luck. I hope you can make a go of it."

His parting words were not very reassuring. It will take more than luck, Peter thought to himself, to survive on land such as this.

Peter and his family carefully followed the directions they had been given. After two hours they came to a farm exactly like the one the clerk had described. They drove along the dusty road that surrounded it before coming to what appeared to have been a driveway. They turned in and followed it to its end. And sure enough, there was the cistern the clerk had mentioned. They removed the boards that covered it, looked down into the deep hole, and were pleased to find water almost to the top.

"This must be our farm," Peter announced. He found a sickle among the tools on the wagon, and told the boys to begin clearing weeds from an area large enough for pitching the tent he had bought. By nightfall the tent was ready for occupancy. Sticks of wood and dried weeds were gathered for an open fire. Beans and bacon were cooked, devoured, and washed down with water from the cistern. The Guenther family spent their first night under the stars on the vast Nebraska prairie.

The first order of business the next day was to clear an area from which they would cut sod for their new home. Sod houses were common on the prairies of the mid-west. The prairie sod was a layer of short grasses held together by an intertwined system of roots upon which even a modern-day engineer could not have improved. Building the houses of sod served a twofold purpose: for one thing, it provided an excellent building material and for another, if the prairie land was to be farmed, the sod had to be broken to get to the tillable soil. The sod was usually broken with hand plows, such as the one Peter had purchased before leaving town. If a plow and team of horses were not available, men resorted to axes and shovels to cut the sod into brick-like pieces.

Slabs of sod were cut six inches thick, a foot wide, and three feet long. The floor of the house was cleared of any sod before the slabs were stacked like bricks to form the walls. Some built their houses with a double thickness of sod, adding to its strength and insulating qualities. When the walls had reached the desired height, a hip roof had to be built. If wood was available, it was placed over the house and additional sod was placed on the boards. If there was no wood, the roof was made of thickets and twigs, and covered with pitch, hoping it would keep out the rain, wind, dust and cold of winter. Such houses were quite durable and, if maintained properly, lasted many years, provided that the cattle didn't get to them and use them for scratching posts.

Peter had helped build such houses back in the old country, so he knew the process well. The one-room house with a single window and earthen floor was ready for occupancy within the month. Getting settled in their humble new home after months of travel was pure luxury for Margaretha. But then she began to think about the long winter months ahead, and the huge amount of food their family would need. So she and the girls planted a fall vegetable garden in the area from which the sod for the house had been removed.

It seemed to Margaretha that the work to be done in their new home was endless: cooking, sewing clothes for the children, mending socks, and a hundred other chores. There were mountains of clothes to be washed, using a scrub board and a large tub of hot water, then hung outside to dry before ironing them with an iron heated on their wood stove. She thought about those cold winter days when the clothes would have to be hung on the line in a blowing wind, with temperatures below zero. She had already learned from living on the steppes in Russia, that they would dry even when frozen.

Margaretha also thought about the Saturday night bathing ritual which was necessary to get everyone ready for Sunday worship. A small tub would have to be placed in an inconspicuous corner of their one-room sod house. Water would have to be carried in from the cistern. The ice that would form over the top of it during the cold of winter would have to be broken before the water could be carried by bucketfuls into the house and heated on the stove. Several of the children would have to share the same bath water. The whole affair would start in the early afternoon and continue until late in the evening, with Peter being the last to bathe.

While Margaretha gave her attention to household chores, Peter's mind centered on other matters: winter shelter for the horses and animals he had bought from a neighbor, and breaking enough of the sod to be able to plant their first crop of wheat the next spring. As he thought about that first year in Nebraska, he worried about whether it would rain enough through the spring and summer to cause the seed to sprout and produce a harvest. And even if the wheat matured for harvest, perhaps a hail storm would wipe it out, and the whole crop would be lost. What then?

Summer quickly turned to winter. Their first snow came early that year. The cold penetrated their house and the shelter Peter had built for the animals. By mid-winter they experienced their first blizzard – snow coming down so thick and blowing so hard that it resulted in a complete white-out. No one could see more than a few feet in any direction. It was foolish to wander from the house under such conditions. The only way to get to the animal shelter was to run a rope from the house to the shelter, something Peter had had the foresight to do before winter set in, and hold on to the rope while making one's way between the two. The Guenthers had heard of neighbors who had frozen to death because they had been working in the field when a sudden blizzard blew across the prairie and they could not find their way home.

When such blizzards hit, farm families were completely isolated. Margaretha grumbled on days when the children were under her feet all day because of the weather. She also worried about what they would do if they would need a doctor when such storms came. They had never heard of telephones, since the first one had been invented in 1876, just eight years ago. Bathrooms were unheard of in most sod houses. No one wanted to think about having to use an outhouse in such weather.

In spite of the many hardships Peter and Margaretha faced, they had a happy family life. God blessed them with three more children during the years they lived in Nebraska. Death, however, was not unfamiliar to them. Besides the two children they had lost to death in Russia, one of their children, little two-year old Maria, was laid to rest there in Nebraska. A year later, in January of 1891, Peter's beloved Margaretha, died at the age of 41, after only nineteen years of marriage. The most heart wrenching task Peter had faced to this point in his life was to dig yet another grave, leaving his beloved helpmate on the frozen prairie.

As Peter grieved the loss of his young wife, he soon realized that without a mother, the task of caring for his eight remaining children was more than he could handle. Heinrich, the youngest, was just five months old. One night Heinrich lay in his crib crying as Peter helplessly stood by. A few days later, with tears in his own eyes, he made a decision he would later deeply regret.

In the face of Margaretha's untimely death, Peter had to deal with the pain, grief, and hardships of prairie life alone. He had heard of a community in Butler County, Kansas where several of *his own people* had settled. Soon after Margaretha died, Peter decided to move his family to the new community. When asked by his neighbors why he was moving, he finally admitted only to himself that his main motivation for the move was to find a new wife and mother for his children. A move to Kansas was worth the hardships involved in pulling up stakes and making a new beginning.

The farm on which the family settled in Kansas was again miles from nowhere. The earth was of heavy black soil, but good for wheat. The roads in the rainy season, however, turned to clay. Hence one would see the warning sign on many rural roads in Kansas, *Choose your rut carefully because you will be in it for the next ten miles.*

Peter believed it was an answer to his prayers that one day he met a young woman, Katharina Isaak. It was as though he had stumbled upon a vein of gold! He was twenty-two years older than she, but was convinced that God had His hand in helping him find her. Her beauty, no doubt, helped lead him to that decision. He soon took courage and proposed marriage. Peter was forty-five years old. Katharina was just twenty-three and knew that Peter already had a large family. But love prevailed and she accepted his proposal. On March 3, 1892, they were married, and happiness descended upon them like a cloud of morning dew on the green of the spring wheat growing in the field.

Just a year after the happy union of the couple, Peter indicated an interest in another move, this one south to the Oklahoma Territories. The possibility of this move evoked a response in his young bride that the newly-wedded couple would have to resolve before they would be able to continue their journey through life.

The road Peter was to propose to his family would include unexpected twists and turns, filled with triumph and tragedy, and would finally answer the question of what happened to little Heinrich who, as an infant had been put into the care of relatives. It would also show how the paths of the Guenthers and the Jantzes (now going by the name Janzen) would ultimately cross.

But before we proceed to follow the Guenthers on their journey, we need to catch up with the Janzen family from the time it disembarked ship in the New York harbor.

Peter and Margaretha Peters Guenther

Peter and second wife,
Katherina Isaak Guenther

Chapter 6
Moundridge

It was a crisp November day in 1874 when Heinrich and Helena Thomas Janzen, together with their seven children (ages 1 to 11), set foot on the soil of what would become their new home in a strange land. They had successfully crossed the Atlantic ocean. The daunting challenge of negotiating the streets of New York City was too intimidating to even think about, but they realized there was no turning back. The city had to be conquered. As head of his family, Heinrich realized he had to take charge, but deep within his being was the same wrenching sensation he had experienced at sea at the height of a storm.

The family's destination, together with that of several other immigrants from Karolswalde, was McPherson County, Kansas. Before leaving the famous city of New York, they would need to replenish their supply of food and other provisions, then find their way to the train depot that would take them halfway across the continent. Unfortunately, no one in their contingent spoke a word of English. None had any idea of what to expect as they faced the adventure which awaited them.

As the Janzen family made its way down the gangplank of the ship, Heinrich and Helena looked out over the waterfront, aware that New York City was known all over Europe for its magnificent buildings designed by famous architects, department stores that covered whole city blocks, and neighborhoods of opulent homes of its sophisticated, fashionable citizens. The waterfront bore no resemblance to what they had heard about the city.

Instead, what they saw was a cesspool of the vulgar and repulsive. The streets leading from the harbor were lined with tenement buildings plastered with huge handbills. Vendors were like squatters who set up their booths down the middle of the streets, selling anything from underwear and overalls to fruits and vegetables too ripe to eat. Liquor flowed freely in the beer halls and gambling dens. Houses of prostitution were too numerous to count. Most streets were mud holes that were miles long. The stench from the raw sewage that ran down the streets was overwhelming. Tracts of land, waiting to be developed, were overgrown with weeds and underbrush. Horse-drawn buggies and wagons wound their way carelessly through the ugliness of the narrow roadways, often colliding with pedestrians who got in their way.

For the most part, New York was still a frontier city. People on the waterfront swarmed the open-air bazaars, some seriously making deals with the vendors, some leisurely sitting on apple crates drinking the latest brews imported from Europe. Others, like Heinrich and Helena, anxiously wandered about, searching desperately for help. How would they ever find their way through the clutter and confusion of the waterfront to the Grand Central Depot, to buy train passage, first to Chicago and then to Kansas?

About the time the Janzen family reached New York, another family from Karolswalde, Peter and Eva Koehn and their five children (ages 13 to 23), made their way across the Atlantic. Like the Janzen family, their destination was also McPherson County, Kansas. The families had been neighbors in Karolswalde. Their children had played together. However, when the decision was made by the Karolswalde colony to migrate to America, these two families traveled to different European countries and port cities, crossed the Atlantic on different ships, and reached America at different ports. The Koehn family arrived thirty-eight days later than the Janzen family. In spite of having gone their separate ways, they both ended up in a little town few had ever heard of – Moundridge, McPherson County, Kansas. The day they found each other in their new homeland they embraced and wept. God had protected and provided for all of them throughout the long journey.

Heinrich remembered the handbill he carried in the hip pocket of his overalls. He got it out and reread it carefully once more as it described the wonders of the State of Kansas and all the benefits available to an immigrant to that State.

On January 29, 1861, Kansas became the thirty-fourth State to join the Union. A year later, Congress passed the Homestead Act which offered unappropriated public lands in the State of Kansas to any citizen or alien who filed a declaration of intention to become a citizen. He or she had to be twenty-one years of age or the head of a family. A tract of 160 acres or less could be acquired without cost if the resident lived on the land and cultivated it for a period of five years.

The Karolswalde Mennonites got to Kansas too late to take advantage of the Homestead Act. But Heinrich heard that the Government provided huge land grants to railroad companies that would provide rail service to these isolated rural communities as they sprang up across the plains. Although several railroad companies vied for these grants, the Atchison, Topeka and Santa Fe (AT&SF) became the dominant train to cross the State of Kansas. It connected with other main lines in Chicago, ran southwest through the heartland of the new State, and ultimately linked Chicago with California. It was estimated that by 1872, the AT&SF had been given grants of land totaling three million acres. The land was worthless unless there were farm products to be transported to eastern markets. So the railroad company began looking for farmers. It built long barrack-like houses where the newcomers could stay until they could erect their own homes and offered land at dirt cheap prices.

So, as Mennonite farmers fled Russia, they came to Kansas. It is estimated that 5,000 immigrants had come to central Kansas by 1874. Now, the Mennonites from the village of Karolswalde, Volhynia, were about to join them.

Most of the Karolwalde Mennonites had little or no money by the time they got to their new home. Heinrich Janzen had been able to convert what little money he had brought with him from Russia into six American dollars. Peter Koehn fared little better. They were able to get a fresh start only with the help of relatives and members of the Mennonite Church. Some of the immigrants moved into the *long-houses* the AT&SF had built along the railroad. The Janzen family rented a small farm known as the Rose Place along Turkey Creek, northwest of Moundridge. The Koehns secured farm land near by.

The first winter the immigrants spent in Kansas stretched their endurance to the limit. It was too late in the season to plant gardens, so

Note: Moundridge was about fifteen miles northwest of Newton, Kansas, a main railroad depot and maintenance yard for the AT&SF. The depot also included a "roundhouse," a huge circular platform with tracks running in four directions – like a large "plus sign." A train engine was moved on to the platform. The platform was then turned in the new direction the switchman wanted the train to travel, and connected it with the cars waiting to be moved.

all of their food had to be bought or given to them by relatives, friends, or sympathetic neighbors. Snow covered the landscape through most of the winter. Firewood to stoke their cookstoves and heat their cheaply built houses was scarce. But these immigrants from Karolswalde had become accustomed to the harsh realities of pioneer life.

As spring approached and the ground thawed, the pioneers began to plow the soil of the prairie land. Their first priority was to till enough ground for a spring vegetable garden, then to prepare as much land as they could for a crop of wheat and corn. The soil was black and heavy, but rich. They were certain that with the proper amount of rain their small farms would yield a bountiful harvest.

There was a time when the church had been the central focus of most Mennonite communities. During their early pioneer years, it seemed impossible to survive the harsh, rigorous life of an immigrant without the encouragement of the brothers and sisters of the Church. But the Karolswalde Mennonites had a different story to tell. Church life in the old country had stagnated. The long and tedious church services were meaningless. The Church was no longer important or necessary. Many of them simply dropped out. Now, in coming to their new homeland, the Church seemed even less vital to their daily life. Just trying to survive the hardships as pioneers in a new land consumed all of the time and energy they could muster. However, many of the Karolswalde immigrants, including the Janzens and Koehns, eventually discovered the Emmanuel Church (General Conference Mennonite) in the community of Canton, Kansas, and made it their church home. A note in the family records indicates that Eva Koehn was buried in the cemetery next to this church. Another note in the same record, makes reference to the fact that several members of the Janzen family did not become believers until much later in life. Even though both families attended church from time to time, it would take a serious crisis to bring the Janzen family back to God and into the full fellowship of the church.

Living in the same community and attending the same church, it was inevitable that love would one day blossom between the young people as they grew into adulthood. And so it was that Jacob, the second oldest son of Heinrich and Helena Janzen, began courting Karolina Koehn, the youngest daughter of Peter and Eva Koehn. Twelve years after coming to America, Jacob and Karolina were married. The day was May 23, 1886. The young couple made their home with Jacob's parents.

"A big mistake," Karolina said.

But it was the only way the couple could survive. The Janzen house was long and narrow, with a kitchen at each end, ideally suited for two families. However, there was constant friction and competition between Mother Janzen and her new daughter-in-law, Karolina. For instance, both tried to outdo each other in keeping their stoves polished. Jacob's siblings noted the rivalry with contempt. The old adage proved itself to be true, *No house is big enough for two families.* In spite of the annoyances of living in the same house, they also discovered that they needed each other. Every hand was required to meet the demands of farm life on the prairie. For the Janzen women it meant washing the mountains of clothes on a scrub board with water carried from the creek and heated on their cook stoves. They would then need to be hung out to dry even when the Kansas wind incessantly blew more strongly than the breath of a dragon. They were responsible for countless chores including preparing three meals a day for a family that was always hungry. The men in the Janzen family had all they could do to plow, cultivate, and seed the land with one team of horses and one plow between Heinrich and his married son, Jacob; milk the cows; feed the pigs and chickens; and on and on.

All the hard work slowly paid off. Both the Janzen and Koehn families survived the rigors of pioneer life. It also had its pleasant moments: time to tell stories and laugh, to sit around the table and plan for the future, time to go to church and visit neighbors. The day also came when Jacob and Karolina were blessed with a baby girl, whom they named Helena, born February 28, 1887.

While living in the same house with Jacob's parents, little Helena became a great joy to her grandmother, who took great pride in the fact that her first grandchild had been given her name. It was impossible for Grandma to ignore this beautiful, energetic, and sometimes feisty girl. Young Helena was encouraged by her Grandma to spend a lot of time playing in her end of the house. She was given special treats and sat in a highchair while eating meals at Grandma's table. The special attention Helena received from her grandmother also eventually became a source of friction between Grandma and her daughter-in-law. Karolina decided one day that giving little Helena a good spanking was in order. It apparently solved the problem of Helena wanting to be on Grandma's end of the house.

Jacob and Karolina Janzen continued to live with his parents in the Moundridge community until 1889. The day came when Karolina said, "One can live with her in-laws only so long!"

It was time for Jacob and Karolina to find a home of their own, but not before another child, Elizabeth, had been added to their family. They finally settled on a farm in Lehigh about ten miles north of Moundridge where they lived for just one year.

From Lehigh they moved to Butler County, Kansas, and rented a farm which was fourteen miles west of El Dorado, the county seat. A large number of Mennonite families, including the Peter Guenthers, moved to Butler County in the early eighteen-nineties. Churches were established. More virgin prairie land was tilled. More wheat and corn were grown. God blessed the Janzen family with two more children.

The Janzen farm lay at the edge of a creek where black walnut trees grew wild. The children found that the walnuts made great toys. Real toys bought in a store were unheard of in the Janzen family. They gathered walnuts and played *marbles* or hid them like Easter eggs. After they were through playing with them, mother Janzen roasted them in the oven. The family spent long evenings cracking walnuts and enjoying the tasty morsels. The shells were saved for fuel for the stove.

Jacob took pride in his beautiful bay horses,

Note: Jacob and Karolina's first son, Peter, was born in Lehigh. At the same time another couple by the name of Mr. and Mrs. Heinrich F. Janzen (not related to the Heinrich F. Janzen in our story above) was living in the Hillsboro area. This Mr. and Mrs. Janzen were blessed with a daughter whom they named Katherine. Years later Peter Janzen and Katherine Janzen were married and had a son, William. Twenty years later, Tabor College was established in Hillsboro, just six miles east of Lehigh where William was born. Soon after the college opened its doors William became Professor of Chemistry at Tabor College, a position he held throughout his teaching career.

and on those rare hours when he could take the time away from the farm work, he loved to ride one of them across the prairie. In the fall of the year, when the Canadian geese migrated south, he carried his twelve caliber shotgun with him. He was an expert marksman and often brought home a goose or two. Karolina cleaned them carefully, picking out the pin feathers. Roasted goose with sweet potatoes was a real treat for the family.

There was a railroad track just one half mile south of the Janzen farm. By late summer the corn in their field was ripe for harvest. One day, while Jacob and his son, Peter, had gone into town to take care of some business, mother Janzen said to her three daughters, Helena, Elizabeth and Karolina,

"We need to go and get some of the ears of corn for supper."

While they were walking among the tall stalks, they noticed two men making their way toward their house. They apparently were tramps who had gotten off the train and had noticed the farmhouse. As they approached the house it appeared to them that no one was home. They went in, helped themselves to what-ever food they wanted, and left.

The men did not realize that mother Janzen and the children were watching them from the corn-field. Naturally, the Janzen family was scared to death. They waited until they thought the men were gone. Mother Janzen slowly approached the house keeping her eyes wide open, looking from side to side while the children stood at a distance. When she got to the door she slowly opened it, trying not to make a sound, lest the men were still inside. She carefully made her way from room to room, looking in every corner and under every bed. After she was convinced that the men were no longer in the house she went back outside and carefully knocked on the

Note: The records indicate that it was during the life span of Heinrich and Helena that the name of the Jantz family was changed to Janzen. Forms of the name appearing in the records also include Jantzi and Jantzen. As I continue the story, the name Janzen will be used in referring to the family until another fascinating event changes the name once more.

door of the outhouse. No one there. The last place they could be was the storm cellar, twenty feet from the house. She slowly lifted the cellar door and found the cellar empty. She finally concluded that the men were gone and gave the children an all-clear signal. They went back into the house to take an inventory of what the men might have taken. Among other things, they discovered that they had taken father Janzen's prized gold pocket watch. When Jacob and Peter returned home and heard what had happened they were relieved that the family was safe but angry about the loss of Jacob's prized possession.

In early 1893, word came to the Mennonites of Butler County that parcels of good prairie land were available for homesteading in the Oklahoma Territories. After discussing the matter with Karolina and with his parents who still lived in Moundridge, it was decided that Jacob and his father, Heinrich, should mount their Bay Draft horses and ride the two-hundred-and-fifty miles south to search out the land. Karolina was fearful of having her beloved husband make the dangerous journey. She had heard stories of savage Indians and gangs of bandits attacking traveling pioneers. A tear dropped from her eye as she watched Jacob ride into the distance until he disappeared from sight.

Karolina, together with relatives and neighbors, waited nervously and impatiently for the return of Jacob and his father. When they finally returned, the family gathered for a long discussion about the benefits of another move and another start in pioneer living. The decision was finally made in favor of the Oklahoma Territories. The move, however, would not be made until 1894, a year after several other Mennonite families from Butler County had already settled in the Territories. It would be compensated with important spiritual victories, and a daughter's romantic involvement, but not without trials and hardships.

Chapter 7
The Oklahoma Land Runs

On April 30, 1803, the United States Government purchased more than 800,000 square miles of land from France. This land extended from the Mississippi River to the Rocky Mountains, and from the Gulf of Mexico to the Canadian border. The sale came to be known as the Louisiana Purchase and brought the entire land area under the sovereign control of the United States. The price paid for this enormous piece of real estate was $15 million.

For centuries, the great plains, rich with grass land, had been the home of great herds of buffalo and other wildlife. Native Americans roamed freely across this land as hunter-gatherers and depended on the buffalo for their main source of food and clothing. They followed these herds, moving south in winter and north in the summer.

After the War of 1812, a small portion of the Louisiana Purchase was designated as Indian Territory. The Territory was what is now the State of Oklahoma and parts of Kansas and Nebraska. It was the intention of the U.S. government to move Native American Nations (usually referred to as the Five Civilized Indian Nations) then living east of the Mississippi River, to land west of the River in what had become the Indian Territory. Each of these tribes was assigned to a designated *Reservation* within the Territory. The goal of the government was to make room in the southeastern states for white settlers who were demanding more and more land for their huge plantations. Treaties were made with these Native American Nations, promising free land and food west of the Mississippi River in exchange for the lands they had been occupying. Beginning in the eighteen-thirties, tens of thousands of native people were forcibly uprooted and driven on foot to the new Indian Territory. The relocation of such huge numbers of people turned out to be a tragic story in American history. The journey became known as the *Trail of Tears*, since as many as two of every five Native Americans died along the way.

Several Native American tribes other than the Five Civilized Indian Nations that had been relocated, had freely roamed the ranges of the Louisiana Purchase for centuries. These tribes continued to claim ownership of the land in spite of what the U.S. Government told them about having bought the land from the French.

In the late eighteen-hundreds white settlers were beginning to demand land west of the Mississippi. The Government had already bowed to their greedy appetites by giving them the land of the Five Civilized Indian Nations east of the River. Now, the goal of the United States Government was to establish Reservations and to confine the tribes that had roamed up and down the Purchase. Before the Government had completed its plan of relocation, the entire Indian Territory had been cut up into Reservations, and what is now the State of Oklahoma, could have been declared the *Indian Capital of America*. To the chagrin of the Government, many of the Native Americans refused to settle on their designated Reservation. Fierce wars followed. Before they were subdued, the land had been stained by the blood of thousands of Indians. The Government's failure to peacefully relocate many of these Native Americans left huge areas of prairie land in the Territory uninhabited.

As white people continued to expand westward, they put pressure on the U.S. Government to open the Indian Territory to homesteading. The Government finally conceded, purchasing large tracts of land for almost nothing from the various Native American Tribes.

The land was surveyed and laid out in 160-acre homesteads. Since there was such a great demand for this land, it was decided that it be made available to homesteaders by means of *Land Runs*. Millions of acres in various parts of the Territory were opened to potential home-steaders by this method of land distribution.

It should be noted that on May 2, 1890, the Federal government passed the Organic Act by which it changed the name of the *Indian Territory* to *Oklahoma Territories* and enlarged it to include what was then known as *No Man's Land* (now the Oklahoma panhandle) and what is now the State of Oklahoma, including Greer County in the southwest.

Five runs were organized between 1889 and 1895. The government announced when and where the runs would be held. The 1893 Cherokee Land Run of six million acres was the largest and the most famous.

In 1866, the Cheyenne-Arapaho Indian Reservation had been set aside and designated as the home for these tribes. At the time, these two tribes had an estimated three to four thousand members that were reported to be among the most fierce and warlike Indians in North America. White men and Indians were on the war path for most of the years between 1866 and 1893. The Indians were ultimately disarmed, and an agreement was reached giving every member of the two tribes, regardless of age or sex, a tract of 160 acres. The remainder of the land was sold to the U.S. Government and opened to white settlers.

The Government proclaimed that the third of the five runs would be held on April 19, 1892. Although the proclamation was made just a week before the event, an estimated 25,000 would-be settlers gathered at twelve o'clock noon for the great Cheyenne-Arapaho country land run. They came from all directions by whatever means available. By this time, train travel was available deep into the Oklahoma Territories, but many came on foot, race horses, plow horses, wagons, buggies, or even bicycles.

All would-be runners lined up along the northern border of the Reservation as they waited impatiently for the gunshot that would signal the beginning of the Run. The goal for most of them was the Washita River Valley, because it contained the best and richest land in the Territories. As in the previous and subsequent Runs, greedy and impatient men and women crossed the border before the time set for the Run, and earned the title of *Sooners*. The myth persists to this day that this is the reason Oklahoma is known as the *Sooner State*.

In spite of the fact that thousands had participated in the Cheyenne-Arapaho Run, many of them turned back when they realized how wild and rough the raw prairie really was and how demanding life would be. Moreover, they were told they would have to begin developing a homestead within six months of the Run dates and live on the homestead for five years before they could claim title to it. Consequently, hundreds of tracts of land were not claimed or settled until almost the end of the century. This provided an unprecedented opportunity for Mennonite settlers to claim much of this inhospitable land (eventually be-coming known as *Tornado Alley*) and build a rich, wholesome community for those with the stamina to endure.

In 1889, the year of the first of the Oklahoma Land Runs, a missionary by the name of J. J. Kliewer opened a Mission Station among the Arapaho Indians who lived along the Wash-ita River in an area known as Shelly. The Station was located five miles west and two miles south of what is now the town of Corn, in Washita County, Oklahoma. While living in the area, Kliewer witnessed the Cheyenne-Arapaho Land Run. He observed that after the Run, much of the land was still unclaimed. He was probably the missionary who sent word to the German-Russian Mennonites in Butler County, Kansas, encouraging them to move to the Washita Valley, stake a claim, and settle in the area.

Records show that by the fall of 1893, forty Mennonite families moved to the area, with others coming within the next two years.

A rather interesting development resulted from the influx of the Mennonites: the Arapahos gradually moved away. With the Indians gone, Mr. Kliewer's Mission Station was closed in the year 1900.

Chapter 8
Oklahoma Homestead

Several weeks after Peter Guenther had brought up the matter of a move from Butler County, Kansas to the Oklahoma Territories, Katharina decided it was time to speak her mind about it. She said, "Peter, we have just gotten started here on this farm. How can you even consider moving two-hundred and fifty miles south with me, your new wife, and all your children?"

Suddenly she felt a flash of anger deep within her – an anger that caused her words to flow as hot as an oven with an open door. After a while her voice grew softer, and more tender. "If you want to know, Peter," she continued, "I just discovered that I am carrying our first child, who will be born about the time you are talking about making the move."

Peter was completely dumbfounded, first by Katharina's reaction to the proposed move, but even more by the news that he would be a father for the twelfth time. He was silent for a long time – for days, in fact. It was Peter's characteristic way of dealing with disagreements. The tension between the two of them continued to mount until the third evening, when Katharina could no longer deal with it. She said, "Peter, we must talk."

After supper that night, Peter called the family together. He needed to explain why he felt the move was not only desirable, but necessary. When he bought the farm here in Kansas, he could do so only by borrowing a great deal of money. At the time he bought it the price of wheat was good and they were able to sell their first harvest at a profit. Since then, growing wheat had become unprofitable. The prediction was that the next crop would be worth only twelve cents a bushel. It would be almost impossible for them to stay here, have enough money to live on and make their mortgage payment. If they stayed, they would most likely lose everything. "If we stay, we will lose everything we have, including our house and land. If we move to the Territories we will have free land. We can sell our land here in Butler county, pay off our mortgage and be free from debt." Even though the price of wheat or corn would be low, perhaps they would at least have their land and be able to survive.

News in those day was not flashed on radio waves and televisions screens. In remote areas of the country, like Kansas, it often took weeks or months to find out what was happening in New York or other parts of the country. So at first Peter did not understand why the price of wheat had suddenly tumbled. But as prices continued to decline he ultimately learned about what was called "The Great Depression of 1893" that had engulfed the nation. (Years later, historians compared it in its severity to the Depression of 1929.) Banks and businesses failed. The stock market went into shock. One fourth of the nations's railroads went into bankruptcy. Farmers, especially in the Midwestern States of the Dakotas, Nebraska, and Kansas, lost their farms.

It was estimated that four million people nationwide lost their jobs. Bread and soup lines in the cities grew longer. The unemployed had few alternatives but to do something as drastic as fight with each other for the few jobs that were available. Some men and husbands, in their desperation to find food, left their families and became *tramps*. They fanned out across the countryside, catching rides on freight trains to more prosperous neighborhoods where they knocked on back doors asking if they could chop wood or do some other chore in exchange for food.

News about the devastating effect of the Depression reached the Peter Guenther family only in bits and pieces. But as it did, a move to the Territories pressed down upon them with ever increasing urgency. It did not take long for Katharina to agree to the move.

After Peter had explained the financial crisis confronting his family he said, "I have given much thought and prayer to this matter. I realize how much hard work is involved in such a move, but I do not see that we have a choice. We have the opportunity of a lifetime to settle on good, rich land we can one day call our own. This land has never seen the blade of a plow, or the foundation of a house. After a strenuous move we will have to live in very primitive conditions for a while, but we have done it before, and I believe we can do it again."

It had been nine long, hard years since Peter and his family had come to America. However, God had blessed and prospered them materially to the extent that they had a significant accumulation of household goods, several fine horses, essential farm equipment (including two wagons) and a buggy. With so much to be moved, the undertaking was not a simple one. Everything would have to be moved in one 250-mile trip.

When the time came for the big move, the farm implements (plows, harrow and corn planter) were loaded onto one wagon. Dishes, pots and pans, clothes, tables and chairs, benches and enough food items to see them through the long winter ahead were loaded onto the other. Seven head of cattle had to be driven on foot. A chicken coop with several chickens was bolted to the side of one of the wagons. After everything was loaded, a team of horses was hitched to each wagon. The younger children, together with some food items and water, were loaded onto the buggy, which was pulled by one horse.

Peter had already warned his tender new wife, Katharina, that she would have to drive the buggy. Just months before the move, she had given birth to Abraham, her first child born to this union and was pregnant with their second. Little Abraham was laid on blankets just beneath the buggy seat.

Peter then laid out a plan for each family member's responsibility. Margaret, his oldest child, age 19, would sit up in the buggy seat beside her stepmother, ready to help drive if needed. Anna and Katharina would ride in the back of the buggy. Peter B., the oldest son age 16, and according to custom, only carried the initial B instead of a full middle name, would drive one of the wagons. The horses were a bit spirited, but they would settle down after a day or two of heavy drawing. Aganatha, age 14, would be in the driver's seat with Peter B. Daniel, age 13, and Johann, age 11, would herd the cattle. Peter would drive the other wagon and lead the way.

The family of ten, including parents, started their move on a warm summer day in 1893. It would mean traveling the dusty but famous Chisholm Trail which had already been well-defined by cattlemen. Their goal was to average ten to twelve miles a day. Three major rivers would have to be forded. One, the Cimarron, had a reputation for its quicksand – loose, wet, deep sand deposits in which a person or heavy object might easily be engulfed. Peter worried about crossing the river from the day they started the move. One of the three to be crossed, the Canadian River, was wide and could only be forded when the water was low. If a heavy thunderous rain storm hit, as it often did that time of the year, it could delay the move for days or weeks.

Herding the seven head of cattle meant that the two boys, Daniel and Johann, would be walking most of the way to their new home. But walking twelve miles a day was really no challenge to them. They had walked that far following a harrow and horses on the farm since they were small kids.

The family started each day with a hearty breakfast – but not before taking time to read a Scripture passage and have a prayer. The cows had to be milked, the livestock watered and fed. Camp had to be broken before they could get on their way. They stopped to rest for lunch. As the sun was setting in the west, they set up camp for the night. The women were in charge of making a supper of fried potatoes or beans with ham or bacon. The men took care of the livestock, greased the wagon wheels, checked to make sure none of the *traces* showed signs of excessive wear, and made repairs of the harnesses as needed. They committed each day to God to provide for their safety and give them good weather. They reached their destination in less than a month.

The very next day, after arriving, Peter sought out the nearest land office (probably in Cloud Chief, the seat of Washita County at the time) to find out what tracts of land were still available. He was directed to a tract one mile east and three miles north of what is now the town of Corn in Oklahoma.

After walking with his sons across the tract of land from corner to corner, he took a shovel which he had brought along, turned over a shovel full of sod and said to his boys, "The sod is thick and the soil is rich, but I have never seen soil colored deep red. It is as if stained by the blood of a million buffaloes."

Peter also noted that the land was not flat, as he had expected prairie land to be. A ravine ran through it from southwest to northeast. After completing a thorough inspection of the acreage, he and the boys decided the tract would be suitable for farming. He immediately made his way back to the land office and on September 16, 1893, signed the necessary papers as a homesteader. (This was, coincidentally, just one day before the famous Cherokee Land Run on the northern border of the Oklahoma Territories.)

When the family arrived on the acreage they had agreed to homestead, there was no house to move into, no barn, not even a shelter for the night. So the first order of business for the Guenther family was to build another sod house.

> Note: After a homesteader had lived on his tract of land and developed it for a period of at least five years he was eligible for a Trust Deed guaranteeing that the land was his free and clear. I have in my files, a copy of the Deed issued to Peter Guenther dated "the second day of September, in the year of our Lord, One Thousand nine hundred and two." The deed is signed by T. [Theodore] Roosevelt, President of the United States from 1901 to 1909.

Peter and Katharina's house was a one-room structure with one window and a door. The floor was just plain dirt. The entire family shared this one room home, furnished with a stove, crude table and chairs and mats for sleeping. The girls slept in a loft that was built on one end of the room. Since this was tornado country, Peter built a storm cellar near the house – a dugout covered with sod. Some of the boys used this as a sleeping room. An outhouse

187

PATENT RECORD.

(Form 4-404.)

This instrument was filed for Record the _25_ day of _Nov_ A.D. 19_02_ at _11⁵⁰_ o'clock _a._ M.

and duly Recorded in Book _One_ of _Patents_ at Page _187_

C. T. Murrel

Register of Deeds.

By _G. W. Wheeler_

THE UNITED STATES OF AMERICA.

TO ALL TO WHOM THESE PRESENTS SHALL COME, GREETING:

HOMESTEAD CERTIFICATE NO. _5843_   WHEREAS, There has been deposited in the General Land Office of the United

APPLICATION _7922_   States a Certificate of the Register of the Land Office at ....

Oklahoma — _Oklahoma_

whereby it appears that pursuant to the Act of Congress approved 20th of May, 1862, "To secure Homesteads to actual Settlers on the Public Domain," and the acts supplemented thereto, the claim of ....

Peter Günther

has been established and duly consummated, in conformity to law, for the _South East quarter of Section fifteen in Township eleven North of Range fifteen West of Indian Meridian in Oklahoma Containing one hundred and sixty acres_

according to the Official Plat of the survey of the said land, returned to the General Land Office by the Surveyor General:

NOW KNOW YE, That there is, therefore, granted by the United States unto the said _Peter Günther_

the tract of land above described, to have and to hold the said tract of land, with the appurtenances thereof, unto the said _Peter Günther_ and to _his_ heirs and assigns forever.

IN TESTIMONY WHEREOF, I, _Theodore Roosevelt_ President of the United States of America, have caused these letters to be made Patent and the Seal of the General Land Office to be hereto affixed.

GIVEN under my hand, at the City of Washington, the _Second_ day of _September_, in the year of our Lord One Thousand _Nine_ Hundred and _two_, and of the Independence of the United States the One Hundred and _twenty seventh_

BY THE PRESIDENT, _T. Roosevelt_

By _F. M. McKean_ Secretary.

C. W. Brush

Recorder of the General Land Office.

Oklahoma

Recorded Vol _77_, Page _231_

Peter Guenther's Grant Deed to Homestead in Corn, Oklahoma

would have been a desirable addition to the farmstead, but this would have to come later. The thick sod walls actually served as excellent insulation, keeping out the heat of summer and the cold of winter. Insects and other varmints often found the house inviting. Spiders, rats, and rattlesnakes were common visitors. Smoke from the stove was often stifling.

Peter hired a rig for drilling a well in the ravine. A windmill was built above the well and supplied water for the household and the livestock. Water had to be carried from the well to the house and was used for drinking, cooking, washing clothes, and bathing. Wood was scarce on the prairie, so buffalo or cow chips were gathered from the land and used as fuel. The odor from the chips was a bit overwhelming until the family got used to it.

The Saturday night bath during the cold winter was definitely one of the more challenging aspects of life on the prairie. The water had to be carried in buckets from the creek which ran through the ravine (and later, from the well), and up the hill to where the house stood. It was then heated in a large metal utensil that covered half the stove. Bathing was done in a round metal tub placed in a secluded corner of the house.

As in coming to Nebraska, getting through that first winter was the Guenther family's greatest challenge. Food for the large family was scarce. They had to butcher one of the cattle for meat. Wheat for flour and corn for cornmeal were rationed. Milk from the cows provided butter and cottage cheese. Katharina had learned to make a yogurt-like food called clabber milk. In the spring they planted a garden in the small area they had cleared of sod for the building of their permanent home.

Peter Guenther with children borne by Katharina. Left to Right: Lydia, Helen, Samuel, Esther, Father Peter, David, Emil, Isaac.

During the winter months, the men built a sod barn for the livestock. They broke more of the prairie sod in preparation for the first planting of wheat and corn. There was no thought of school for any of the children during those first years. All hands were needed just to survive. In the meantime the family settled into the rigors of homesteading. Although it seemed like the winds blew continuously and the spring and summer months threatened their home with tornadoes, God graciously provided their needs. Rain to water the crops came at the right time. That first summer the land yielded an abundant harvest. Peter loved his new wife Katharina deeply. As the children got older they found spouses from among the other Mennonite settlers in the community and started life on their own.

But even as the older ones married and left home, additional children were born. Baby Martha was born that first winter after they arrived in the Territories and died eight months later. Salome was born two years later and died just before she was two years old. Abraham, the first child of Peter and Katharina, died that same year. Once again, the adversity of primitive life exacted its measure of grief. Peter was very familiar with the verse in the Bible which promised that God would never test him above what he was able to bear (I Corinthians 10:13), but there were times he wished God would not trust him quite so much. For Katharina to lose her first three children in such a short time was a grief from which she would never recover.

Chapter 9
A Father's Grief

It was now 1907. The Peter Guenther family had been able to move out of their sod house and into a new large home built of wood. Farming operations were in the hands of Peter's sons. The family had settled down to a normal routine of life, and Peter was able to turn his attention to a matter that had been troubling him since leaving Nebraska.

Peter's eleventh child with his first wife, Margaretha, was named Heinrich. Margaretha died soon after Heinrich was born. From the day Heinrich was born he was a sickly child. Peter soon realized that, without a mother for his children, he had neither the strength nor ability to care for this infant. He, therefore, gave Heinrich into the custody of an uncle, Peter Peters, and his wife Elisabeth, a childless couple who lived in Henderson, Nebraska. They were people he trusted completely. When he could, he rode his horse eighty miles from Petersburg to Henderson to visit his son. During these rare visits he was pleased to note that Aunt Elisabeth had nursed his frail baby into a strong, healthy boy.

On one such visit Peter rode up to Uncle Peter's house only to find it empty. Completely bewildered and wondering where the family might be, he began asking neighbors, "What has happened to the Peters family? Their house is empty. Where have they gone? Do you know where I might find them?"

Peter slowly pieced the story together. Uncle Peter and Aunt Elisabeth had moved to South Dakota and taken little Heinrich with them. Much later he learned that from South Dakota they had moved north into Canada. In the spring of 1907 Peter received a lead indicating that they had settled down in Hepburn, Saskatchewan. He decided it was time to find his long lost son, now seventeen years old.

One day Uncle Peter and Aunt Elisabeth received word that a stranger was in the area and would like to visit them. To get to the Peters' farm this stranger had to cross the Saskatchewan River. There was no bridge or ferry across the river, and the ice on the river was just breaking up after a cold winter. Heinrich (now going by the name of Henry) was told by his foster father to take a boat, row across the river, and pick up this stranger. Crossing the river at that time of year was very dangerous but Henry succeeded in his assignment. Henry's foster parents suspected who this stranger was, but of course, Henry did not.

Once the stranger reached the Peters home it didn't take long for the stranger to tell Henry: "My name is Peter Guenther. I am your father."

Upon hearing this, seventeen year old Henry was dumbfounded! "What? I don't know you. I have never seen you. You can't be my father! My father and mother are standing right here in front of me. These are the only parents I have ever known."

Peter Guenther tried to explain: "You are my son. Soon after you were born, your mother died. I already had eight other children to care for. I didn't know how I could take care of you. Your Uncle Peter and Aunt Elisabeth offered to take care of you for a while. I have been trying all these years to find you. Now here you are. I have married a new wife and now have a mother for my children. I would like to take you home to live with the rest of my family."

Henry refused to believe such a wild tale. It simply could not be true. And even if it was, why would he want to leave his Papa and Momma to live with a family of which he had never heard? Papa and Momma had taken care of him all these years. They loved him and had raised him in the fear of God. They had given him everything he had needed, even a share of their farm.

"No, Brother Guenther. I will stay here with Papa and Momma, the only parents I have ever known," said Henry.

Peter Guenther tried his best to persuade Henry to come and be part the rest of his family. He tried to explain: "You are my son. I am your real father. I can take care of you now. You belong to me. At least come with me and meet your other brothers and sisters!"

His pleading was to no avail. Sadly, with the grief of a broken heart, he slowly turned away, leaving his beloved son behind as he made his way back across the river and home. He would never see his son Henry again.[1]

Peter boarded a train for the long trip back to Oklahoma. He had a lot of time to think about the years since he had brought his family to America. He had experienced

the hardships of pioneer life,
the primitive living conditions,
the years of drought.

Peter thought about the time he was caught in a blizzard while on the back forty of his farm, snow blowing so hard and swift that he did not know if he would find his way back home. He thought about the hard life his dear wife, Margaretha, had endured – working from dawn to late into the night just to take care of the family. No medical help, except a mid-wife, was available in giving birth to eleven children. He had often wondered whether this was the cause of her premature death. Perhaps he should have stayed in Russia where he had prospered materially; where medical help was more readily available when he left; where he was surrounded by an established church.

And yet he thought to himself, *God has so graciously provided since coming to this new land*. His family, after all, was his greatest blessing. His home was warmed by the laughter of children who were growing up to be decent, loving, and God-fearing. The sacrifices of homesteading on the bleak prairie had been worth it, especially since coming to Oklahoma. He had so much for which to be thankful.

Peter was, however, shaken to the depths of his soul when he realized Henry was lost to him forever. What had he done? Why had he not foreseen the possibility of what happened? Had he demanded too much of his beautiful wife? Perhaps he could have given a little more energy to raising this beautiful child himself.

His thoughts about his family were only interrupted by the frequent stops the train made on his way home. After the train was moving again he returned to the quiet, contemplative spirit that was so much a part of who he was. He relived the grief of the death of Margaretha. At the same time he rejoiced in his good fortune of finding Katharina. But even those first years with her were not without sorrow. Since marrying her, the first three of their children died in infancy. So, together with the loss of three children with his first wife, and

---

[1]This true story is based on notes written by the Peters family and Helena Gunther.

the loss of three children with his second wife, he had buried six children. As grievous as it was, he now had to consider Henry as lost to him as well.

By the time the train neared the station in Oklahoma City, Peter realized that he was coming home to a family of thirteen children. Four of these were grown and married by this time. Deep in thought, he was very much aware that each child was a gift from God to be treasured above all things, and love for children, no matter how many there are, never runs out. In the quiet moments at journey's end he offered a prayer for each of them knowing, at the same time, that the death of any one of them was a loss from which he would never recover. Nor could he have foreseen the additional grief he would face later that year.

On the spring day in which Peter returned home from his long journey to Saskatchewan, he anxiously peered over the horizon as he approached home. His concern was the condition of the wheat he had sown the previous fall. Farmers in Oklahoma depended entirely upon rain to produce a successful harvest. Peter had already observed that many of the fields in the surrounding area were suffering from a lack of rain. The first glimpse of his north forty confirmed his worst fears. Most of the tender shoots were bent over – some had already turned brown. There would probably be no wheat crop this year. This had not been the first crop failure the farmers of the area had experienced since breaking the prairie sod thirteen years ago. Perhaps God would be merciful and send enough rain for the corn and sorghum crops yet to be planted that spring.

Spring turned to summer. Rains were sparse; barely enough to produce a meager crop of the sorghum he had planted. They would have to depend on the garden they had planted to see them through the next winter. It would have to be watered by buckets carried from the well. Peter called his family together one Sunday afternoon. "This will be another time of testing our faith," he said. "The loss of my son, Henry, was already more than I thought I could bear. The drought is testing all of us in another way. We cannot turn our backs on God when hard times come. Otherwise we would have forsaken Him long ago. No, we must trust Him more, allowing our faith to grow." He was not aware that 1907 would hold another test for this family. Three-year old Sara died in August of that summer.

To add to his cup of grief, Peter's second wife, Katharina, died November 8, 1911, at the early age of 42. They had been married just nineteen years – the same number of years as his marriage with his first wife. She lived to be just one year older than his first wife. His cup of grief now overflowed.

By day Peter followed the single shear plow with his team of horses, spending many hours thinking over the past; praising God for the blessings of family and the provision of spiritual and material needs; but also grieving the loss of his first wife, and then the second; feeling the pain of placing those seven children into their graves; knowing Henry would never come back. As he walked behind the plow his mind was absorbed by the intense sorrow he felt in the depth of his soul. He knew that his grief would need to find a voice, otherwise he could no longer bear the burden. In the quiet evenings, after the children were asleep, Peter often took his pen and quill and composed poetry.[2]

---

[2]Many of these original poems, written in German script, are preserved in a journal in my files. Several were translated by Dr. Larry Warkentin, a great grandson of Peter, and published in a book together with his own poems *Conversations with the Past*, by Larry Warkentin.

One evening Peter wrote this poem, which so poignantly describes his feelings in the death of so many of his family members. In the first seven verses of this poem Peter describes in graphic detail the reality of the pain of losing spouse and child. I will include just the final victorious conclusion he comes to in the face of such bereavements.[3]

At The Deathbed Of A Loved One

For he who dies in faith believing
  If freed from guilt through Christ the King.
This truth sustains us, when we're grieving,
  "O haughty death, where is thy sting?"

Such times as this should set us thinking
  That man is mortal and must die,
And on our knees in penance sinking
  There claim God's grace through Christ on high.

Then when our last word has been spoken
  This hope our loved ones will sustain.
Their hearts may bleed, but not be broken
  Though we are gone and they remain.

–Peter Günther, Circa 1912

On January 18, 1914, three years after Katharina died, Peter married for the third time. Maria Ratzlaff was the daughter of Jacob and Elizabeth Janzen Sawatsky. Maria had married Peter Ratzlaff in 1880. They had ten children. Peter Ratzlaff died in 1913. A year later, Maria Sawatsky Ratzlaff left her family behind to marry Peter Guenther.

The following is an article Peter wrote five years before his death. It appeared in the *Vorwärts*, a weekly German newspaper, published in Hillsboro, Kansas.

Weatherford, Okla.,
27 April, 1922
Dear Vorwärts,
    I would like to send a sign of life and some information about the way things are going to my friends and acquaintances and maybe also to my sister, Mrs. Reinhard Hiebert, nee Anna Günther, of

Note: What a treasure Peter found in this woman who, at the age of 56, took on the responsibility of his family. Peter had twenty-two offspring with his marriages, first to Margaretha Peters, and then to Katharina Isaak. Of these, seven died in infancy or early life and one was lost to foster parents. By the year 1913, when he and Maria Sawatsky Ratzlaff were married, seven of his children were married and living on their own. But that still left seven young Guenther children to care for. In marrying Maria Ratzlaff, Peter Guenther could now count thirty-two offspring, including the ten Ratzlaff stepchildren.

---

[3]The entire poem can be found in the book *Conversations with the Past*, by Larry Warkentin.

Prangenau, but who since moved to Podolsk in Samara. Recently, when I could not sleep one night, I was preoccupied, thinking especially about heaven that seemed to be so near. It suddenly was as though I saw Jesus ascend from earth to heaven. In spirit I was far away at the Mount of Olives where the ascension of Jesus took place. When He arrived in heaven the Father made room on His throne so that Jesus could sit next to Him. Then I was reminded of the words that Jesus once spoke: *"He who overcomes, I will grant to him to sit down with Me on My throne, as I also overcame and sat down with My Father on His throne"* [Rev. 3:21]. A precious promise we have. Not tribulation, not fear, not hunger will there be, but joy and bliss will take hold of us up there. Pain and sorrow will have to vanish.

I have endured much hardship, especially when the good Lord took my dear wife from me. Those were painful times for me as well as for my children who now had to be without a mother. Everything was lonely and forsaken. My feelings often drove me to my knees and I cried to God for light. Everything was so dark. But one must learn to know the Lord more intimately. Fortunately I had a dear neighbor, John Berg, who now lives near Herbert, Saskatchewan. At that time we both lived in Boone County, Nebraska. We often prayed and sang together and found joy that way. Even in sorrow one can attain joy and have the Lord Jesus at one's side to guide us. *"Light is sown for the righteous, and gladness for the upright in heart"* [Ps. 97:11]. There is much that I remember and much that I have retained as a blessing in my heart.

A year and three months later it so happened that I, together with my family, moved to Butler County, Kansas and there, again, I found a helpmate in Katharina Isaak at my neighbor, Abr. Isaak. Over a period of nineteen years we shared sorrows and blessings from the Lord in the spiritual as well as in the material realm. All too soon these nineteen years also ended when the Lord took my second wife from my side and I was again alone with my children which she and I had had together. The oldest daughter was eleven years. It was, again, a very difficult time. Many prayers ascended to our dear Lord so that my deep sorrow could be driven from my heart. Fortunately, my daughter, Anna, although she lived seven miles away, came to spend one day each week to take care of the laundry without ever complaining. It also happened quite frequently when I came home from town on Saturdays, that my neighbor's wife, Sister Shapansky, had come over to assist my children with their work. *"Inasmuch as ye have done it unto one of the least of these my brethren, ye have done it unto me"* said Jesus. Often when I came to church on Sunday, the sisters asked, "Brother, do you need anything we can help with such as sewing or washing?" That was like balm to my wounded heart! I was so thankful for such kindness.

In that way we managed two years and three months; but as a family without a mother, I saw the loss in my children, and now the dear Lord again had to come to my rescue. I prayed and the Lord heard. He directed me to Buhler, Kansas where the dear Sister Ratzlaff lived. She had taken care of her bedridden husband, Peter, for ten years and now lived alone in the house of her children, the Heinrich Cornelsens. Since we were somewhat acquainted from years past, the idea came to me to ask her whether she would be willing to assume responsibility for such a family as mine. She was willing to accept and now we have already spent eight years together sharing hardships and joys and still believe that the dear Lord has brought us together and that we will spend the rest of our lives with each other. *"The Lord hath done great things for us; whereof we are glad"* [Ps. 126:3].

On February 24, 1922, it has been fifty years since my first wedding. Many people celebrate their golden wedding when they have been married for fifty years but I think to have been married three times in fifty years is worthy of more gold. Much has to be received from above which glows like gold from the New Jerusalem. It has to be much purer and brighter. One always has to look away from self unto Jesus the author and finisher of our faith. After fifty years this day was of special importance to me. On this day I was reading the Bible and everything was so quiet in the house. My dear wife and Lydia [a daughter] were busy with other things. In the afternoon Lydia came and brought me a letter from David Shapansky who had been my neighbor in Oklahoma for twenty years. He and I had often shared our joys and sorrows together, spent time in prayer, and now he greeted me with Psalm 7. My son, John, came with a poem and Psalm 71 and my daughter also congratulated me with a poem. All three from California. That was gold and much fine gold! Even though it was quiet in the house my heart rejoiced with gratitude and looked up to Jesus expressing words of the Bible: "Words are silver but silence is gold." [Editorial note: quote not actually in the Bible]. In such quietness one can stay close to Jesus leaving no room for anything else. I believe when John leaned on the breast of Jesus there was no space between him and Jesus and that is how one can lean against the breast of Jesus even today. How heavenly does the inward man become. Is that not sufficient gold to celebrate fifty years of struggle since that first wedding day? Now my dear friends and acquaintances, I greet you on my 70th birthday. Move on with courage until we have overcome! Someday we will be rewarded for having fought the good fight, for the pure in heart shall see God.[4]

–Peter Gűnther

Peter Guenther was my grandfather on my father's side. He died at the age of eighty and was buried in the Corn, Oklahoma, cemetery. See Appendix B.

[4] I found this article in Peter's journal written in Gothic German script. My thanks to Hans and Frieda Kasdorf for translating it.

Chapter 10
Janzen's New Home

After the decision was made by the Janzen family to move from Kansas (chapter six), Jacob returned to the Oklahoma Territories in 1893 to file a claim for homesteading one of the many parcels still available among the Cheyenne-Arapaho people. With the help of a friend who had already filed a claim and knew which land in Washita county might still be available, Jacob found an acreage he decided would be suitable for farming. The tract was four miles southwest (one mile east of the Washita River) of what is now the town of Corn, Oklahoma.

The next day Jacob rode out to the land office in the town of Cloud Chief to file the necessary papers for the quarter section he hoped to homestead. When he returned he showed them to his friend who carefully looked them over and exclaimed, "They have spelled your name wrong, Jacob! The name on these papers is *Johnson*, not Janzen."

"No, not really," Jacob groaned in disbelief. "How can it be?" he said to his friend in Low German. "The clerk in the recording office asked me what my name was, and I told him as clearly as I could. He must have misunderstood me. He didn't ask me to spell it out. Could it be that he had never heard the name *Janzen* before and thought I said *Johnson*?"

Early the next morning, Jacob returned to Cloud Chief to see if he could correct the error. He was told it was too late. The papers had already been sent to Guthrie, the city which was then the seat of government for the Oklahoma Territories.[1]

As he rode back to his home in Kansas, he was annoyed with himself for not having caught the error, but also afraid that if he had tried to pursue the issue of making the correction he might lose his land. When he told Karolina what had happened, she was more than just a little upset. She kept saying to Jacob, "Are you telling me that from now on we will be known as the *Johnson* family? How could you have made such a mistake? Why did you not check the papers before you left that land office? How are we going to explain this to our relatives and neighbors? Some will think we changed it because we want to be thought of as *English* people rather than Germans. Think of all the people we will have to notify that our name has been changed."

Jacob tried again and again to help Karolina understand that there was nothing he could do. It would be impossible to make the correction now. "I know I was careless. I should have done this, and I should have done that. But it's too late. We just have to live with our new name. We have no choice." After weeks of arguing back and forth, discussing the matter up and down, raising their voices one day, and calmly contemplating the change the next, it was finally decided to live with the name *Johnson*.

All settlers knew, that according to government regulations, they would lose their homesteads within six months from the time of filing unless there was evidence of work being done on the land. Jacob and Karolina were not able to pull up stakes in Kansas until a year after filing their claim, so Jacob made several trips from Kansas to build a sod house and prepare for the family's move.

---

[1]This is at least one account of how the family name, from that time on, became Johnson, as it is to this day.

The move from Kansas was made with horses and wagons. Jacob took pride in owning the best horses in the county. Draft horses were thought to be best suited for both riding and working the fields. The most popular of the breed were the Clydesdales. Jacob's horses were probably not Clydesdales, but were beautiful Bays, strong enough to pull several tons of cargo on wagons fifteen to twenty feet long. Jacob and Karolina and family, like the Guenther family before them, made the trek from Kansas along the Chisholm Trail, fording the same dangerous rivers as they made their way to their new home.

The farm on which the Johnsons settled clung to the edge of Coffee Creek, with a ravine making its way right through the middle of the acreage. Jacob had built their sod house on the brow of the hill to prevent the possibility of the Creek flooding it during heavy rain storms. The house consisted of one room with a dirt floor. A curtain separated the kitchen and eating area from the sleeping area. A loft was cleverly built on one end of the house. A potbelly stove kept the whole house warm during the cold months of winter. At the time Jacob and Karolina lived in this small house they had six children. The four girls slept in the loft, while Peter and baby Jacob slept on the main floor with their parents.

Over the years, God blessed Jacob and Karolina with twelve children. All grew to adulthood except little Maria who died at age two, just two years after the family moved to the Corn community.

The family slowly accumulated the usual farm animals. These provided much of the milk, butter, eggs and meat for their table. The Johnson children all learned to work while very young: milking and feeding the cows, gathering eggs, feeding the chickens and hogs, helping in the fields.

In the meantime, Jacob and his boys began breaking the prairie sod of deep rooted buffalo grass and experimenting with the kinds of crops that would do best in the rich red soil. They soon discovered that sorghum, a crop from which molasses was made, did well. The Johnson family not only grew the crop, but started processing molasses from it, a process that was very labor-intensive. After the sorghum crop was ready for harvesting, each stalk was stripped of its leaves and the head of seeds cut off. The seeds could be fed to the hogs or chickens. The stalks, which could be from six to 12 feet long and two inches in diameter at their base, were cut as close to the ground as possible. The canes were then loaded onto a wagon and taken to a press where the juice was squeezed out. The Johnson's press was homemade and powered by horses walking in a circle, turning the wheels of the press. The juice was then poured into large iron kettles and a fire built under them slowly brought the juice to a boil and it turned into a syrup of just the right consistency. All the while, the kettle had to be stirred and tended.

Karolina Koehn Johnson, 1861-1917

Karolina did the cooking. She took great pride in making the best molasses in the county. No one else was allowed to touch her kettles. So she stood by the stove, built specially for the purpose, for hours, sometimes late into the night, tending the syrup. When the cooking process was completed, the clear brown liquid was cooled and stored in fifty gallon barrels in an outdoor cellar until it was sold. The result was a sweet syrup good for many sweetening purposes, but was especially good on home-made biscuits. This would have been a profitable venture except for the years of drought when there were no crops to be harvested.

Helena, the oldest in the family, learned to work in the field with horses while still very young. She often spent the day following the plow or cultivator with a team of horses. She once said that working the fields with horses at her young age was something she never complained about. She thought of it as a normal part of farm life.

She remembered well the day she was working on the back forty, preparing the field for a crop of sorghum. The acreage was just over the crest of a hill where no one from the house could see her and she could see no one. If an accident happened it would go unnoticed. One day she was working the field with a harrow and a team of four horses. Holding the eight lines of the horses' harnesses in her little hands, she diligently followed the harrow until she felt like her short legs would not carry her another step. It was late in the day when she came to the end of the field and made the mistake of turning too short. As she did, one end

The Jacob and Karolina Johnson Family.
Left to Right, Back Row: Carrie, Jacob I., Peter, Helena, Elizabeth and Susanna.
Front Row: Katie, Henry, Father Jacob, David, Mother Karolina, Eva and Lydia.

of the harrow flipped over and flew high into the air, landing on the horses' backs. She was paralyzed with fear knowing that when something like this happened, the horses would usually panic and start running with no one to stop them. Instead, the horses just stood there, but both Helena and the horses were shaking like leaves in the Oklahoma wind. After she had recovered from her fright she slowly and carefully approached the horses,

Johnson Family home in Corn, Oklahoma

lifted the harrow off their backs, untangled it, and continued harrowing. She said later, "It was a miracle; God was watching over me that day."

Eighteen-Ninety-Five was a drought year in Oklahoma. The years of drought affected all the pioneers in the area, but it was especially difficult for Jacob and Karolina. They had come a year later than many of the other Mennonite homesteaders and had not had time to establish themselves. The drought was so serious that the church in Corn organized cottage prayer meetings to pray for rain. Although Jacob and Karolina were not Christians at the time, they took part in the prayer meetings. It is not known whether the prayer meetings

Tent Revival held by the Mennonite Brethren Church in Corn, Oklahoma

brought rain, but it is a matter of record that soon thereafter, Jacob and Karolina opened their hearts to Jesus Christ during a tent revival meeting held by the Corn Church. Two years later they were baptized by Elder Isaac Harms and were accepted as members of the Corn Mennonite Brethren Church.

Jacob and Karolina's conversion led to a whole new lifestyle for the Johnson family. Church now became a major focus of their lives. In spite of the long hours in the fields and in homemaking, they found time to set aside that first day of the week for worship and for the renewal of their spiritual and physical well being. They could not understand how it happened, but it seemed as if they got more done working six days a week than seven.

In addition to the 160 acre homestead the Johnsons farmed, they also rented land from their Arapaho Indian neighbors who were not farmers, and were glad to be able to rent out the160 acre parcels the government had given them. The Johnsons soon befriended many of their Indian neighbors. Jacob was gifted in music and had learned to play the guitar, harmonica, and other instruments. The family often spent evenings singing together while Jacob played an instrument. On Sunday afternoons they went to their neighboring Indian villages where they sat among them, singing Gospel hymns, and playing instruments. Their audience was always pleased to have them come. Jacob often made the comment, "We were told that these were the most savage and wild Indians in the west. Now they are our friends, and we have the privilege of sharing the Gospel with them."

The Johnson family lived in the Oklahoma Territories fourteen years. During that time the seat of government had moved from Guthrie to Oklahoma City, and in 1907 the Territories gained statehood. A year later Jacob stood at another crossroad in his life's journey. Jacob did not think they could economically survive another year of crop failure. He had heard that there was good, rich land available in Michigan. His older brother Cornelius and his family together with several other Mennonite families had already made the move to a rural area near Nolan, in Roscommon County.

One evening Jacob proposed to Karolina the possibility of a move to Michigan. She immediately became very skeptical about such a huge undertaking. After weeks of thinking and praying and letters from Cornelius, Karolina finally agreed. Jacob immediately called his family together and announced, "It's time for us to pull up stakes here in Oklahoma. I have heard that there are several Mennonite families moving to Michigan. Your mother and I believe we ought to join them."

"Michigan?" the whole family asked in shock. "Where is Michigan?"

Johnson Family home in Corn, Oklahoma.
Note the guitar and the phonograph with two horns.

Papa pulled out a map, pointed to the general area to which they would be moving, and with an impatient manner said, "Here – far to the north, near the Canadian border. Do you see it on the map?"

"Why Michigan?" the children cried like they usually did when they were being told something they did not want to hear. "All our friends are here. How about our classes in school? This is where most of us were born. We don't want to move to a new place." They offered a dozen reasons why they thought moving was a bad idea.

With a stern and serious voice Papa said, "We have planted fourteen crops here in Oklahoma, and harvested only seven. I am told that in Michigan there are no crop failures. Mama and I feel God is leading us to make this move and we would like to have the support of all our children. Think and pray about it."

The children sat in shocked silence as they began to think about all the changes such a move would involve. They soon started to think of the move as an exciting adventure. Helena however spoke up one day, "You can move if you must, but I will stay here in Corn. I am twenty-one years old. I will find work here and live with friends."

What her father did not know was that Helena had discovered that a handsome young man from church was in love with her. This young man had not, however, actually expressed his love in a tangible way. She was concerned that she would probably lose him if she moved away. She also knew that her family needed her. Would her rebellious spirit prevail?

Jacob and Carolina Johnson

Chapter 11
A Far Away Wooded Land

In February of 1908, the Johnson family said goodbye to their many friends in Oklahoma and boarded the train that transported immigrant families together with their household items and farm animals. It would take them to their new home in Nolan, Michigan. In spite of finding it hard to break ties with her friends in Corn, Helena had decided to move with them.

They arrived in the small lumber town of West Branch where Cornelius and other members of his family met them with sleds and horses. Their household goods were loaded onto the larger sleds while Jacob, Karolina and their children crowded onto a smaller one. They were on their way to their new home twenty miles to the south. It was snowing so hard that they could not see a trace of a road, nor the rugged countryside of underbrush and huge stumps of trees.

The entourage was about half way to its destination when a single-tree broke – a serious problem.[1] It was like breaking the drive shaft from a car's engine to its wheels. Everything came to a standstill. So there they were, in the middle of a Michigan snow storm, with no help in sight. For these Oklahomans, accustomed to temperatures near one-hundred degrees in the summer, the cold and snow were almost unbearable.

However, with the ingenuity of experienced pioneers, the men found a tree branch of hardwood, got out their pocket knives, and whittled a new single-tree while the rest of the folks took shelter under a large broken tree limb. Before long the procession of sleds was again on its way. At last they arrived at the newly-built two-story home of Uncle Cornelius Janzen where they were greeted with Aunt Mary's warm smile and a table loaded with food for the hungry travelers.

Jacob and Peter Johnson
pulling out a tree stump in Michigan.

When Jacob made the decision to move his family to the far north, he did not realize that Michigan would have pioneering challenges of its own. The move was, in itself, a monumental task. A new home would have to be built. The long, cold winters and mountains of snow would have to be endured. And that was only the beginning. The area to which Jacob intended to move was heavily forested and the land, although fertile, was permeated with rocks. The trees would need to be

---

[1]A single-tree is a wooden bar about two feet long, swung at the center from a hitch on the sled and hooked at either end to the traces of a horse's harness.

Jacob and Karolina Johnson's home in Nolan, Michigan

cut down and their stumps removed one by one.   After the ground was cleared, the surface rocks would need to be picked up, put on a wagon and hauled away. Each spring thaw would push new rocks to the surface of the farm land and would need to be gathered again. There were so many stones piled in a long line that eventually they formed a rock fence along the border of their farm.

Jacob and Karolina's small, two-story house was built with the help of relatives and neighbors. The lower floor included a kitchen and bedroom for Mom and Dad. The upper floor had two bedrooms; one for the girls and one for the boys. They, of course, had no electricity or telephone. Water had to be hauled in on wagons and stored in fifty gallon barrels near the house.

Nolan, Michigan, School House

Logs harvested from Johnson farm in Nolan, Michigan

There was a small country school house about a half mile from the Johnson's new home. The fifteen Mennonite families that had located in the area used the schoolhouse on Sundays as their place of worship. They were soon joined by pioneers of German Baptist descent and formed an organized church.

The German families that had moved to the Nolan area had large families. The parents of these families soon realized that these children would need an education and Christian training. After the Johnson family was settled, Helena was asked to teach these children the Bible and the German language. She also taught them to sing in four-part harmony. They soon formed a choir which sang at the church's revival meetings.

Clearing the land of trees and pulling the huge stumps so it could be farmed occupied the daylight hours of the men that first winter. Jacob learned from his more experienced neighbors that the only way to remove the stumps was to use dynamite. So one cold winter morning they opened their first keg of dynamite only to find it was frozen. They were advised by their neighbors that it could be thawed by putting it in the oven of the kitchen stove. Following these instructions, Jacob spread the sticks of dynamite out on a large baking pan and put them in the kitchen oven, closed the door and added more wood to the firebox. He then left the house to take care of some chores, forgetting about the dynamite in the oven.

In the meantime Karolina came into the kitchen carrying two buckets of water from the barrel outside the house. She immediately detected a strange odor and smoke coming from her oven. The moment she opened the oven door, the dynamite burst into flames. At the risk of her life she threw the water she was carrying into the oven. It kept the dynamite from exploding. The flames, however, quickly spread into other parts of the kitchen.

While all this was happening, the menfolk were busy with other chores in the barn when Peter, the oldest son in the family, happened to glance up.

"Our house is on fire!" Peter yelled at the top of his voice.

The men immediately dropped everything they were doing and ran to the house. Flames could be seen through the window shooting up from the kitchen stove to the ceiling.

Their first concern was for mother and the girls who had immediately vacated the house and were standing in the yard looking with awe and disbelief as they watched the house quickly being engulfed with flames. Attempts were made to draw more water from the water barrels nearby, but everyone soon realized that their efforts were in vain.

At the risk of their lives, Jacob and the older boys broke through the front door and rescued a few items of furniture. But by this time the precious reed organ, around which the family had gathered so often to sing had begun to succumb to the red-hot fire. The flames soon found the stairwell, engulfing the entire house and destroying most of the furniture upstairs and down, including their clothing and bedding. All the family could do was stand by and watch in shocked disbelief as the fire finally burned itself out. It appeared that there was nothing left of their home except a few lonely pieces of furniture they had rescued earlier. With tears streaming down her face Karolina cried, "It is all gone. Everything we have worked so hard to accumulate to make life easier is destroyed." She then remembered that she had stored some bedding in her sister-in-law's house. But that brought little comfort compared to the tragic loss which mocked her as she stood watching.

Helena, in one of her journals, wrote about the results of the fire:

I had nothing left than what I had on and one dress downstairs in the wash. That day I had even forgotten my watch, all my pictures from Korn, Oklahoma – pictures I had received in the Academy and from friends. Everything was gone in smoke. Also some money I had saved from teaching. We found a few melted pieces of gold from my watch and chain. The watch had been a Christmas gift from Dad.

The Johnson family stayed with relatives that night. The next day the relatives and members of the church the Johnsons attended were at the scene of the horrible disaster. They helped salvage what they could, cleared away the parts of the house that were beyond repair, and helped rebuild it, using lumber from the trees surrounding the farmstead.

Jacob soon realized that his moment of carelessness would follow him the rest of his life. Karolina never recovered from the affects of the disaster. Soon thereafter her health began to deteriorate. With few tests available to diagnose her symptoms, the doctor suggested it was probably cancer. If it was cancer there were few options available for treatment. Many believed that surgery was absolutely the worst option, because once doctors started cutting a tumor, it would only spread. Several suggested home remedies like drinking grape juice and eating nuts and other fruit. Karolina tried them all, but her health continued to deteriorate. Since there were few medications available, her pain was, at times, almost unbearable. Her doctor suggested that perhaps a drier climate and higher elevation might help.

During this time the family had heard that a group of Mennonites was moving to the farming community of Texline, Texas. The town was located on the border of New Mexico and the most remote northwest corner of the Texas Panhandle. It was about as far removed from any big city as a mid-western prairie town could be, and had no medical facilities, doctors, schools or churches. But with an elevation of 3,500 feet and a dry climate, it matched exactly what Karolina's doctor had suggested. Jacob had learned that the land was rich and well-suited for farming corn, maize, and sorghum – the same crops he had farmed in Oklahoma. They had endured the hardships of pioneer life before, and they could do it again.

After nine years in Michigan, while America was fighting World War I in Europe,

Jacob and Karolina were fighting their own battle, racing against time to see if the spread of Karolina's cancer could be halted. One day in 1917 they loaded the few household items they had replaced after the fire, and their farm equipment, onto an immigrant train and began to make their way to their new farmstead in Texline, Texas. It was a sad day for the family as it left behind their beautiful northland home and their brothers and sisters from their church. The parents and their youngest child, Eva, boarded a train for the long trip south. Three of the older sons, and daughters Katharina and Lydia, traveled in the family's one-year-old car. Peter and the four oldest girls in the family had already married. Susanna, age 19, stayed behind in Michigan.

Those who traveled by car had no maps for the trip of more than 1,200 miles, so they had to ask for directions from one town to the next. Even though it was a new car, they had several flat tires due to many rough roads. They had to fix the flats themselves. They decided to extravagantly spend one night in a hotel at the cost of $3.00.

By the time of the move, Elizabeth, the second oldest of the Johnson children, had married Peter Rogalsky. The young family was living in Corn, Oklahoma. Upon hearing of Karolina's health condition, they decided to join the family in Texline, making the move by covered wagon. They cooked their own food each day. One morning Elizabeth made pancakes (a real treat) but happened to drop them on the ground before they got onto each one's plate. It was really no problem. She simply washed then off and re-fried them. Smothered in the home-made sorghum molasses, they were as delicious as ever. As they slowly made their way across the prairie they sometimes stopped at farm houses for water and feed for the horses. Many times they were invited to spend the night; others simply turned them away. Although it was a trip of more than 400 miles, they arrived at their new home just two hours after the car from Michigan got there.

While in Texline, the Johnson family relived all the hardships of pioneer life they had experienced in their previous moves: building new homes and barns, opening the prairie sod for the first time, planting new crops. Lumber

Peter Rogalsky marries
Elizabeth Johnson

and materials had to be hauled from stores more than fifty miles away. Water wells, more than 300 feet deep, had to be drilled. Even then, many wells were dry, so water had to be hauled from neighboring wells to meet the needs of the family and livestock. Because of the scarcity of water, there was no indoor bathroom, neither was there any electricity. The wind blew days without end. It was said that if a heavy chain was hung from a pole, the wind was often so strong the chain flew horizontal to the ground, as if it were a flag.

Mennonite Brethren families from all parts of the mid-west continued to move to the Texline community for the next fifteen years. They eventually organized a Mennonite church. As time and money allowed, the men came together to build a meeting house. Because of the strong winds, most of the building was underground like a basement with only about three feet above ground for windows to let in the light. Many houses were built in the same fashion.

A ten-year drought across much of Arkansas, Oklahoma and the Texas panhandle began in 1920. By that time much of the prairie land in these states had been opened for farming. The drought, together with high winds, created what came to be known as the Dust Bowl days. The wind blew for days, stirring up the open top soil. The dust in the air became so heavy at times that no matter how these pioneers tried to keep it out of their homes, it found its way inside. They tried stuffing sheets or clothing into the cracks around the windows and doors. The dust still found its way inside. Outside, the dust was so thick that if a farmer was caught out on the back forty, there was a chance he would not be able to find his way home.

As the drought continued across the mid-western states year after year, crop failures caused many thousands of farmers to lose their farms. Many moved to California. John Steinbeck, in his book, *Grapes of Wrath*, tells the story accurately. Among those who moved elsewhere were the Mennonites of Texline, Texas. The church closed its doors in 1940.

As indicated earlier, the reason the Johnson family moved from Michigan to Texline was because of Karolina's health problems. Even if the drier climate and higher elevation might have improved her health condition, the move came too late. In the weeks that followed Karolina began to feel the effects of her prolonged illness. It is said the night the family dog went to her bed and shook hands with her, as if to say goodbye. On that night of May 6, 1917, at the age of fifty-five, just a month after they had made the move, the family gathered around her bed as they wept, sang hymns and prayed. As she passed into the presence of the Lord she whispered words from a familiar hymn, *"O Mein Jesu, Du bist's wert! Meine Seele jauchzt Dir zu,"* (O My Jesus, My soul delights in Thee).

There were no undertakers or burial grounds in the area. The next day Jacob built a coffin of pine boards while the boys dug a grave in a corner of Elizabeth and Peter Rogalsky's farm. There was no church leader to perform a funeral service so the family and neighbors gathered around the grave site as Jacob read passages from the Bible, spoke a few words, and committed her body to the grave with the confident assurance of the resurrection of all who believe in Jesus Christ as their Savior and a glorious reunion in heaven.[2]

Jacob grieved deeply for his dear wife of thirty-one years. He also soon realized that he could not care for his family and do all the work demanded of a pioneer in a strange, new land. God graciously brought him together with widow Anna Funk Bartel, age forty-four. She had given birth to ten children before her husband had died. Her children were grown and on their own by this time. Jacob and Anna were married December 23, 1917, in Boyd, Oklahoma, eight months after Karolina died.

In spite of having found a new spouse, things were never the same for Jacob. His grief could not be assuaged. On February 11, 1920, just shy of three years after Karolina died, Jacob passed into the presence of his Savior, at the age of fifty-five (as had Karolina). As he did so, Jacob H. Johnson heard in the distant Texas wind the words from the hymn Karolina had whispered two years earlier.

---

[2]Karolina's grave was later moved to the Texline cemetery.

Tenderly you look at me.
Calling that I come and see;
Calling, I may come to you and see.

From this world, Lord, rend me loose;
Make my faith and trust increase,
Grant to me a faithful mind,
Take me wholly, Lord, I'm Thine.
--Text: M. Gurke, Translator: Hans Kasdorf

Jacob was buried beside his beloved Karolina in the Texline cemetery. He and Karolina Koehn Johnson were my grandparents on my mother's side. (See Appendix A)

Headstone at grave of Jacob H.
and Corlina Johnson, Texline, Texas.

Anna Funk Bartel Johnson (second
wife) and Jacob H. Johnson.

Chapter 12
Looking Back – Life in the Town of Corn

The community which became known as Corn, Oklahoma, was indeed at the edge of civilization in the 1890s. It was originally a part of the Oklahoma Territories. Those who homesteaded around Corn were almost all German Mennonites from South Russia who had migrated to Kansas and from there to the Corn vicinity. These people spoke *High German* in their church services and *Plautdietsch* (Low German, the vernacular of North Germany) in their homes, on the street, or while visiting with relatives.

In its beginning, the town was known as Korn, spelled with a "K" since that was the way corn (a field crop) was spelled in German. It is said that the town was given its name by a government agent who chose to have a post office built there. The agent noticed that a small patch of corn had been planted next to the new post office and decided the town should be called Korn, the way it was spelled in German. Spell it Korn or Corn. It did not matter until World War I when America went to war with Germany. Americans of German descent, opting not to go to war or bear arms, were not very popular at that moment in history. That is when the town fathers changed the spelling from Korn to Corn.

The open prairie of Washita county to which the Mennonites came wore a facade of tough, impenetrable grass. It had been trampled by the feet of a million buffalo over hundreds of years and defied being rooted up and turned over by even the most determined and resolute pioneers. The average farmer would have given up in an attempt to tame the soil. But not these German-Russian Mennonite settlers. They had tackled the unrelenting grasslands of Kansas and Nebraska and had won. They would bring the rebellious buffalo grass of the Oklahoma Territories under their control. And when they did, they would discover a rich red soil beneath its thick facade, which when sown with the hard, red wheat seed brought from Russia, would yield crops that multiplied one-hundredfold.

The battle against the tough grass was won acre by acre as one homesteader, and then another, gave himself to the conflict. With nothing more than a crude plow and a team of horses they tackled the back-breaking task of preparing the soil for planting. Eventually thousands of acres of wheat, corn, sorghum, and other crops spread across the prairie and produced some of the highest yielding crops in the territory.

The settlers learned, after a few planting seasons, that a major obstacle for a good harvest was the weather. A good crop depended entirely on getting the right amount of rain at the right time. The mid-western weather was as indifferent to producing good harvests as a turtle was to crossing the road. The rain might come in great abundance and flood the crops, or it might not come at all. And even if it did come as needed, and raise the hopes of the farmers by producing a beautiful field of ripening grain, a hailstorm could come the night before harvest and wipe out the entire crop. During the first fifteen years only about half the crops planted by the homesteaders produced a harvest.

The spring of the year usually brought its share of turbulent weather. It was not uncommon for the weather to bring drenching thunderstorms, hail the size of baseballs, lightning striking a man working in the field, or a tornado ripping across the landscape and destroying everything in its path. Washita County soon came to be known as *Tornado Alley*.

These weather storms were feared and dreaded by all, but were completely out of the control of any man.

In spite of the incredibly hard work involved in preparing the land for farming, the unstable weather, and the years of drought, the persistent settlers endured and put down family roots as deep as those of a mighty oak. What was it that sustained them during those tough early years? Grandpa Peter Guenther would have said it was the Mennonite Church. Life was hard on the prairie. The years of drought took an enormous financial toll on the homesteaders. The lack of medical care resulted in the premature deaths of children and adults alike. As in former generations, the church stood in the gap to help with financial burdens and to meet the emotional, social, and spiritual needs of the people. The church encouraged its people to look beyond their immediate hardships and problems, to look up to God in praise for His blessings, and to express their faith with joy and in singing.

Almost as soon as these Mennonite families arrived in Washita County in 1893, they began church meetings in the sod homes they had built for themselves. They met for Sunday morning and evening services, and for prayer meetings on Wednesday nights. The first sixteen Mennonite Brethren families that initially moved to Corn soon drew up a formal charter in which they pledged to band together as a church for worship, fellowship, and mission. The church was legally incorporated in 1901.

They built their first meetinghouse in 1894, a year after the pioneers began to arrive. It was a sod-dugout, dug by hand four feet below ground level and standing four feet above ground level. Its size was forty feet east and west, and twenty feet north and south. They used only enough lumber to support the sod roof. The dugout had a few small windows, and a door at each end. The men used the west door, and the women entered from the east. The interior included a platform and pulpit for the preacher and the choir, and wooden benches for the congregation. This, their first meeting- house, was dedicated on Thanksgiving Day in 1894. The total cash outlay was $25.00.

Dug-out Meeting House of the Corn Mennonite Brethren Church

The Church, defined as the people who made up its congregation, and its meetinghouse, became the focus of the Corn community. Many of its members sacrificed the necessities of daily living to maintain their meetinghouse as a vital presence among them. Their first crude dugout was soon too small to accommodate the increasing number of new homesteaders. Four years later, it was replaced by a wood frame structure. In 1918 a new, larger building was erected and served the congregation until 1949. On January 16, 1949, it was destroyed by fire. The congregation immediately banded together to construct a building of brick and mortar that would seat up to 1,000 persons, and stood high enough to be seen from miles around. From its humble beginnings, this Mennonite Brethren Church became a beacon of the light of the Gospel in what became the town of Corn.

The Peter Guenther family (my grandparents on my father's side) came to Washita County when the Territory was opened to homesteaders in 1893. They immediately became active members of the Mennonite Brethren church. Grandfather Peter became one of its first deacons. In those days a deacon was ordained for life, so Peter continued in this strong leadership role the remainder of his life. Because of his own experience in the loss of his first two spouses and several children, he had a special place in his heart for ministering to the widows and orphans, a service to which he gave himself with dedication and love. As a deacon, he also assisted in the open air baptismal services conducted on a regular basis by the church.

One of the stories of Peter's deaconing years has been passed on to my generation. In those days most Mennonite Brethren churches used wine in the service of Communion. Deacon Guenther, so the story goes, was "keeper of the wine." As we all know, that part of Oklahoma was subject to tornado weather. Every family built a *storm cellar* close to their house. Peter decided that his storm cellar would be an excellent place to store and hide the Communion wine. Unfortunately, word ultimately leaked out as to the location of this hiding place. One Sunday night, while everyone else was in the meetinghouse, some of the young people from the church visited Deacon Guenther's farm and raided the storm cellar. The next day the church called a special meeting to deal with the villainous culprits who had committed this unspeakable wickedness. It was decided at the same meeting, that henceforth just plain grape juice would replace wine at all Communion services.

The Corn Church held a strong conviction that the education of their children in their own church school was important. So in 1902 the Church opened its doors to the Corn Bible Academy, a preparatory school including elementary and high school grade levels. By this time, Jacob and Karolina Johnson (my grandparents on my mother's side) had become active members of the Corn Church. So when the Academy opened, one of its first students was their oldest child, Helena. She was already eight years old by this time. But no matter. Even if the Academy had been opened earlier, Helena was needed at home to help with the chores, school or no school.

In 1903, ten years after the first homesteaders arrived, and a year after Corn Bible Academy was opened, the main street of the township of Corn came to life. As indicated above, the town became the site of a United States post office. Various businesses followed, including a grocery store, a hardware store, and a café. Corn soon became the business hub of the farming community. A printing press began publishing a weekly newspaper. Gas stations were opened as motorized vehicles became popular. My uncle, Peter B. Guenther, opened a milk and cream store and bought the café which he and his wife, Elisabeth, operated for many years.

Through the years, the town of Corn, and its farming environs, continued to thrive. Farms grew larger and more productive. Farm equipment was modernized. But, alas, Washita County ran out of land. And because of bigger tractors, seeders, and harvesters, fewer farmers were needed. In spite of it all, the town of Corn has remained the hub of its farm community to the day of this writing. The café is still open. The printing office still publishes its weekly newspaper. Corn Bible Academy still has its doors open. The cemetery still opens its grave sites to those who have gone to be with the Lord.

Peter Guenther died November 17, 1927, at the age of 80, just fifteen days after I was born. I was not privileged to see or know my most remarkable Grandfather. Peter's body was buried in the Mennonite Brethren church cemetery in Corn, Oklahoma, but his soul now dwells in the mansion prepared for him in the presence of his Lord and Savior, Jesus Christ.

Corn Bible Academy, 1905.

Chapter 13
Summary of Part I

"We are on a spiritual journey. Journeys don't go around the block. That's known territory. Journeys infer distance and often take us to new, challenging, scary, surprising, beautiful and exciting places. Are we willing to go on this journey or do we want to continue circling the comfortable, dependable, maybe even boring block? Might we miss perceiving how the glory of the Lord can be expressed innovatively in this complex world?

"The scriptures tell us Jesus went on a journey. He set his face as a flint and headed for Jerusalem. Sometimes our journeys take us where we don't want to go, but we know that a fellow traveler is with us and will guide us into all truth and even unto death. 'Call unto me and I will show you new and hidden things which you have not known before,' (Jeremiah 33:3).'"
–Margaret Gray Towne, from *Honest to Genesis*

Prussia, Russia, America. It was an incredible journey, encircling half the globe, involving as many as eight generations, and spanning four centuries. Each crossroad in the journey involved new beginnings and presented new and difficult challenges.

Even the generation which ultimately reached America's shores soon realized that the road ahead was fraught with unprecedented peril. Nebraska, Kansas, Oklahoma, Michigan and Texas, all States in which my grandparents sojourned, were in many ways more demanding than the ones they had left behind in the old country.

For each generation, it meant leaving behind parents, spouses and children because of death. Each loved one left behind was like a freshly etched grave stone buried in the hard, cold earth. They were there somewhere, but could not be seen, or found, or taken along.

Ties had to be broken with extended family, beloved brothers and sisters in the church, trusted friends and neighbors. Each one was left like a valued garment from one's closet, not missed until it is needed, but too late to retrieve.

Each new beginning left a feeling of emptiness; someone and something was missing. It was like striking out across the hot desert without water, or being lost in a dense forest without food or compass.

The path they chose at each crossroad finally led to a predetermined destination where:

> new ground was broken,
> > new homes were built,
> > > new seeds were sown,
> > > > new churches were planted,
> > > > > new ties with friends and neighbors were made.

So life went on: through shadow and sunshine, through sorrow and joy, through trial and triumph, through poverty and plenty. Each new dwelling place had its own challenges; no two were the same.

So the question I have asked over and over is, "Why? What was it that drove my forebearers from place to place like wandering nomads, or perhaps more like Abraham, in search of a *'city that has foundations?'"* Hebrews 11:10 (NLT).

Perhaps the underlying reason for their sojourn was a burning desire for freedom to express their faith according to their understanding of the Scriptures. For this they were willing either to lay down their lives or migrate from country to country. The light for their journey was carried in a torch which was fueled by a high view of God and the Scriptures, the need for confessing Jesus Christ as Savior, and living a life consistent with their faith. Yes, some stumbled and faltered along the way, but there were always those who picked up the torch, even when its flame seemed almost extinguished, and handed it off to the next generation.

For their journey they packed the basic essentials, not money or material things, but faith, hope, courage and determination. They had armed themselves, not with armor or shield, but with the very fabric of any strong culture: undisputable moral values, a vibrant church, a commitment to strong family life, and hard work. Their conduct and lifestyle spoke a clearer message than their words. Their message has sounded across the years and speaks to us today. ...

"Those who are wise
Will take all this to heart,
They will see in our history
The faithful love of the Lord,"
(Psalm 107:48 NLT).

As I look back and reread the history of the countries from which my ancestors sojourned, especially in Poland and Russia, I have drawn the conclusion that my forefathers made the right choices. By leaving when they did they were spared the inevitable loss of religious freedom, persecution, and starvation experienced by many who stayed behind. As pioneers in America, they experienced indescribable hardship, but their persistence, steadfastness of purpose, and hard work eventually produced a harvest of spiritual and material prosperity of which I and my family became the beneficiaries. For this I am eternally grateful.

Appendix A
Peter Jantz – John Wesley Gunther Family Tree*

1. Peter Jantz Note: Deacon in Przechowka congregation
     Spouse, _____ _____ (not known)
     b. 1650, Przechowka, Prussia
     d. _____ _____
    2. Cornels Jantz
         Spouse, _____ _____
         b. Abt. 1680, Przechowka, Prussia
         d. _____ _____, Przechowka, Prussia
        3. Jan Jantz
             (Spouse: Ancka Decker)
             b. Abt. 1705, Schoeness, Grosswerder, Prussia
             d. _____ _____
            4. **Cornelius "Cornels" Jantz**
                 (Spouse: Trudcke Machitgahls)
                 b. 5 Dec. 1739, Schoensee, Grossweder, Prussia
                 d. 6 Aug. 1803, Jeziorka, Prussia
5. **Peter Jantz**
     Spouse, _____ _____
     b. 4 Oct. 1766, Jeziorka, Prussia
     d. 10 Sept. 1835, _____ _____
    6. Tobias Jantz
         (Spouse: **Sara Koehn**)
         b. 18 Jul. 1801, Jadvinin, Vohlynia (West Russia) Note: Migration to Russia
         d. 4 Aug. 1846, _____ _____
        7. **Heinrich F. Jantz (Janzen)**, Note: Name Change
             (Spouse: **Helena Thomas**)
             b. 23 Aug. 1839, Karolswalde, Vohlynia
             d. 18 Mar. 1905, Corn Oklahoma, Note: Migration to USA
            8. **Jacob H Janzen (Johnson)**, Note: Name Change
                 (Spouse: **Karolina Koehn**)
                 b. 11 Feb. 1865, Karolswalde, Vohlynia
                 d. 11 Feb. 1920 Texline, Texas
9. **Helena Janzen (Johnson)**
     (Spouse: John P. Guenther)
     b. 28 Feb. 1887, Moundridge, Kansas
     d. 26 Feb. 1975, Reedley, California
    10. John Wesley Gunther
         (Spouse: Beverly Jane Gunther)
         b. 2 Nov. 1927, Kerman, California

*Source: Grandma 4, Genealogical Registry and Database of Mennonite Ancestry, California Mennonite Historical Society, 2002

Note: Names in bold print prominent in my story. –J. Wesley Gunther

Appendix B
Johann Guenther (1826) to Roger William Gunther*

1. Johann Guenther
   (Spouse: Helena Goertzen)
   b. 29 Aug. 1826 (Probably, Molotschna Colony, South Russia)
   d. Probably 1900

2. Children	Born	Died
Maria Guenther	5 Jan. 1842	6 Jan. 1842
Agenatha Guenther	15 Apr. 1844	_____ _____ (Not Known)
Katharina Guenther	30 Oct. 1845	22 Nov. 1850
Peter Guenther**	5 Sep. 1847	17 Nov. 1927
Susanna Guenther	3 Dec. 1849	12 Nov. 1852
Eva Guenther	23 Dec. 1851	5 Apr. 1852
Susanna II Guenther	2 Feb. 1853	_____ 1953
Heinrich Guenther	15 Jul. 1855	(and died)
Elisabeth Guenther**	10 Jan. 1857	_____ _____ (Married Jacob Klass)
Daughter, No Name	23 Jul. 1859	
Son, No Name	8 Dec. 1860	
Annie Guenther**	_____ 1861	_____ _____ (Married a Hiebert)
No Name Daughter	_____ 1866	(and died)

2. Peter Guenther
   (Spouse: Margaretha Peters; 2nd, Katherina Isaak; 3rd, Maria Sawatsky)
   b. 5 Sep. 1847, Ladekop, Molotschna, South Russia
   d. 17 Nov. 1927   Note: Migrated to USA 7 Jun. 1884

3. Johann P. Guenther (John P. Gunther)
   (Spouse: Helena Janzen (Johnson))
   b. 28 Aug. 1882, Prangenau, Moloschna, South Russia
   d. 18 Mar. 1972, Reedley, California

4.	Born	Died
Johanes Gunther	4 Oct. 1909	21 Dec. 1911
Jacob Gunther	16 May 1911	22 Oct. 1994
Alma Gunther	15 Jun. 1912	2 Jul. 2001
Caroline Gunther	16 Aug. 1913	15 Nov. 2006
Martha Gunther	13 Oct. 1915	19 Sep. 1934
Marie Gunther	13 May 1917	22 Sep. 2001
Ernest Gunther	1 Nov. 1918	1 Jun. 1992
Peter Gunther	22 Mar. 1920	7 Feb. 1992
Lydia Gunther	14 Jul. 1921	22 Nov. 2003
Eva Gunther	22 Nov. 1922	23 Jul. 2005
Rubena Gunther	9 Aug. 1924	
J. Wesley Gunther	2 Nov. 1927	

Raymond Gunther	28 Dec. 1928	12 Jun. 1984
Roger Gunther	24 May 1933	14 Aug. 1933
(As of September 1, 2009)		

*Sources: Grandma 4, Genealogical Registry and Database of Mennonite Ancestry, California Mennonite Historical Society, Fresno, California, 2002, and Files of Helena Johnson Gunther in John P. Gunther Archives, John Wesley Gunther, Fresno, California,
**Names of children in bold print are adult survivors of Johann and Helena Guenther

Part II

Joy in the Morning

"Weeping may last for the night,
But joy cometh in the morning"
Psalm 30:5

Introduction to Part II

After graduating from Immanuel High School, my fiancee Beverly Friesen and I attended Tabor College in Hillsboro, Kansas. After three semesters at Tabor we decided to get married. But before we could do so we had to earn some money. So during the spring and summer of 1948, I had the happy privilege of farming with my father, hoping to earn the money I needed to get married and then go back to school. Dad and I had come to an agreement that he would share the profits of the year's crop in exchange for my working the farm with him for ten months. As it turned out, these were the most enjoyable ten months of my growing up years. We spent a lot of time together, talking about many things while working the fields, milking the cows, and doing other chores.

German was my Dad's native language. His parents and the people in his church and neighborhood all spoke German. When they came to America in the 1880s and lived in Nebraska, they didn't have much of an opportunity to go to school to learn a new language.

One day I asked him, "Dad, how did you learn English?"

Dad replied in near perfect English and without an accent. "We spoke only German in our home and church during the years I was growing up. We had learned a little English when we got together and played games with our neighbor's children. When I was old enough to attend school, my older brother Dan and I rode a horse to the schoolhouse during the cold winter days when we could not work on the farm. There were about twenty-five students in a small, one-room schoolhouse, seven miles from where we lived. We were not allowed to speak anything but English at school, so it was hard for us. But it was in that little one-room schoolhouse that I learned to speak, read and write a little. Then our family moved to Kansas and I was never able to continue my English education. From the time we were very small children, we all had to work on the farm. By the time I was of school age, I had already learned to milk cows, feed the chickens and hogs, ride a horse, and work the fields with a team of horses."

Note: After farming those ten months with my father, he handed me a check one day for my share of the crop – $500. I took it and said thank you, never questioning whether it was a fair share, or asking to see the books. He had provided my room and board during those months. I had never lacked for anything. He even allowed me to fill the tank of my car with gas at his gas pump (which was on the farm yard), never questioning how much I used. I always trusted my father to do the right thing in such matters. That is the way he lived his whole life. Beverly and I were married on July 9th of that year (1948). The $500 was enough to pay my share of the wedding expenses, go on a short honeymoon, set up a home (rent free) in the little two-room apartment situated on my father's yard, and get us off to school in Los Angeles in November of that year.

"That is unbelievable," I said. "So what you are telling me is that you went to school for only parts of three years and, yet, your English is near perfect."

Dad continued, "My father was convinced that it was more important to learn how to be a good farmer than to receive a formal education, but learning English is something I continued working at all my life. I practiced it whenever I could: when I went to town to do business, when we got together with friends and, most importantly, after you children went to school and came home speaking English. I listened to you and practiced whenever I could."

"You learned well," I said to my father.

In 1954 my mother bought a game called Scrabble. The popularity of the game had swept across America just a few years earlier. Mom had heard that by using little blocks of wood with letters of the alphabet on them, words could be formed by placing them on a game board. The idea intrigued her because, at age 66, she was still trying to master the English language. All her children were grown and married by then. So during the long winter evenings when she and Dad were home alone, Mother got out her Scrabble game and, with a dictionary at her side, put words together, often until late into the night after Dad had gone to bed. In this and other ways she tried, from her early youth until the day she died, to become proficient in the English language.

"German," she said in her broken English, "was the only language we speak, read or write at home in years I grow up."

She said, "We speak High German when we go to church. We sing, pray and read Bible in High German. Church leaders preach sermons in High German. When we come home we speak Low German (*Plautdietsch*). Except for a few English words, my parents did not know any other language. Learning to speak, read and write in English was something I work at all my life."

Learning English was apparently much harder for my mother than for my father. Mother was also a member of a pioneering family. Being the oldest in her family she had to learn many of the outdoor skills that the boys learned. In addition, she had to learn to cook, clean the house, and help take care of her younger brothers and sisters. In her early years, most of her neighbors were of German descent, so they spoke German when they got together. The family went to church occasionally, but everyone spoke German there as well.

During the years she lived with her family in Michigan, she was asked to teach the young children of families in their small church. She taught elementary subjects and singing – all in the German language. Throughout her adult life she taught the Bible in Sunday School classes for both the young and old and again, most of them in the German language. In spite of the demands of being the mother of a large family, she found time to study the Bible and always came to her classes well prepared.

One day I asked her, "If you didn't learn English in school, and it was not spoken at home or church, how were you ever able to learn English at all?"

"When I was teacher I listen to children when they learn to speak English. When you, my own children, come home from school and speak English, I practice. I say words and sentences I hear from you. I never stop trying to improve. At night I sit with my children and they teach me to write.

In these, and in many other ways, Mom slowly absorbed the English language. For instance, when Dad finally bought a radio in 1935, Mom started listening to radio programs when Dad and all of us children were at work or school. Later in life she finally admitted that on those days when she was home alone she listened to soap operas, the most popular form of daytime radio entertainment in the 1930s and 1940s. Arthur Godfrey was the most popular radio talk show host of the day but he never topped the ratings of such soap operas as *Today's Children*, *The Guiding Light*, *Ma Perkins*, and *Stella Dallas*. She said, "These radio programs help me learn English." (*The Guiding Light* started airing on radio in 1937. It switched to televison in the 1950s. After 72 years, it aired its last program in August of 2009, becoming, to this date, the longest continuously running soap opera in American history.)

In the late 1950s, when Dad brought home their first television set, she was often caught sneaking into their den in the middle of the afternoon, not to take a nap, but to watch *Edge of Night*, a popular soap opera of the day. We all knew she listened to and watched these soaps, not to learn English, but because she enjoyed the programs. We had to admit, though, that they probably did help her English.

Even though Mother spoke English without hesitation when necessary, she found it very difficult to pray in English. Praying in German was her last holdout, the thing she found most difficult to give up, probably because praying is a very intimate way of speaking and she could only bare her soul in her native language. Not that she had any religious scruples about praying in English, but it was only in her later years that she dared to pray in English.

She said, "English is hard. I try every way I can to learn."

Most people whose native language is something other than English seem to concur with my mother's conclusion about learning the language. Perhaps this is one reason:

Why English Is So Hard
We'll begin with a *box*, and the plural is *boxes*;
> But the plural of *ox* should be *oxes*, not *oxen*.
Then one fowl is *goose*, but two are called *geese*;
> Yet the plural of *moose* should never be *meese*.
You may find a lone *mouse* or a whole lot of *mice*,
> But the plural of *house* is *houses*, not *hice*.
If the plural of *man* is always called *men*,
> Why shouldn't the plural of *pan* be called *pen*?
The *cow* in the plural may be *cows* or *kine*,
> But the plural of *vow* is *vows*, not *vine*.
And I speak of a *foot*, and you show me your *feet*,
> But I give you a *boot* – would a pair be called *beet*?
If one is a *tooth* and a whole set are *teeth*,
> Why shouldn't the plural of *booth* be called *beeth*?
If the singular is *this*, and the plural is *these*,
> Should the plural of *kiss* be nicknamed *kese*?
Then one may be *that*, and three may be *those*,
> Yet the plural of *hat* would never be *hose*.
We speak of a *brother*, and also of *brethren*,
> But though we say *mother*, we never say *methren*.
The masculine pronouns are *he*, *his*, and *him*,
> But imagine the feminine *she*, *shis*, and *shim*!
So our English, I think you will all agree,
> Is the trickiest language you ever did see.
>   –Eugene A. Nida, *Learning a Foreign Language*

Mom actually had good penmanship when she wrote something in longhand. I found a copy of something she wrote and it amazes me to realize how beautiful her writing was.

In her later years Dad bought Mom a small portable typewriter. With it she began writing letters and stories, using the hunt and peck system. Some of those earliest stories were a bit difficult to decipher. From the time she got the typewriter she depended on it to do her writing. Most of the files she left behind are written on that typewriter. As I have poured over these stories I found that it is not difficult to tell her early work from the later. Her typing definitely improved over the years.

Before Mother died, she left dozens of pages of vital information and charming stories recounting the past. She wrote dozens of travelogues, collected and typed her favorite recipes, drew up family trees, and kept records of births, baptisms, and deaths. Her journals include information about her seven or eight life-threatening surgeries, the year and model of the various Studebaker cars Dad bought, our family reunions (including who was there and who was not), and wedding anniversary celebrations. She wrote intimately about how it felt to lose two infant sons and one eighteen-year-old daughter. Her stories included the joys of motherhood as well as the hardships of poverty. She left a scrapbook (possibly the forerunner of present-day scrapbooking) with pictures she pasted onto each page with typed stories in English between them, telling what life was like in the good ole days.

While Mother worked so hard at learning English, my deepest regret is that we children did not make an earnest effort to learn her beautiful German language. Sadly, in one generation, we lost it. Although I can understand some of it, I can not speak, read, nor write it, not even the Plautdietsch we spoke at home during my growing up years. Although my son, Jeffery, studied German in college, I lament the fact that I did not even try to pass it on to my children.

I will be forever grateful that my mother never gave up on speaking, reading or writing in the English language. Most of the information for Parts I and II of my story is based on material Mother typed and retyped, stories she told and retold. I will attempt to retell them once more in the pages that follow.

Thank you, Mom. Your loving son, *Vesley*.

Author's footnote: The setting for the chapter that follows is taken out of chronological sequence. You will note that it is written in the form of an interview I had with my parents at the time of their fiftieth wedding anniversary. After that I will go back in time to tell their story in the sequence in which they experienced life, from the days they married and began life together.

The W is pronounced like a V in German. Mom never learned to form the "W" when speaking English, so I was always Vesley instead of Wesley. In telling her story, I will try to retain her speaking and writing style as much as possible. Except when she calls my name, I will use the "w" where my mother would have pronounced a "v."

Dad and Mom, as we children lovingly referred to them, technically were not my mother and father until the eventful day I was born, which was not until near the end of this part of my story. I have chosen, therefore, to refer to them as John and Lena up to the day I actually became a family member.

Chapter 14
The Wedding

One day when I stopped to visit my mom and dad at their home in Reedley, California, my Mom and Dad were making final plans for the celebration of their fiftieth wedding anniversary. My wife Beverly and I had come from Enid, Oklahoma, to join the family for the celebration.

Always ready to tell a story, my mother said, "Vesley, I want to tell you the story of our fifty years marriage."

Mom had written and rewritten the story several times and each version was a bit different, which was typical of her storytelling. She loved to tell stories about the past, and I had heard this one before. But I sat down and politely listened again.

"I start by telling about my grandfather," she said in her broken English. I knew I was in for a long one, so I settled back in my chair at the kitchen table in their home at 12 Rupert Street, Reedley, California, where they had lived since moving off the farm. I had armed myself with a cup of coffee and a couple of mom's homemade cookies.

"My grandparents were born in Karolswalde, Russia," she began. "In 1874, they migrate to America and settle near the town of Moundridge, Kansas, where many of *our people* (meaning Mennonites) settled when they come to America. My father, Jacob Jantz was his name at that time. It later changed to Janzen and then to Johnson. I just nine years old when the family come to Moundridge. Another family that come from Russia the same time was the Peter Koehns. They had a daughter named Karolina. In 1886, Jacob Jantz and Karolina Koehn got married. I was their first child, born February 28, 1887, in Moundridge, Kansas." (This paragraph is typical of my Mother's English).

Note: When the adults of past generations got together, which they did frequently, they spent whole afternoons or evenings telling and retelling their stories. Children were often present and listened. After they had heard the same stories several times, they knew the stories as well as their adult parents did. Years later they, in turn, told them to their children. And so the stories were handed down from generation to generation with surprising accuracy. Today, this oral tradition has largely passed from the scene, as books and other media have taken the place of storytelling.

"Are you listening, Vesley?" Mom asked as I bit into my second cookie.

Realizing I had heard all these details before, I said, "Yes, Mother, I am listening to every word you are saying."

She continued, "In 1894, my parents move to Corn, Oklahoma. They were saved during cottage prayer meetings, baptized, and become members of the big Mennonite Brethren church a few years after they moved to Corn. From then on they go to church regular and take children to Sunday school. In Sunday school, we learn to read and write in German. Our teacher used a 𝕵𝖊𝖚𝖊𝖘 𝕬 - 𝕭 - 𝕮 - 𝕭𝖚𝖈𝖍 𝖋ü𝖗 𝕾𝖔𝖓𝖓𝖙𝖆𝖌𝖘-𝕾𝖈𝖍𝖚𝖑𝖊𝖓 (*Jesus A.B.C. Book for Sunday School*). I still have the book. I give it to you."[1]

---

[1]The sixty-three page book, published in 1876, is in the Gunther archives. Each letter of the alphabet is illustrated with a religious symbol. The book includes short stories and poems.

"I not go to school til the family moved to Corn, Oklahoma in 1894. When I was eight years old, my papa let me go to the Sparta Grade School. On the first day, Papa take time from working on the farm to walk me to school. After that I walk alone. I walk four miles over crooked paths and roads that were muddy in spring, dusty in fall, and big snowdrifts in winter. The first winter I go to school in heavy snow. Sometimes I could stay with grandparents. They live only one mile from school. My brothers and sisters grumble because, besides their own, they had to do my chores on those days."

"As I was growing up, I had to work hard to help in the house and with the farm work. But in 1902 our church started a Bible School, at first called the Washita Gemeinde Schule (Washita Church School) and then the Corn Bible Academy. Subjects were taught in German and English. I was one of the first students, but already I was fifteen years old. I went to school one year. The next year I stay home to help with the farm work so my sister Lizzie can go to school. But I go back the next two years and in the first graduating class."

"Why I am telling you this, Vesley, is because your father, John Gunther, was in Bible School the first day it started. He was a bachelor, twenty years old, and rented a farm. In the winter months he did not have so much work on the farm, so he decided to go to school when he had time. Well, the very first day of school, the eyes of that young man, John Gunther, fell on a student with a red flowered dress. Upon inquiring, he found that her name was Lena Johnson and thought to himself, truly the "King's Daughter is all glorious within" – even the gossiping angels peeked out of heaven to see how I should fall for thee. John told me that years later."

Upon hearing such beautiful words, I suddenly sat straight up in my chair. I could not believe my dad would ever have been capable of such romantic sentiments. Perhaps, I thought to myself, the reason he started school at age twenty was not so much to get an education as to find a young lady who might marry him. I had never heard this part of the story.

"Keep talking," I told Mom, "This is getting very interesting. How long was it before he told you how he felt about you?"

Corn Bible Academy's First Graduating Class, Helena Johnson on the right.

"He kept it hidden from me for six long years! But his love never vanished," my mother said. "John was very quiet about things like this, so he never said anything to anyone about his feelings for me. It was not until the day he heard the Johnson family was going to move to Michigan, and Lena was going with them, that he decided it was time to do something about his feelings for me. He still not sure he had courage to make known to me his love. It happened this way: Professor J.F. Duerksen, from the Academy, noticed that John seemed to pay a lot of attention to Lena Johnson, even though he never even talked to her. One day Professor Duerksen takes John aside and tells him he felt Lena would be a good wife for him. John was so encouraged that, instead of going to church on a Sunday night soon after this and sing in choir, he stay home and writes a letter, telling of his love for me."

"Dad, did you actually skip church to write such a letter?" I asked. Dad just kept quiet and let Mom keep talking.

"The next morning," Mom said, "instead of mailing his letter right there in Corn, John got on his horse and rode ten miles to the town of Colony to mail it. Why? He hoped that if his love would not accept his proposal, no one would know."

After days of anxious waiting John finally received his answer: "Dear John," I wrote, "It cannot be now. I must go with my family. There is work for me in the far-away wooded land. If it is God's will, He will lead us together some day."

"But that, obviously, was not the end of the story," I said.

"No," my mother continued, "On the last evening before our family left for Michigan, John paid a visit to our home and made known to my parents that he loved me and hoped I would consent to be his wife. He asked if they would give their blessing to his proposal for marriage."

"And what did your parents say about Dad's proposal?" I asked.

Mom answered my question before Dad could open his mouth, "They said they knew John was honest, hardworking man, and good Christian. If it is God's will for their daughter to marry him, they will not stand in the way."

"Were you okay with their answer? It seems to me it left things up in the air. It was neither a yes or a no," I said to Dad. He still had nothing to add.

"So your family moved to Michigan, and you went with them, leaving Dad behind?" I asked in anticipation of what Mom would say next. "As I recall, you moved in February of 1908. How did you ever get together?"

"After we left, John write letters to me. In these letters he tells me he will come to Michigan to take me back to Corn as his bride. I kept those letters hid from my parents because, if they knew, they would tell me not to answer – they did not want to lose their oldest daughter. But I wrote back in secret and told John I would wait till he came."

"So how long was it before you had the courage to go and claim your bride?" I asked Dad.

For the first time during our visit in their kitchen that morning, Dad finally spoke up. "Your mother encouraged me to come as soon as possible. The farm work was less demanding in winter after the wheat had been sown. So I wrote your mama and told her I would come in December (less than a year after they had moved). Mom finally had the courage to let her parents know that I would be coming with the intention of marrying her before returning home."

Mom broke in and continued the story. "My parents know they could not stop us from getting married, but did little to help me prepare for his visit, much less make plans for a wedding. John kept his word and with just one satchel in hand, takes train in Oklahoma to Michigan. He come to West Branch the day before Christmas. My Papa hated it that he would have to go by horse and sleigh through deep snow to meet John. When he got to the depot, the train was late because of deep snow it had to plow through in Michigan winter. Waiting for the train did not make my Papa happy. So when the train finally came, he greeted John with cold handshake. With satchel in hand, John got on the sleigh with my Papa for the trip back home. Both were men of few words, so had little to say."

> Note: West Branch was a little town on the upper Michigan peninsula, forty miles straight west of Lake Huron. The twenty mile route from the Johnson's home generally followed the Middle Branch of the West Branch River.

"When the men finally got home, I was anxiously waiting for them," Mom said. "It was a happy time for me. In his arms, I said, 'At last you come to take me with you, John. I will go wherever you take me if only I can be with you.' I spend so many lonely hours in our separation."

I was intrigued by the romantic flavor of Mom's story, as I got up for a second cup of coffee. I had never heard either of them talk about their intimate feelings for each other. It just was not like them to talk to their children in such a manner.

"How did your parents and their family respond to all this show of affection?" I asked.

Disregarding my question, Mom continued, "That was on Friday, Christmas Eve. We had to eat supper in a hurry and get ready for the church meeting. We were a mile from meetinghouse, so instead of harnessing horses and hitching them to the sleigh, we all walk through packed snow on the road. It was beautiful, walking under a clear, starry sky, with the moon shining on the fresh snow. John and I walk behind the rest and hold hands.

"We had a regular Christmas program. The children recited their pieces, short poems and Bible verses they memorized. The choir I taught to sing in four parts sing a song. Together we sing carols in German: I at the organ. Church leader Heinrich F. Janzen gave a sermon."

"The next day was Sunday; we were in meetinghouse again to noon. During the morning meeting John and I were announced to be married. 'The wedding,' the church leader said, 'will be Friday afternoon [January 1, 1909] at the home of Brother and Sister Jacob Johnson. All invited.'"

When church was out that morning, we ride to my parent's house on a fine one-horse sleigh covered with jingle bells – one John rented for this. The bells ring joyfully as the proud groom–to–be drove away from the meetinghouse on the sparkling, crusty snow."

"When we come home from church that Sunday, my mama fix a big chicken dinner. After the announcement dinner, the groom placed a gold engagement band on the bride's finger. I wear this ring to this day."

"In afternoon, Mama and Papa, and John and me, we go to sit in the parlor to plan for wedding. The most important was to get marriage license. For this we had to go to the county seat in Roscommon. The first part of the trip had to be made by horse and sleigh. The snow was still so deep, and no roads could be seen. But the next day John, my Papa and my

Uncle Cornelius put on heavy fur coats for the journey. They first had to retrace their route to West Branch where Papa had gone to get John from the train just three days before."

At this point my father broke in again to continue the story. "We got to West Branch just in time to catch the train going another twenty-five miles north to the county seat. When we got there it so happened that we met the County Clerk at the train depot. I told him I needed a marriage license because I was getting married in a few days. To my surprise, the clerk was very willing to help."

He said, "Come to the courthouse with me, and I will give you a license while the train turns around for its trip back to West Branch."

"In just a few minutes, I had my marriage license in my pocket as we boarded the train to go back to where our horses and sleigh were waiting for the trip back home. We did not get home until 11:00 o'clock, but that was alright. Having had such good fortune in finding the clerk just when we needed him, we had made the trip in one day, and I teasingly told my father-in-law-to-be, 'It must be God's will that Lena and I get married.' He did not appreciate my humor. We were welcomed home by the family with a hearty meal and went to bed with thankful hearts."[2]

My mother continued her story. "The same morning the men went to get the license, Mama and my sisters start to make food for the wedding. How did it all get done I do not know. It was good thing that Mama taught us girls to sew. I sewed my own wedding gown on treadle machine, late into the night by kerosene lamp. I first go with Mama to Gladwin to buy material – light, white wool. The skirt was eight–gore circle, reaching only to the shoes. The blouse was with high neckline collar, trimmed with lace down the front. The skirt also trimmed with lace. I buy white shoes and silk hose to wear with the dress. My mama bought two small bouquets of imitation flower, one for John and one for me."

"During the week, while I was busy getting ready for the wedding, my family visited with John to get better acquainted. John helped my Papa on the farm, clearing land for farming. My Mama and sisters cooked and baked food for the meal that would follow the wedding. The day of the wedding came too fast. It was New Year's afternoon and very cold outside. Seventy guests crowded into my parents' house."

"The wedding ceremony was led by church leader, Heinrich F. Janzen (not related to either of the other two Heinrich F. Janzens previously mentioned in my story). John and I stand while Brother Janzen read from the Bible and give a sermon. We promise to live together as husband and wife until death. We were then announced married by law as Mr. and Mrs. John P. Gunther."

I learned, while sitting in Mom and Dad's kitchen, drinking my third cup of coffee, that after the ceremony, the usual food prepared for such a wedding (Zwieback, home cured ham, sausage, plum pudding, and cakes of several kinds) was put on the table. The guests enjoyed the feast and visited the rest of the afternoon until it was time for them to go home to do their evening chores.

That evening the Johnson family gathered in the parlor and with the new Mrs. John Gunther at the organ, spent the evening singing their favorite hymns and songs.

The next day the newly married couple borrowed Papa's horse and sleigh to go into Gladwin to have their wedding pictures taken.

---

[2]The original marriage license is in the Gunther archives.

John P. and Helena Johnson Gunther's
Wedding picture

Chapter 15
The Newlyweds

The newly married couple stayed with the bride's parents for the two weeks following the wedding. There was discussion about where John and Lena should make their home – in Oklahoma or in Michigan. Things got rather tense during those two weeks. Lena's father insisted that he needed them to help with the farm. He even offered to help them build a house and rent some land. John finally told them it was a settled matter. They must return to Corn where he had already established a home and farm and where there was much work to do. Mama and Papa Johnson, and other family members, shed many tears as the couple boarded the train for the trip back to Oklahoma. Everyone knew it would be a long time before they would see each other again.

John and Lena's long-distance courtship of less than a year (with one living in Oklahoma and the other in Michigan) had consisted of writing letters back and forth. Such a courtship was not conducive to learning to know each other very well. My readers will recall that John did not make known his love for Lena back there in Corn until just the night before the Johnson family moved to Michigan. The train trip south to Oklahoma was their first opportunity to be alone and to get better acquainted.

Lena soon learned that John was a shy man of few words. But the twinkle in his blue eyes bespoke his warm, quiet, and personable disposition. He had a quick wit and loved to tease. She had already noticed this about him during the time they had spent with her parents, when he had occasionally teased Lena's father and her two sisters.

John soon learned that Lena was one who could talk endlessly. She kept the conversation going even when she was the only one listening. She was more serious minded and let John know that his humor, for the most part, was unnecessary. Not only her mind and mouth but also her hands were usually in high gear. As he watched her during those days spent in her parents' home, he had thought to himself that she could get more done in a day than most women do in three. He had also noticed that her temperament matched the rest of her personality. If she got angry, which she did quite often, she let everyone know about it.

As the train slowly made its way south, the young couple learned more about the basic personality traits each of them brought into their marriage. Being very much in love, they talked about many things, all in the Low German language since this was their native tongue and none of their fellow passengers would understand what they were talking about – they hoped.

Lena wanted to know what to expect when they arrived in their new home. How far was their farm from the town of Corn? In what kind of house were they going to live? Had the wheat crop for the coming spring been planted? What kind of neighbors would they have? Had John stored up enough food for the winter? And on and on.

John patiently listened to her questions but acted as if he had not heard a word his new bride had said, which annoyed her to no end. After they had more or less exhausted their discussion about what to expect about life in Corn, they got on to more personal matters.

Lena said, "John, I know you were saved, and you are a baptized member of the Corn Mennonite Brethren Church. I was at the baptism and saw you. I remember you singing in the church choir. You could not do that if you were not a church member. Tell me how you got saved."

At this point, John decided it was time for him to open up and start talking. He said, "Our family moved to Corn in 1893. The Corn church began Sunday morning meetings from the day several of us Mennonite families moved into the area. Two years later the church held a tent revival meeting. For two weeks, all of us went to the meetings. One night, when I was thirteen years old, I went forward during the altar call and was saved (See the end of Chapter 26 for what this means). A few months later, July 21, 1895, I was baptized together with thirty-one other young converts by Elder Peter Neufeld, one of the church's first pastors."[1]

Corn Mennonite Brethren Church Immersion Baptism Service in the Washita River

While the newlyweds held hands (since they were sure no one on the train would recognize them), Lena said, "Now I will tell you my story. As a young girl, when we still lived in Kansas, I liked Sunday school. On Saturday afternoons, I stayed with friends who lived close to the church. On Sunday mornings there was a preaching meeting. I have lunch at a friend's house and then went to Sunday school. When our family moved to Corn in 1894, my parents were not saved, so we did not go to church. A few years later, they were saved and we all went to church together. It was not until 1905, when I was eighteen years old, that I got saved and was baptized in the Washita River, with twenty-six other souls, by Pastor Abraham Richert."

---

[1]In those days Pastors were unpaid, and most earned their living by farming.

It was on the third, and last, day of their trip back home that Lena bravely brought up a subject neither of them had ever talked about, nor wanted to. She said, "John, I think we should talk about the future. ...about. ...about. ...family. John, do you like children?"

"Why. ...why do you ask?" John replied.

"Well, you come from a big family, and I sometimes wonder if you hated it, that you had so many younger brothers and sisters, and so you would not like children."

John, as usual, was silent for a long time before he answered, "I like children! How can we be a family without children?"

"Have you thought about how many children we should have? One, two, or maybe three?" Lena persisted. "John, why do you not answer me?" Lena was getting exasperated.

He said, "I am thinking. I am thinking. Maybe twelve, like Jacob in the Bible."

"Twelve!" Lena almost went into a dead faint. "Jacob had twelve children, but he had them with two wives, and two handmaids! I hope that is not what you are thinking? Do you expect me, your one and only wife, to give birth to twelve children?"

"Yes, a perfect dozen. And I think the twelfth one will be our finest." There was humor in John's voice as he said it. He had actually never seriously considered exactly how many children they should have.

Lena had not yet learned to recognize John's humor. This time she was the one who sat in stunned silence. She had taken John seriously and was aggravated with his careless manner. "I do not think I can bear twelve children."

For the rest of the trip both John and Lena sat in a tense silence, not only because of their discussion about family, but also because they were nearly home. Both were anticipating how the other might respond when they drove onto the yard of the farmhouse John had prepared for them.

It was early morning when their train pulled into the depot in Oklahoma City. After a restless sleep on the hard wooden seats of their coach, they pulled back the window coverings to find the ground covered with snow. John had arranged for his oldest brother, Peter B., to meet them at the depot and drive them the eighty miles southwest to the town of Corn. Sure enough, Peter was there with a team of two strong horses hitched to a wagon with a horse and buggy with sleigh bells attached to the canopy behind it for the special occasion. The wagon was needed to haul the crates of personal items Lena had brought with her. It would be a long, hard day's drive through the soft snow to Corn.

The winter sun was about to set when the entourage drove down the driveway and stopped in front of John's humble but tidy house four miles east of the town of Corn, the house he intended to be the couple's new home. Peter B. helped unload the crates from the wagon and deposited them on the front porch of the house before hurrying off to his own home where his wife would be waiting for him.

When John was sure the two of them were alone, he went to the front door, opened it and went inside, asking Lena to wait outside until he came back. He quickly lit some candles and a kerosene lamp he had trimmed before leaving for Michigan. When he returned to the porch, he told her to close her eyes; then in a very chivalrous manner, picked up his bride in his long, strong arms, and carried her over the threshold, put her on her feet, and told her to open her eyes.

It was the most romantic moment Lena could have imagined. For the first time, she was truly speechless – and very pleased with what she saw. John lit a fire in the potbellied stove while Lena examined her new home. The warmth of the fire soon filled the house and began to kindle a bond between them, a bond that would only grow stronger as the years passed. Before retiring they knelt beside their bed and thanked God for His protection and provision.

The next morning was very cold, with temperatures hovering near zero. John went out to do the chores while Lena made her first breakfast in their new home. Before partaking, John got out his Bible and read a Psalm, then prayed a prayer of thanksgiving for the blessing of love and hearth and home, a practice they continued the rest of their lives.

Lena was anxious to see the rest of the farm. So as soon as the breakfast dishes were cleared away, John took his wife on a tour of the barnyard. He showed her his four handsome horses in their barn stalls, the three milking cows, the hog he had fattened for butchering, and the chickens in the hen house. He showed her the granary full of corn–everything they would need to see them through their first winter, and beyond.

"The wheat field," he said, "was planted last fall, and when the weather turns warmer it will begin to green up and grow to maturity."

Before the morning was over, both John and Lena were in their work clothes and began to tackle the dozens of jobs every good farm demanded. Within a few weeks they were ready, with the help of neighbors, to butcher the 400-pound hog. It provided them with hams and bacon (cured in John's homemade smokehouse), pork chops and ribs, pickled pig's feet, sausages, and a variety of other delicacies. The fat was rendered in a huge cast-iron cauldron (*meagropa, in Low German*) and produced sixteen gallons of lard plus gallons of "cracklings." Nothing was wasted. Every morsel was tasty and satisfying to the palate.

Married life was good.

Chapter 16
Farming Corn

The wheat John had planted a few months before going up to Michigan to marry his beloved had wintered well, and by early spring it appeared that it would produce a bumper crop. It was a variety of wheat the Mennonites had brought with them in their emigration from Russia and was known by various names: hard wheat, winter wheat, Red Turkey Wheat (because Turkey was probably the first country to develop this strain of wheat) and most often as hard red winter wheat. It usually commanded a high price in the market place. When ground into flour, the product was favored over other varieties by bakers and consumers.

As they had watched the beautiful green fields of grain grow toward maturity that first spring, John explained to Lena, in fluent Low German, that the proper name of the wheat was of little consequence.

"It is a variety," John said, "which is planted in the months of September and October and is very hard, as opposed to wheat planted in the spring which is usually softer. Once it has sprouted, it remains dormant through the cold winter months, and is not harvested in Oklahoma until June of the next year. This wheat withstands drought, severe cold, and grows equally well in high or low altitudes. As you well know, my dear, we depend on God's blessing for all our crops; a little snow in winter and occasional rains during the spring months. Then, as the sun warms the earth in early spring, this wheat breaks out of its dormancy and the livestock can graze on it for several weeks before it begins to head out."

Lena was impressed, as any young bride would have been, at her husband's knowledge of wheat husbandry as well as several other crops grown in the area. It seemed to her that he knew just about everything one needed to know about all aspects of farming, including the care of livestock. As they stood looking out over the ripening grain that spring morning, Lena looked up at his slender, muscular, six-foot frame, proud as a peacock to be his wife, and asked, "How many bushels to the acre can we expect from the crop this year?"

"One of the best things about this variety of wheat," John said, "is its high yield – up to twenty-five to thirty bushels to the acre. If the rains continue until near harvest time, and the crop is not damaged by hail, hard wind or, God forbid, a tornado, we should have a great harvest this year." Raising his eyes and looking into the deep blue of the morning sky he said, "Lord God grant it."

Note: With the development of new varieties of hard wheat, modern technology, the use of fertilizers and insecticides, farmers in the early twenty-first century expect their harvests to produce from forty to sixty bushels to the acre. One farmer recently reported an 81.2 bushel yield.

"I have to admit that I become a little anxious waiting for the harvest at this time of year," John said. "There is always the possibility of a change in weather that overnight could destroy the most hopeful prospects of an abundant yield." As if speaking prophetically, one morning in late May, John and Lena awoke to another perfect day for ripening of the grain. By mid-afternoon they noticed a few gray clouds on the horizon to the southwest. It was not long before the clouds grew into a bank of billowy thunder heads. They knew in an instant that a storm was on its way. The first thing they did was to get the cattle and horses from the pasture into the barn. They could already hear the thunder begin to rumble in the distance.

By the time John and Lena were safely in their house they were surrounded by heavy black clouds. The distant sound of thunder, like the rumble of an angry giant, could be heard piercing the usual silence of the prairie. Lightning spat from cloud to cloud, lighting up the afternoon sky. "This is tornado weather," John said to Lena. The wind quickly picked up to a velocity near fifty miles an hour. The young couple could do nothing but stand at the kitchen window, while they prayed and waited with bated breath. Would their beautiful wheat crop, for which they had such high hopes, be destroyed in minutes by hail? Heavy rain began to inundate their farm. Their eyes were riveted on one queer looking cloud with a short tail. "It looks like the start of a tornado, and we have no storm cellar," Lena lamented. They both moved away from the window and stood in the doorway to their bedroom as they watched with a sigh of relief as the cloud finally passed. The storm subsided within the hour. The rain had done no damage to their wheat. They paused to kneel in a prayer of thanksgiving to God. The next day they heard that scattered farms in the area had been slightly damaged by hail.

Harvest time for John and Lena arrived in early June of 1909. At that point in the history of harvesting grain, the first phase of the harvesting process was to cut the wheat with a binding machine drawn by a team of horses. The machine cut and tied the stalks of wheat into bundles that were then moved onto a cradle on the side of the binder. The cradle could hold several bundles which were dropped in one spot when the operator tripped a lever. Farm hands then came along and stacked each drop of bundles, grain heads up, into shocks. After several days of drying in the sun the wheat was ready for threshing.

The custom of the day for the threshing process was for several neighboring farm families, including men, women and children, to come together to form a threshing crew. The crew moved from one farm to the next until the grain of each of the participating farmers was harvested. This joint effort was sometimes called a *threshing bee*. John had carefully planned and prepared for the day his wheat would be harvested.

A typical
threshing
bee.

The exciting day started at sunup. Each member of the crew was assigned a job. Some loaded the bundles of wheat onto horse-drawn wagons. The drivers took the loads from the field to the threshing ring where a threshing machine separated the grain from the stalk. The threshing machine was powered by a huge steam engine. The steam engine and the threshing machine were connected by a ten-inch belt and driven by a pulley on each machine.

The engine, much like that of a steam-powered locomotive, only smaller, was fired with coal. It was the job of the first men to arrive on the job each morning to fill the boiler with water and start the fire in the huge firebox of the engine. After the boiler got its steam, the crew was ready to thresh wheat. One person was assigned the job of shoveling coal to keep the fire burning, and the boiler filled with water to maintain steam for running the engine. Two men pitched the bundles of wheat from the wagons onto the deck of the machine. Two stood on the deck to feed the bundles into the thresher. Others tended the wheat kernels as they were thrust from the machine onto a pile below. Some were responsible for removing the chaff and straw from the back of the thresher. It was a hot and dirty job, with straw and chaff blowing in all directions and smoke spewing out of the steam engine; but it was harvest time! The sweat, dirt, and smoke added to the excitement of the day.

While the threshing crew, including women and older children, hauled the bundles of wheat and worked the machines, a crew of women prepared a huge meal for the hungry threshing crew. As they gathered around tables set up in the shade of the Gunther's giant elm tree, they gave thanks to God for the abundance of His provision. Mealtimes were the highlight of the day as the men swapped stories of harvests past and the women gossiped about the goings on in the neighborhood. How many days of intense labor were required depended on the size of the farm.

The day the threshing was completed on the Gunther farm and evening faded into the darkness of night, John and Lena knelt in their kitchen with grateful hearts, giving praise to their loving heavenly Father for the gift of the abundance of the land.

The next day, the crew continued to another farm until everyone's wheat had been threshed. However, the back breaking work involved in harvesting was not complete until the grain had been delivered to the nearest elevator and sold. El Reno, Oklahoma, the elevator nearest the Corn community, was sixty miles to the northeast. The wheat had to be loaded with scoop-shovels onto wagons, then pulled by teams of four horses along rough dirt roads with dangerous up and down grades, and even through creeks and river beds. For the Corn farmers, this also meant crossing the wide Canadian River, which had its headwaters high in the Rocky Mountains. By the time the river got to that part of Oklahoma, it was too wide to ford

Note: Grain elevators are round structures often called silos, perhaps 60 or 70 feet high, connected one to the other like beehives, built for the purpose of storing and transferring grain to railroad cars to be shipped to flour mills. In the early twentieth century many of them were built of wood, but later they were built of steel and concrete. By the time my father harvested wheat, these elevators could be seen in almost every town in the mid-west served by a railroad. The reason they are called elevators is because small buckets, attached to a conveyor belt, scoop the grain from a pit on the ground level, fill them with grain, and carry it to the top of the silo where it is dumped into a bin.

for most of the year as its waters rushed eastward and emptied into the Mississippi River. A rickety bridge had been built near El Reno, but both crossing the great river by bridge or fording it caused farmers untold trouble and anxiety. From time to time, a man was killed while crossing this river with his load of wheat. Wagons and horses with their loads of grain were often lost to the swift current below. A heavy rain, not uncommon during that time of the year, could delay the crossing for days or even weeks. The rain made it necessary for farmers to camp by the river and wait for the water to recede.

It took two strong men to take a load of grain to the elevator, so John and his older brother Dan, who also farmed wheat in Corn, worked togther. If there were no breakdowns along the way, the round trip from Corn to El Reno took from five to six days. After delivering the wheat to the elevator, John usually bought a load of lumber at a lumberyard in El Reno and hauled it back home to sell to the other farmers, who always seemed to need a new supply.

While John was on these trips, Lena stayed behind to take care of the farm and livestock. These were anxious days for her, as she awaited the return of her beloved. She was, at times, reminded of sailors' wives waiting nervously and impatiently for the return of their men who had been at sea for months at a time; she then thought to herself, compared to theirs, my burden is light.

In the spring of the first year of their marriage, John had planted a small acreage of corn and milo. By the time these crops were harvested later that summer, it was time to prepare the soil for another crop of wheat.

Summer quickly turned to fall. God had blessed John and Lena with material abundance. On October 4 of that first year, God added another kind of blessing, the birth of their first child, Johanes. "He was a handsome child, strong and healthy," Lena wrote in her journal. "John and I were so proud of him." It was the custom of the day to dress small boys in fancy dresses. When Johanes was a year old, his mother used her new Singer treadle sewing machine to make him an exquisite dress trimmed with lace. The proud parents then dressed him in his new gown and took him to a studio in Oklahoma City for a professional photograph.

Johanes soon won his way into the hearts of his parents. Years later, his mother, vividly remembering the happiness he brought them, wrote in

Helena Gunther and son Johanes

one of her journals, "*He had spunk and loved to do things to tease us, a characteristic he undoubtedly inherited from his father.*" She continued in her journal, saying that she remembered two things in particular. One summer day Johanes, standing on a chair near the kitchen sink, asked for a Zwieback. With his mother's permission he reached out and took one out of the breadbox. Before eating it, he folded his hands and thoughtfully thanked the Lord. On another occasion, he was near the table in the next room. His mother saw him from the corner of her eye, raising one finger. He had apparently done something bad, so he was lecturing his bad finger, telling it never to do that bad thing again.

When Johanes was about a year old, Lena's parents came from Michigan to visit. It was a joyful visit, except for one incident. His mother wrote in her journal:

> *Our little boy had the habit that before he could fall asleep, either his mother or father had to rub his hands. Well, one night while my parents were visiting, my husband decided this habit should be broken, so he gave our son a good spanking, put him in his bed and left that poor boy to cry himself to sleep. My heart was almost broken, and I asked myself why my husband had to do this while my folks were staying with us. He could have waited till they were gone. And I told him so! That's when the devil brings trouble between a couple. But we forgot about it.*

On May 16, 1911, God blessed John and Lena with another son, Jakob. Anyone could see at a glance from the day he was born that Jakob looked like his father, whereas Johanes looked like his mother. But then, it soon became apparent that their temperaments were reversed – Johanes had the temperament of his father and Jakob that of his mother. These two angelic boys brought great joy to Papa and Mama.

That joy, however, later turned to anxiety. When Johanes was nearly two years old, he developed diphtheria and pneumonia, two common childhood diseases for which there was no effective medication at that time. Little Johanes had to be quarantined. Only his mother was allowed to care for him. She herself was continually at risk of being infected. The isolation was almost more than the boy's father could endure, but he knew that if he joined his wife and son, he would be at risk of contracting the illness as well.

Jakob was almost four months old when Johanes contracted diphtheria. John and Lena's greatest concern was that little Jakob would also come down with the condition. "How are we going to keep Jakob safe?" Lena asked. "Even though the wheat has been planted for next year's crop, I know there is always work to be done. I cannot take care of both children. First caring for Johanes, and then coming into the kitchen and caring for Jakob, I could easily carry the disease from one to the other."

After earnest prayer about it, John said, "Do not worry, my dear Lena, the farm work can wait. I will take time off to care for Jakob while you care for Johanes. We will get bottles, and I will feed him milk from the cows (his mother had been breastfeeding him). I will change his diapers, put him down for his naps and put him to bed at night. We will get by."

As it turned out, neighbors who were members of their church came to help with the farm work during the time of quarantine. The women brought food and helped with the washing and ironing. The whole church was in prayer. John and Lena gave their full attention to taking care of their two boys. They were hopeful that if little Johanes's condition would improve during this time he would make a full recovery. Instead, his condition only seemed to get worse. Retelling the story years later, my mother said that Johanes also had contracted lock-jaw (a tetanus infection), from which he suffered intensely. It was as if his jaws were frozen shut. She could hardly feed him anymore. He died on December 21, 1911, just four days before Christmas, at age two years, two months and seventeen days.

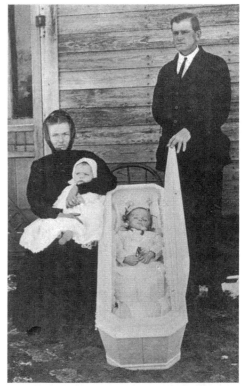

The church continued to surround the Gunthers with prayer. A funeral service led by Elder Abraham Richert was held in the meetinghouse. The choir, of which both John and Lena were members, sang several songs. Strengthened and comforted by their church, John built a small wooden coffin and lovingly, but with much grief, buried little Johanes in the parcel of ground the Corn Mennonite Brethren Church had set aside as their church cemetery.

Christmas that year was the saddest day of John and Lena's life. Since Johanes' death, their tears ran like water over dry land, and the land was never satisfied. They, however, had the strong consolation that their handsome little boy was in heaven with Jesus. After a Christmas morning service at the church, John's extended family shared a variety of Christmas food as they gathered in Grandpa Peter Guenther's home. After the meal, the family gathered around the

Lena holding baby Jakob (Jack), Johanes in his coffin, and father John Gunther.

pump organ played by Lena, and sang Christmas songs and read from the Scriptures. It all seemed like a dream to John and Lena. Years later they told their pastor that without the support of church and family, they were not sure they could have endured this trial of their faith. Even so, they could not leave behind the wound of spirit the loss of their firstborn had inflicted.

John continued to raise wheat, corn and milo on his farm. But one day he came across a bulletin from the Oklahoma Agricultural Experiment Station. The bulletin was dated 1908, and read:

> "Cotton is a banner crop in Oklahoma. This crop has been tested for several years in succession in the two territories, and the practical grower has reached the conclusion that cotton can be cultivated with profit in the new state."

John was intrigued by the information published by the Experiment Station at Oklahoma A&M College (now Oklahoma State University) and authored by L.A. Moorhouse and J.F. Nicholson. In the spring of 1912 he decided to give cotton a try. All he needed was cotton plates in exchange for corn plates in the bottom of the canisters of his corn planter, and he would be all set to plant his first crop of cotton. The venture turned out to be such a success that growing cotton became a lifetime passion.

After their marriage, John and Lena lived in the Corn area a total of six years. During that time their first daughter, Elma Maria, later spelled Alma, was born on June 15, 1912. They both felt that with two children, Jakob and Elma, their family was complete. Little did they know. They noticed that the temperament of each of their children was different. Jakob was often jealous of his little sister, who was suddenly robbing him of Mama and Papa's attention. On the other hand, he had a free spirit that allowed him to take things in stride. They soon discovered that Elma was a child with a strong will and great determination. When push came to shove, she usually did the shoving.

Raising two children, they decided, was a full-time job! They loved their children intensely and took seriously the responsibility of training them in the fear of the Lord. Something told them that the first two or three years in a child's life were the most important. Whatever time and energy it took, they were willing to pay the price for getting their family off to a good start. Even on those nights when John had been plowing in the field all day and was bone tired, he took time to play on the floor with their beautiful children. Before going to bed each night, John and Lena read the Bible and knelt in prayer with their children beside them. The children learned both Low and High German perfectly, and John saw to it that they would also begin to learn English.

During the years the young couple lived in Oklahoma, they experienced two years of drought. Their crops hardly paid the rent on their farm. They simply could not get ahead financially. Besides, the death of their firstborn left a wound in their hearts they could not dispel. It seemed that everything in their home and on the farm was a vivid, daily reminder of that tragic loss. Perhaps it was time for them to move on. They found what looked like greener pastures in Kansas. In fact, the green pastures looked so good that they gave little thought to seeking God's guidance about the move. If they made a move, would it be a good one?

Only time would tell.

Chapter 17
Coldwater

Coldwater, located thirty miles north of the Kansas/Oklahoma border, is one of just three small towns in the entire county of Comanche. In the early days it was Indian country, where buffalo roamed by the thousands. By the late nineteenth century the Native Americans had been rounded up and forced to move to designated reservations so their land could be opened by the United States Government and parceled out to white homesteaders. This part of Kansas was so rough and rugged that most of the homesteaders who came to farm the land soon abandoned their 160-acre farms, leaving fences, windmills, and small shanties behind.

The town of Coldwater was typical of many of the hamlets of the wild west in the early days. It had a saloon, horse stable, blacksmith shop, and a sheriff's office. The sound of gunshots from raiding bandits was not uncommon.

The road running through the town was a mud hole when it rained, a dust bowl when it did not. The same was true of the roads and lanes running into the countryside in every direction from the center of town. The terrain in that part of Kansas consisted of rolling hills with hardly a flat piece of land suitable for farming. To the south of the town was an area known as the Seven Canyons. Actually, they were rolling hills. To get to Coldwater from the south, the traveler had to climb one side of the hill and coast down the other – seven times. It was treacherous landscape for anyone traveling by horse and wagon.

In years past, several General Conference Mennonite families had homesteaded the prairie land near the town and formed a rural church. Those first settlers must have been a determined group to have had enough courage even to begin to make this land their home. Little wonder that they soon moved on. The town, however, has survived the adversities of those early years.

During the six years that John and Lena Gunther lived in Oklahoma, they had hoped they could one day afford to buy the farm they had been renting. The years of drought had wiped out their savings and dashed their hopes. The value of the land had inflated. There was never enough money to qualify for a mortgage loan. In 1912 John heard that land could be bought in Comanche

Note: Perhaps some of my readers would consider retiring in present day Coldwater. The majority of its citizens are of German extraction. The town has a 0.0% unemployment rate. The divorce rate is 10% compared to the national rate of 50 to 60%. Between 1997 and 2004, the city issued one building permit. The median price of a house is significantly below the State average (even more significantly below home prices on the east or west coasts). The average age of the residents is significantly above the State average. The length of stay after arriving is above the State average. Population (771 as of this writing) is significantly below the State average. The nearest big city is Wichita, just 140 miles to the east. The town has a hospital, an airport, seven churches, and boasts a beautiful 250-acre man-made lake.

County, Kansas, for almost nothing. One day he suggested to Lena that perhaps they should consider a move to Coldwater.

Lena was dumbfounded. "John, what are you saying?" The idea of leaving Corn and moving to the state where she was born had never occurred to her. "I will have to think about that a long time," she told John.

As Lena began to consider the possibility of such a move, she was in a dilemma – torn between a desire to stay where they were, and a need to leave Corn. On the one hand, the prospect of leaving their beautiful farm and home, their church, their family and friends and moving to the wild west was almost more than she could bear. On the other hand, it was here in Corn that her heart and soul had been, as it were, wrenched from her. She could not forget those days she had spent trying to nurse little Johanes back to health after he had come down with diphtheria. Finally, she could only watch as his precious life broke into the sunlight of his eternal home. She knew her little boy was with Jesus, but the grief of being separated from him was sometimes almost more than she could bear. Perhaps she would find a balm for her bereavement if she and John left Corn and started anew in another place.

As they talked to each other in Low German, Lena said, "John, there is a part of me that wants to leave this place and never come back again. But I also know what it is like to start on land never farmed before. When I think of how hard my parents worked to clear a small piece of land in Michigan, and build a house and barn, John, I think we cannot do this. In Michigan, we children were old enough to help get started. Our relatives and neighbors helped us. We now have two small children. They need me. I cannot help on the farm. We will have no relatives to help us. We will be strangers in a strange land. But I also know that Corn has bad memories I must leave behind."

John said, "I struggle with the same memories. I am thinking that it would be good for both of us if we could move to a place where we would not be reminded of our great sorrow. But making a new start strikes me with a sense of foreboding. I can't sleep at night when I think about what it will take. In many ways, it would be easier to stay here and trust God to provide for us even though it seems so hopeless, but it appears that we have no future here. The land in Kansas is cheap. I am told that the acreage we are considering has been farmed before and even has a house into which we can move. With God's help, maybe we can make it work."

John and Lena had made a pact early in their marriage: they would never make a move like this unless they were in agreement. It was a rule they applied to every important decision in their journey through life. Both of them knew that before they could leave their farm in Corn, they would both have to commit to the rigors of a new start.

It was one of those drought years in Oklahoma. John and Lena would have no wheat crop to harvest. They decided to purchase a farm on the prairie near Coldwater, sight unseen. Plans were set in motion for the move. In the spring of 1913, John and Lena sold their livestock and much of their farm equipment, loaded a big wagon with as many household items and farm implements as it would hold, and set out for Kansas.

John hitched their four strongest horses to the wagon and their more spirited horse to their buggy. Little two-year-old Jakob would ride with his father on the wagon seat high above the backs of the horses. Lena would drive the buggy with Elma, just a year old, placed in a basket that had been strapped to the buggy's seat. In this way, they would make the hazardous 150-mile journey over mostly dirt roads to their new home. Spring rains were common in that part of the prairie. The roads were often a quagmire of mud and deep ruts. They would not pass through any big cities. They would have to stop at the small farm towns scattered here and there to replenish food supplies and find feed and water for the horses.

The day they left Corn was a sad day for both John and Lena. Both had grown up and gone to school there. John left his brothers, sisters and beloved aging father behind and would probably not see them again. For both, Corn had been home. They were leaving so much of what had enriched their lives.

Things went smoothly on the first day of their journey. The road was dry and dusty, but they were able to cover a longer distance than expected. They set up camp on the open prairie that first night. As soon as they had eaten supper and put everything in its place for the next day, Lena and the children lay down on several layers of quilts she had brought along. Being dead tired, they were soon asleep.

John went to check on the horses one more time before lying down beside his beloved. Sleep did not come easily for him. He stared into the sky brightened by a full moon and millions of stars and marveled at the vastness of God's creation. As he did so, he began to wonder whether he had made a big mistake in taking his small family into unknown territory for mere economic reasons. He spent the night praying and asking God for a sign that they had made the right decision. It was almost morning before he finally fell into a deep sleep. He had received no sign from God that night.

The second day was another good travel day. Being the private man that he was, John did not share with Lena his struggle with God on the previous night. Toward evening the sojourners began looking for a suitable place to camp. In the distance, Lena thought she saw what looked like a farmstead. When they got there they decided to stop and ask for hay and water for their horses. As they approached, the farmer and his family were standing in their yard, looking them over. No one was aiming a gun at them, so John was emboldened to say why they had stopped. He found out later that the members of the farm family had been talking to each other about what a pitiful sight stood before them – a man and his wife along with two small children, apparently intent on making a new start on this wild and inhospitable prairie. To the Gunther's amazement, the farmer's wife invited them for supper, while her husband offered to help care for the horses. They even invited them to spend the night in their barn. As far as John was concerned, this was the sign from God he had been asking for the night before.

Toward evening on the third day of their journey, they looked to the southwest and saw the familiar thunder heads on the horizon. They quickly looked for a place to camp, unhitched the horses, tied them to a scrub tree nearby, and threw a large canvas over the buggy. The sky was almost dark as night before the four of them were settled in the tiny buggy. Thunder rolled and lightning flashed. Little Elma drew herself closer into her mother's bosom. The winds picked up. The heavens opened and unleashed a torrent of rain. Water leaked through the tiny holes in the canvas. The downpour was so heavy that, in spite of the canvas, the clothing of all four was soaked. The children shivered from the cold. The travelers would have to spend the night among the mud puddles of the open prairie.

After the storm had passed, John was soon out of the buggy looking for a place to set up their small tent. He and little Jakob scrounged for bits and pieces of wood which, by now, were soaked. Only with great difficulty did John get a little fire going while Lena changed the children into dry clothing. The wet clothes were hung on a primitive trellis of sticks near the fire. Jakob and Elma played in the puddles, splashing mud on each other until their mother sat them down by the fire and said, "Now, don't move until I say you can." They knew what that meant. They ate a cold supper of beans and Zwieback. As night fell, they could hear the howl of the coyotes in the distance. Fearful of the sound, Jakob ran to his father's side. In spite of the coyotes, the mud and the cold, the four of them were covered with warm, dry quilts and soon sound asleep, except for John who was still asking God if he was doing the right thing.

By the fifth day of their move, the Gunther family had crossed the border from Oklahoma into Kansas. The following is an edited version of a story from one of Lena's journals.

John and Lena had come to that place in their journey referred to earlier as the Seven Canyons. They had just passed over the brow of the highest of the canyon hills when the horse pulling Lena's buggy started to run downhill. Before she knew it, the horse was at a full gallop and she had completely lost control. She held on to the basket, with Elma inside, as best she could. She was sure the buggy would tip over as they came around a curve in the road. The only thing that saved them was the incline of the next canyon slope. The horse finally slowed down. Fortunately, mother and daughter survived the incident unscathed.

The next day John went to the Land Office in the little town of Coldwater and, on a map, located the acreage they had bought. With directions in hand, the newest Coldwater pioneer family found the farm and house, just as John had assured Lena they would. It was a small, one room house where the family of four cooked, ate and slept. Jakob and Elma were mighty happy to be off those wagons and able to run and chase each other. The confines of the tiny house were, at times, more than even John or Lena could handle, especially when Jakob started teasing Elma and they scrapped with each other.

During the summer of 1913, John prepared the fields for his first wheat crop in Kansas. With his team of horses, he plowed one furrow at a time, covering a few acres a day. The next day, before the ground got too hard from the hot sun, he harrowed the ground he had plowed the day before. It was a long, slow, and tedious process. But with God sending the right amount of rain through the summer, and John's determination, he got the job done.

As fall turned into winter and their first crop of wheat had been sown, John and Lena found an old abandoned house nearby. They bought it for almost nothing, and with the help of neighbors, moved it next to their own one room house. Even though the two houses were slightly separated from each other, the front part of the new house became John and Lena's *master bedroom*. (Mom does not explain in her journal where Jakob and Elma slept). The back part of the house served as a barn for the horses and storage of the expected spring wheat crop.

The crop was harvested in much the same way it had been harvested in Oklahoma. The neighboring farmers got together to form a threshing bee. John's hard labors paid off; the fields produced an acceptable harvest. Profits from the sale of the wheat would carry the Gunther family through the next year.

August 14 of 1914, however, was a stressful and tense night for John and Lena. Their fourth child was due to be born. They had called for the doctor, but the closer Lena came to giving birth, the more anxious they became. John and Lena soon realized that the doctor would not get there in time to deliver the baby. John had already heated water and collected all manner of towels and clean rags. That night he himself successfully delivered baby Karolina, who became the prettiest and healthiest girl in the county. The doctor never got there.

John and Lena lived in Coldwater just two years. Mom writes in her journal that those years were "blessed times mingled with sorrow and painful experiences." During this time letters began coming from Michigan saying Lena's mother had been diagnosed with cancer. The family urged John and Lena to move to Michigan to help with the care of her mother.

What should they do now?

Chapter 18
Michigan Adventure

They had barely established themselves on the farm in Coldwater. They had bought new farm implements plus cattle, pigs and baby chicks. John had worked hundreds of long, hard days plowing the fields and sowing the wheat. The farming operation was just beginning to show a profit. They had spent many precious hours fixing up their house to make it more livable. The small Mennonite church they had been attending was struggling to keep going in the sparsely settled rural community and needed their help. "How can we leave all this?" John said to Lena as they talked about the pleas coming from Lena's parents in Michigan. "We now have three small children to think about. Karolina is less than a year old."

Lena responded simply and directly, "My parents need us. I think we should move." They began to pray about it. Every evening, as was their custom, they read a chapter from the Bible, then knelt beside their bed as John, and then Lena, poured out their hearts in earnest prayer. Seeking and knowing God's will in this matter was crucial: should they move or should they stay?

One evening after the children had been put to bed, they read in their Bible the story about Paul and Silas on their second missionary journey. These missionaries were in need of guidance from God as to just where this journey should take them. They came to the city of Troas. The Bible records the following:

"That night Paul had a vision. He saw a man from Macedonia in northern Greece, pleading with him, 'Come over here and help us.' So we decided to leave for Macedonia at once, for we could only conclude that God was calling us to preach the Good News there," (Acts 16:9,10 NLT)

Suddenly, as if lightning had struck, it became clear to both John and Lena that God was speaking to them through this passage of Scripture. They had received letters from Lena's father, "Come to Michigan and help us." After reading these verses again, they knelt and told God they believed the verses were His way of telling them to move to Michigan. John was now convinced of God's leading. Then and there they submitted to what they understood to be God's will.

The very next day they began making plans to move. John got out a map and studied it carefully. It would be a journey of more than a thousand miles. Obviously, they could not move with horses and wagon, as they had from Oklahoma to Kansas. John spent many sleepless nights thinking about it. Clearly, they would have to make the trip by train. Upon investigation, he learned that railroad companies offered to transport farm equipment and a certain amount of livestock from one place to another at a reduced rate. Although John had no idea as to how he would get his cattle and equipment the sixty miles from their farm to the nearest train stop, the decision was made to take advantage of this service.

Another concern John had was what to do with the farm he had bought. It would be impossible to sell the farm in such a short time, so they would have to rent it out – if they could find a renter.

It was apparent to both John and Lena that this would be a costly move. During the long nights they thought about how they would have to start over again in the bitterly cold climate of the north. There were times when John was not sure he could face the challenge; perhaps they had misunderstood God's will.

As John talked to Lena about these concerns, it seemed to him that she was taking everything in stride. "It will all work out, John; God will provide," she tried to reassure him.

In early spring John began crating their household goods and clothing. Several men from the Mennonite church offered to haul their equipment and household crates in wagons and to drive their livestock to the AT&SF Railroad rural stop where the train took on water for its steam engine. It would be a two-day undertaking.

In the spring of 1915, the contingent of wagons and livestock moved out of Coldwater in the direction of the train stop. Lena and the children found room to ride in one of the wagons. John helped drive the cattle across the desolate prairie. They camped under the stars that first night and got to their destination as the sun was setting the next day. Since the train was not due to arrive until the next morning, they had to spend a second night in the open. When the train finally arrived the next day, the cattle and farm equipment were loaded onto freight cars. The family found a place in a coach car for the long trip to Chicago and from there to Gladwin, Michigan.

John had wanted to pay the men who helped them move, but they refused to accept his offer. He thanked them profusely for their generosity before he boarded the train. After the train began to move, he and Lena sat back and breathed a prayer of thanksgiving to God for helping them thus far on their journey home. Their farm had even been rented. John was reminded of stories his father had told about leaving Russia and immigrating to America. They had left everything behind to start life again in a new country.

Lena had baked Zwieback and packed them together with packages of German sausage and smoked ham – enough food to get them to their destination. It was not long before little Karolina was crying because she needed to be fed. Jakob and Elma were running up and down the aisle, making a general nuisance of themselves until their father realized they were bothering other passengers. He firmly sat them down on their bench.

During the first night of their journey, Lena began to think deeply about the move they were making. Doubts about whether they had made the right decision in moving overwhelmed her whole being. She thought about all the work that had been involved in preparing for the move, the newly renovated house they had left behind, and the expense of transporting their livestock and farm equipment. The children had been so happy and content as they played at her feet or in the open air of their farmyard each day. She worried that when children the age of her little Jakob and Elma were moved to a new place, they could become cranky

Note: I have never had the opportunity to visit these old homesteads, Nolan and Butman, in Michigan. Neither place is shown in the latest edition of the Rand McNally Atlas. Apparently neither had a post office. I began to wonder if they were real places. Then I found an old map of the area. Both townships are identified (see map).

It should also be noted that when John went to Nolan to marry his bride he had to take the train to West Branch in Roscommon County because Gladwin apparently could not boast having a train running through it at that time. It appears that by the time of this move the train came through Gladwin where John and Lena and family detrained.

and hard to control. A lump formed in her throat as she thought about the kindness of the men who had helped them get to the train stop.

The next day Lena shared her anxious concerns with John. Now it was his turn to try to reassure her that everything would work out. John was aware that such a reversal of roles is common within a strong marriage relationship. He reminded her of what she had said earlier about believing the move was God's will for them. Even though they both felt a great loss in what they had left behind, God would not forsake them. His grace and provision would be sufficient.

The morning they arrived at the Gladwin train depot, Lena's father Jacob and several members of the family were there to meet them. They had brought horses and wagons to transport their household goods and farm equipment. The boys offered to drive the livestock down the muddy road to the Johnson home – some thirty miles from the station. The day was far spent by the time the entourage arrived. Her mother's cancer seemed to have gone into remission, so they spent the first night with Lena's parents.

The Johnson farm was in the Nolan Township of Roscommon County. The forty-acre farm Lena's father had bought for them was actually just across the county line in the township of Butman in Gladwin County. Although the farms of the two families were in different counties, they were within easy riding distance of each other by horse and buggy.

The farm had a house, which John and Lena found ready for them. It was a large two-story house with a kitchen, parlor and bedroom downstairs, plus two bedrooms upstairs. Of course, it had no electricity but did have a fine wood stove for keeping the house warm in winter. Wood for the stove was in abundant supply in the north country, but had to be cut with a handsaw and split with an axe and then carried into the house, an armload at a time. The common saying was that such wood warms a body twice: once while chopping it and once while burning it. All of their water had to be pumped by hand from a well into a large tank protected from the cold of winter and carried by the bucketful into the house. If hot water was needed, it had to be heated on the kitchen stove. The house, pure luxury compared to their house in Kansas, was more than their small family of five required at that time.

Jakob was four years old by this time, Elma three, and Karolina would soon be one. Jakob and Elma were just old enough to play and fight with each other, which they did more than play. As Lena had feared, the move had been unsettling to little Elma. Back in Kansas, her mother had been able to put her down for night and she would immediately fall into a peaceful sleep. Now, when she was put to bed in their new home, she cried herself to sleep every night. It did not seem to do any good for her mother to rock, carry, or spank her. The crying continued for months and aggravated Lena to no end.

The land was, for the most part, unimproved, which meant it would take much hard work before they could actually begin farming. Stumps from trees that had been logged dotted the farm. Rocks, some big and some small, littered the land. Both stumps and rocks would need to be removed before crops could be planted.

The first thing John noticed as he surveyed the forty acres was that the landscape was lush with green grass, especially during the spring months, the time of year they had come to possess the land. "Ideal for cows. We will grow a dairy and sell milk," John said to Lena. A fence had been built by previous owners, but needed repair before the land would be ready for his cows. In the meantime, the cattle and other livestock brought from Kansas were kept in father Jacob Johnson's pasture. The fence would be John's first order of business.

After they had settled into their new home, John went to work on the fence. Within two weeks of arriving in Michigan, he went to a livestock auction yard where he bought six fine milk cows to add to his herd. He then made a trip to Gladwin where he bargained for a wagon (the Kansas wagons had been left behind), buggy, milk pails and cans, a set of hobbles, and a milk strainer. With these bare essentials, John concluded, they were in the dairy business.

Since grass was in abundance, John did not need to immediately buy feed for the cows and horses. He had, however, not given sufficient thought to the fact that he would need to get up before sunrise each morning to milk the cows by hand, and do the same before sunset each evening, seven days a week, 365 days a year. It would take him several hours each day to feed the cows and other livestock, care for the milk, and find a market for it. And he would be tethered to this job for years to come!

John realized, of course, that the grass, while green in the spring, would not be green all summer long, and snow would cover the land all winter. He would immediately need to clear enough land of stumps and rocks to plant and grow Timothy Grass (a perennial grass native to Europe) for making enough hay to last through the long winter ahead. As more land was improved in the following years, he grew a variety of beans, in addition to caring for his dairy.

While John busied himself with his dairy that first spring, Lena plotted an area in which to plant a garden. She convinced John that he needed to take time from his work in the field to harness his horses and plow the land on which she would plant sweet corn, on-

Butman, Michigan, Farm of John and Helena Gunther.
Note home and barn in background.

ions, turnips, cucumbers, beans, and cabbage. She found great delight in gardening. Taking the children with her, she often spent most of the day planting, weeding, and tending her precious vegetables. Some days she forgot to come into the house to prepare lunch, so all John got was a couple slices of homemade bread, a piece of cheese and a glass of milk. The summer days in this north land were long, the nights short, and the soil rich. In less than three months her hard work paid off. One cabbage head weighed twelve pounds. When not in her garden, she was in her kitchen canning and preserving her harvest.

One August morning Lena's father stopped by to visit. He brought with him a hog ready for butchering. A few days later, her father and brothers were back to do the butchering. Her mother's health had improved to the point where she could come along, together with Lena's sisters, to prepare meals for the day. Parts of the hog were put aside for hams and bacon. Other parts were ground for sausage. All these would be cured in the smokehouse John had built. It was a joyful day spent telling stories, laughing and singing while working together and enjoying the abundance God had provided. They were especially happy for Mother Johnson's improved health.

Soon after settling in, John realized he would need a barn large enough to store hay and give shelter to the cows and horses during the five coldest months of winter. He spent many sleepless nights worrying about how he could build a barn and do all the other work that needed to be done. He should not have worried.

It was not long after John and Lena had moved to their new home that they got acquainted with some of their new neighbors and discovered that many of them were of the Amish faith. John had heard the Amish were notorious for their barn raising abilities. Lena suggested he go and talk to one of them to see if they could be hired to build a barn for them. Sure enough, he found them willing and ready. When he asked what it would cost, they told him, "You buy the lumber. The labor will cost you nothing." In fact, they were almost insulted when John told them he was willing to pay them.

One of the Amish men was experienced in the construction of barns. He told John that no blueprints were needed and made a list of what kind of materials to buy. Several days before the raising was to begin, the heavy beams, siding, and metal for the roof were delivered to the building site.

While the men planned the details for building the barn, several of the Amish women came to Lena, who was expecting another baby within a few weeks, and offered to help provide food for the men during the building process. They would need chickens, hams and sausages, which Lena would provide from her pantry. Many of the Amish women offered to bring some of their own freshly canned fruits and vegetables, as well as home-baked bread.

On a Monday morning, in late September of 1915, more than twenty-five Amish men, plus men from Lena's family, gathered on the Gunther farm to begin the barn raising. After it began, the men came back each day to work until the barn was ready for use. At the same time, the Amish women came to help with the preparation of the large amounts of food needed each day. The Amish people sat together with the Gunther and Johnson families at tables and benches set up in the Gunther's yard, where they shared the abundant supply of delicious food and told stories about their sojourns through life. Language was not a barrier, as both the Amish and the Gunther/Johnson families spoke German.

It was a memorable experience for John and Lena. The one thing that impressed them was that the Amish were, in most respects, no different from the other Mennonites they knew. Yes, in some ways they differed in matters of faith. But they practiced their faith with zeal, loved their children, and liked to tell stories, laugh, and enjoy life. John and Lena were moved and inspired by the selfless, giving spirit of these "plain" people who were their neighbors.

In the years that followed, John bought another forty acres of farm land. All this land had to be cleared of tree stumps and rocks. By this time, Lena's brothers had become proficient in the use of dynamite. But pulling the huge tree roots out of the ground after they had been dynamited was another matter. For this task, the family built a tripod of heavy logs and hung a pulley from the top of it. A steel cable was strung through the pulley and attached to a chain. The chain was then slung around the roots of the stump. The other end of the cable was attached to a double-tree and hitched to the harnesses of a team of horses. With the help of the harnessed horses the stump was slowly lifted from its hole and later dragged to the edge of the field. It was a dangerous and backbreaking job.

Clearing rocks from the field was an enormous job. Many of them were so large that a chain had to be slung around them so they could be dragged to the edge pf the field one at a time by a team of horses. The smaller rocks were thrown onto a wagon and unloaded on top of the larger rocks at field's edge. It was not long before a stone fence emerged at the farm's boundary. What frustrated John most of all was that this stone gathering process had to be repeated each year as the winter's frost pushed more and more rocks to the surface.

During the next four years, three more children were born into the Gunther family. Martha blessed their home on October 13 of that busy year of 1915. Maria was born a year and a half later on May 13, 1917. Another year and a half later, on November 1, 1918, Ernest was born. Their mother took great joy in caring for the children – loving, feeding and clothing them. While the children were still very young, she began to teach them to help in the home so they would learn to work. As a crucial part of their training, she taught them to be thankful and obedient. In spite of being dead tired from the day's work, John often spent the evenings romping with the children. Before going to bed, he and Lena read a passage from the Bible by the faint light of their kerosene lamp, then knelt, and prayed – especially for their children.

The little Mennonite Brethren church Lena and her parents had attended while she was still living at home had continued to flourish as other families of similar background moved to the area. John, Lena, and their family attended services faithfully. John and Lena taught Sunday school classes and sang in the choir. It was important to them that their children become accustomed to going to church and Sunday school where they would learn Bible stories and hymns and listen to sermons. It was also imperative that the children get an education and learn to speak and write the English language. When they became old enough, Jakob and Elma began attending the small rural school nearby.

Within less than two years after John and Lena moved to Michigan, Mother Johnson's health began to deteriorate rapidly. So her family decided to move to Texline, Texas, hoping that a drier climate and higher elevation might prolong her life. Suddenly John and Lena were left without extended family or relatives.

As they looked back over their years in Michigan, they counted the blessings of family and church. Lena wrote in her journal, *"The lives of so many dear loved ones, friends, neighbors, and church members had engraved themselves on our hearts."* (She then added a note to her jour-

Pulling a tree stump on Michigan farm, with aid of a tripod and horses.

nal, *"Phrase it different, please."* (I decided I could not phrase better, so I am leaving it the way she wrote it so many years ago.)   The years of intensely demanding work and long winter months had taken a toll on the Gunther family. Perhaps it was time to move on.

The four years in Michigan had, indeed, been an adventure.

Chapter 19
Rosedale

Dietrich Klassen was the principal and his wife, Lena, was a teacher at Corn Bible Academy during the time John Gunther and Lena Johnson were students there back in 1907. The Klassens were said to be excellent teachers and loved by their students, and the school prospered under their leadership. However, after just two years they resigned their positions at the school and moved to California, settling in the rural farming community of Rosedale, northwest of Bakersfield.

In 1919, John and Lena began considering a move from their home in Butman, Michigan. At about this time they received a letter from Mr. Klassen in Bakersfield advising them that good land was available in the Rosedale area and that they should consider moving to California. John and Lena were amazed that they had received his letter at such a fortuitous time. They could only conclude that God had His hand in this correspondence; perhaps this was His way of showing them His will. They began praying about the matter in the same manner in which they had prayed before moving to Michigan.

One day Lena said to John in the English she was trying to learn, "In Michigan God blessed us, but I think about our children. This is not a good place to grow up. *Our people* are moving away. My parents move to Texline. Uncle Cornelius already in California. Always less members in our church. Soon it will close down. Then, how can we give the children spiritual nurture? What chance they have to make living here? John, you work so hard here. You cannot keep this up."

The idea of moving to California was intriguing. Everything they heard sounded like the biblical Canaan – a *"land of milk and honey,"* (Exodus 3:8 KJV). Word was that there were no poor people in California. It was, after all, *The Golden State*! The more they prayed and thought about it, the more convinced they became that they should make the move.

Lena wrote in her journal: *"Once again we sold everything, said goodbye to the many dear ones we had come to love, and with our six children, took a train from Gladwin. Our aim was California."* (Edited quote)

They had saved the wooden crates John had built for their move from Coldwater to Michigan. They packed their household goods into these crates, and were soon on their way. What a journey it was! More than a week on a train, with six restless children to feed and put to sleep at night. Maria was just two years old and not yet potty trained. Ernest, four months old, was also in diapers that had to be changed, washed, and dried on a daily basis. After just two days of travel, their Papa was completely exhausted from trying to keep the children quiet so as not to bother fellow-travelers. In an attempt he said, "Jakob, look at those beautiful horses in the field. Karolina, listen to the sound of the train's whistle as we ride through this town. Elma, repeat the alphabet in English." He finally threw up his hands and said, "This is harder than pulling tree stumps back on the farm!"

On the journey southward, the family was able to arrange a stop to visit Lena's family in Texline, Texas. "The stop in Texline," Lena said, "will help me visualize my parents' home when I think about them later on." Her mother had already died of cancer by that time. Her father had remarried, but she noted his health was also declining. The visit with the family was warm, with a lot of good food to enjoy. They went to see her mother's grave which had been moved from the Rogalskys' farm to the Texline cemetery.

The stopover gave John a respite from having to keep a watchful eye on the children every moment of the day. At that point in their journey John might have said, "Texline looks pretty good to me. We don't have to move to California." But a few days later they re-boarded the train and headed west. During those long days of travel through the deserts of New Mexico, Arizona and California he thought long and hard about the challenge of another new start.

John and Lena had made up their minds that when they finally reached California, they would settle near the small rural town of Shafter where her Uncle Cornelius and family were already living. (It was Uncle Cornelius who had enticed Lena's parents to move to Michigan.) When their train pulled up to the depot in Bakersfield, it was Dietrich Klassen, not Uncle Cornelius, who met them and took them to the Klassen home in Rosedale. Brother Klassen had cleverly arranged for the Gunther family to stay in their home a few days. It would give him just enough time to convince John to buy a forty acre farm he wanted to sell.

Before actually buying the farm, John and Lena looked the forty acres over and noted that the land was quite sandy. After having farmed heavy black or red soil in the mid-west, they thought the light, sandy soil might be a plus, perhaps easier to work. Other farms in the area appeared to have similar soil and were productive. The location was good, just a mile from the small Mennonite Brethren Church. They went to Shafter to visit Uncle Cornelius and get his advice. After praying about it, they bought the farm for $7,000 cash. The sales price included a house with furniture, 10 pigs, four horses, six cows, and a coop full of chickens. The sale was finalized in the fall of 1919. (A good deal, or a big mistake? Perhaps they should have prayed longer.)

> Note: Forty acres is a piece of land that is one-sixteenth of a square mile. In the 1920s, a forty-acre farm in California was usually large enough to support an average family. Considering the size of the Gunther family, they should have had a farm twice that size.

The house on the place was old, with just two bedrooms but a big kitchen. The inside walls had exposed studs, having never been finished with lath and plaster. The outside of the house had never seen a paintbrush. The siding was of clapboard; the roof, scraps of tin. A covered porch extended around two sides of the house. "It is a cracker box – nothing like our nice big house in Michigan," Lena declared. They lived in these cramped quarters for two years. At that point it became necessary, because of their growing family, to convert a part of the porch into another bedroom and a wash room. The kitchen included a wood stove for cooking, baking, and heating water.

The house had no electricity or insulation. It was hot as blazes in the summer and cold as an igloo in winter. But it did have cold running water piped into the kitchen, a luxury they had never had before! A water tank on the southwest corner of the house provided a constant supply for washing and cooking. Water for the weekly Saturday night bath was heated in a big boiler set on top of the cookstove. In summer, the water was warm enough for bathing without being heated.

That first winter, John spent long days of hard work preparing twenty acres of the farm for alfalfa, a crop suited to the climate and general area. He was told there was a good

J.P. Gunther Home in Rosedale, California, 1920.
John is standing in back. Left to right: Marie, Martha, Caroline, Helena
with Ernie on her lap, Jack, and Alma.

market for alfalfa hay in the Los Angeles area where large dairies had sprung up. The other half was prepared for milo that would be fed to the hogs, chickens and cattle.

Having never grown alfalfa, John asked his neighbors for advice on how to prepare the land for seeding, when and how to sow the crop, and how to properly irrigate the crop. The land had to be graded in such a way that irrigation water could run across it from one end to the other. Most farm land in the area was not naturally sloped, so before a farmer could irrigate, he had to have heavy machinery brought in to grade it properly. Fortunately, John and Lena's farm had already been graded.

John learned that before he could sow alfalfa the land had to be prepared with levees – a mound of dirt about ten or twelve inches high formed lengthwise across a piece of farm land. These levees were built about twenty feet apart. Their purpose was to keep the irrigation water from running aimlessly across the land.

The farm implement needed to form these levees in those days was a Fresno scraper drawn by a team of horses. The scraper collected a small amount of dirt as it was dragged across the land, which was then dumped to form the levee. John had not used one of these implements before and soon found that it was hard, tedious, and dangerous work. After a few days behind this scraper, he yearned to be back in Michigan milking cows in the middle of winter.

After the levees were finished and the land harrowed, it was ready for sowing the alfalfa seed. This was a job also done by hand in those days. Several pounds of seed were poured into a pouch-like sack, with a band slung from John's shoulder. As in Bible times, he walked across the land slowly, reaching into the pouch for a hand full of seed and broadcasting it as far as he could. In order to scatter the seed evenly, he first crossed the land walking

A Fresno scraper.

from north to south, then crisscrossing it from east to west.

By the time the seed had been sown that first year, the fall rains began. As fall turned to winter, John and Lena watched as the entire acreage was transformed into what looked like a beautiful green meadow. They were sure they had made the right choice in buying this farm.

Lena planted a spring garden of the usual vegetables. It was ready for harvest by mid-summer. The farm had two trees of pears and two of apricots. They produced a heavy crop of fruit that first summer. Using two-quart jars, she canned fruit from the trees and vegetables from the garden. A two-quart jar held just enough fruit or vegetables for one meal's consumption for their family of eight. She did a little arithmetic and realized she would need at least 300 jars of fruits and vegetables to get the family through the year. The

Note: *"A farmer went out to plant some seed. As he scattered it across the field, some seeds fell on a footpath, and the birds came and ate them. Other seeds fell on shallow soil with underlying rock. The plants sprang up quickly, but they soon wilted beneath the hot sun and dried because the roots had no nourishment in the shallow soil. Other seeds fell among thorns that shot up and choked out the tender blades. But some seeds fell on fertile soil and produced a crop that was thirty, sixty and even a hundred times as much as had been planted."* (Matthew 13: 3-8 NLT).

children were not old enough to assist, so it became a huge job, picking, cleaning, peeling, cooking and canning without any help. The temperature often rose to 105 degrees in the Valley. In addition to the heat outside, the fire in the cookstove inside made the heat almost unbearable. There was not even a breeze to stir the air. She said to Uncle Cornelius one day, "I had no idea it could get so hot in California. It is different in Michigan." But she never complained about the hard work.

Immediately after moving into their Rosedale farm house, the Gunther family began attending the Rosedale Mennonite Brethren Church down the road. The church had been organized in 1909 with 45 members. Two years later it hosted the first District Conference of Mennonite Brethren Churches ever held on the Pacific coast. John and Lena were excited about having a strong church where their children could make friends and learn the Bible. They looked forward to being able to serve the Lord in some way.

In spite of the mountains of work that needed to be done, the family set Sundays aside for going to church, never missing a Sunday. The children had been scrubbed clean the night before. Mama had made sure their *Sunday* clothes were ready to wear. The family got up earlier than usual to get the chores done before breakfast. They walked the mile to church both morning and evening. John, with his strong bass voice, and Lena with her mellow alto, made a welcome addition to the choir. Both were soon asked to teach Sunday school classes. During a time that the church was without a regular pastor, John was asked to be the church leader, and as a layman often preached the morning sermon. Their church, Lena wrote in her journal, was what made all their hard work worthwhile and gave meaning to their lives.

In the fall of that first year, Jakob and Elma were enrolled in public school. Their mother dutifully packed their lunches each morning, made sure their ears were clean, and sent them walking a couple of miles to school. The first World War had ended just the year before, and all German speaking people were very much aware of the stigma of being associated in any way with Germany. When Lena took Jakob and Elma to school to enroll them, she told the teacher to change the spelling of Jakob to *Jacob* and Elma to *Alma*. Whenever she wrote Karolina's name, she changed it to *Caroline*, and Maria to *Marie*. The changes stuck, and the names remained in this Americanized version throughout the children's lives. When Jakob got older, he was called "*Jack*". From that time on, Lena decided their children would be given Americanized names from the day they were born.

In the spring of 1920, the land not planted into alfalfa was seeded with milo. The milo seeds sprouted and the alfalfa grew in the warmth of the spring sun. The Gunther's farm looked like a picture painted by a master artist. John went out to milk the cows each morning, then called Lena to come stand beside him as they proudly viewed their handiwork as it had been blessed by God. All the hard work had been worth it. They would have a profitable harvest that summer.

As everyone knows, in the great San Joaquin Valley, rain stops falling by the end of May or sooner and the sky is cloudless and dry at least until September. As the heat of summer intensifies, the crops can only survive with irrigation: very different from what John and Lena had experienced in the mid-west where the rains from heaven watered their crops all summer long.

When the Gunthers purchased their farm it had a deep water well and pump standing next to a ponding basin. They thought they were ready for irrigating their crops during the dry summer months ahead. In that part of the Great Valley the pump was turned on in the spring and had to run twenty-four hours a day, seven days a week, through the long summer. During the night the water was pumped into a pond. Hopefully, there would be enough water in the pond by morning to irrigate a part of the land each day. The irrigating stopped for the night to allow the pond to be refilled for the next day's watering. This was the way it was supposed to work! But did it?

What John and Lena had not counted on was that the light, sandy soil soaked up the irrigation water faster than it could run to the far end of the field. Their great looking pump had been faking its ability to perform. It simply was not able to bring up enough water for the forty acres of land. There was only one solution, dig another well and buy another pump. "There goes $1,000 of the little money left after buying our farm," Lena groaned. They had to buy water from their neighbor until the new well had been drilled and the pump installed, a huge expense they had not expected.

The new well had been drilled close to the house. Each morning Lena got up and saw the handsome pump through her kitchen window. She decided it was worth the money even though their cash reserves were dwindling so fast it made her very nervous, and she often said so. John seemingly took things in stride. He never said much about money matters. What his family and the people in their church did not understand was that such matters ate at his insides. He carried the burden of breadwinner with deep concern and anxiety. At times he shared these concerns with Lena. They then made them a matter of prayer each evening before they put their tired bodies to rest.

A few weeks after the new pump had been installed and had been running all night, Lena looked out of her kitchen window to admire it and give thanks to God that they had managed to pay for it. As she looked, and looked again, she realized there was no water coming from it. She called John, and together they went to examine the problem. To their horror, they found that the sandy soil had caved in around the pump which by this time was tilted to one side. They immediately called the man who had drilled the well and installed the pump. He came out, pulled the pump out of the well, cleaned the sand out of the well casing, and reinstalled the pump. Before they knew it, the sand had caused the pump to cave in again. After several attempts to stabilize the well and the soil around it, the driller gave them the terrifying news that nothing could be done about it. The well had to be abandoned. Another well would have to be drilled on more stable land some distance from the original pump, and the water piped to the pond. For now, they were back to buying water from their neighbor.

As the alfalfa grew that first summer, John suddenly noticed thousands of weed seedlings germinating among the alfalfa sprouts. He was immediately reminded of the story in the Bible *"some seed fell among thorns,"* (Matthew 13:7 (KJV)). Sand-burs! The vine-like weed produced small grains enclosed in spiny burs, hundreds of them on each vine. "Like hair on a dog," Lena said. Millions of sand-burs covered the field of alfalfa. The burs stuck to anything that touched them, all manner of clothing, a cow's tail, a dog's fur, a rabbit's ear. The sand-burs crept along the ground in their vine-like fashion as rapidly as the tender shoots of alfalfa grew upward. When the alfalfa was cut for hay, the burs were scattered throughout the shocks. Cattle simply turned up their noses at that kind of hay. The Los Angeles market John and Lena had counted on for their harvest would not haul it away even if it had been given to them for free.

They had put so much hard work into preparing the land and sowing the seed.

They had spent so much money on pumps and irrigation.

They had had such high hopes.

The crop was such a failure.

Lena tried her best to salvage the alfalfa. She got up before dawn, put the smaller children into Alma's care, and with a hoe, she and Jacob carefully chopped the root of each vine so as not to scatter the burs. They meticulously stacked them into piles and burned them. They worked this way each morning until the heat of the sun became so intense they could not continue and Mama was needed in the house. There were days when Jacob saw tears streaming down his Mama's cheeks, as she realized this was a losing battle. Each bur that had not been picked up was potentially another vine. They fed what hay they could salvage to their own cows and horses.

By watching every penny they spent, the Gunthers somehow got through that first hot summer and the cold, damp winter that followed. They could not fall back on a Government welfare program for help, and would not have, even if there had been one. They were not about to ask their church for help from the *deacon's fund*. Rather, John and Lena, with their six small children, made do with what they had.

Both John and Lena realized that an adequate water supply was absolutely essential for raising their crops in the summers ahead. The cost of buying water from their neighbors was prohibitive. In spite of the losses they had sustained during their first summer of farming in California, they would need another well. It was drilled the second winter.

On March 20 of 1920, baby Peter was born right there in their tiny, ramshackle house. A doctor came from Bakersfield to deliver him. Peter was a handsome, red-haired boy. "Looks like his father," everyone said. Almost from the day he was born he amused the family with his antics. Lena was reminded of their firstborn, Johanes.

John planted milo and a few acres of cotton the next spring. He had learned the art of raising cotton back in the days when they had lived in Oklahoma and found that the Rosedale area was well suited for this crop. Because of Lena's diligence in rooting out sandburs the year before, the alfalfa did better the second year, but was still not a paying crop.

As the second summer approached and they began irrigating their crops, John began to realize their water supply was still not sufficient for the sandy soil of their farm. The original well was completely inadequate. The new well they had drilled that first summer was a dismal failure. Now they found that the second well they had drilled the previous winter did not produce enough water to meet their need. A third well would have to be drilled!

As one year followed another, the family's cash flow dwindled to a low ebb. Selling some of the cows' milk, a fattened pig now and then, and some of the chicken eggs provided their only cash flow. Somehow there was always enough food, even for another family member.

Lydia was welcomed into the family on July 14, 1921. She was born with a smile on her face. No one was ever disappointed when they came to her cradle to see this angelic strawberry blonde. The smile was always there. By the time she was two years old the smile became infectious laughter. There was no doubt that she was the spittin' image of her father.

A little more than a year later on November 22, 1922, Eva Elizabeth graced John and Lena's home. Her mother noticed almost immediately that she was more serious than her older sister Lydia; quiet and content, a baby easy to care for. Everyone commented about her round face and perfectly blonde hair. "She looks more like her mother," they said.

Less than two years later, on August 9, 1924, the hottest day of summer, Rubena Bernice made herself known as a member of the Gunther family. It was as if the hot weather had affected her temperament. Her older brothers and sisters realized before long that she could not be ignored. Her red hair matched her personality from the day she was born.

With the birth of Rubena, the children in the family rose to a total of ten, not counting John and Lena's firstborn, Johanes, who had died at age two. In spite of dwindling financial resources, they managed to find a bed for each child in what was now a three bedroom house. Through Lena's ingenuity, creative techniques and boundless energy, all ten children were well fed and clothed. All who were old enough were sent to school with their lunches packed. Lena cared for the younger ones while doing her housekeeping: washing, ironing, and cooking, plus going out and working in the fields. The brothers and sisters in the Rosedale church shook their heads and asked, "How does she do it?" None of them suspected that the Gunthers were facing a financial crisis.

Things got to the place where John and Lena needed additional income. Even though the Roaring Twenties were economically robust for most Americans, the farm was not a profitable operation. So in the spring of 1923, John went to chop cotton for his neighbors. Each morning, after he had done his chores, he chopped cotton for several hours during the heat of the day. After two weeks of this work with the glaring sun shining against the reflective white ash soil, he noticed that something was affecting his eyesight. His doctor advised him to wear a blindfold to see if his eyes would heal. Of course he could not work while wearing a blindfold. He could not even help with the chores; so on top of everything else, Mama, together with Jacob's help, did them.

In the meantime, John's eye problems only got worse. He finally was taken to a hospital in Bakersfield where he had to stay for a month while being treated. The eye problem was worrisome for John and Lena and the family. Would he ever see again? If not, how would the family survive with him an invalid? Without a husband and father to work the farm, and to help in caring for the family, what would they do? With only a horse and buggy for traveling, how would Lena get to the hospital more than ten miles away for an occasional visit to see how he was doing? And on top of all that, how would they ever pay the hospital bill plus all the other bills that kept piling up? The family faced a daunting future and Lena knew that only God could help them through this latest crisis.

One evening, after the children had been put to bed, Lena sat alone in the kitchen. The burden of the family's plight engulfed her whole being. She was almost beside herself. Finally, she cried out in prayer to her heavenly Father. She then took her Bible from the table before her and found what had become a familiar passage. She began reading in the German language:

"Fürchte dich nicht, denn ich habe dich erlöst; ich rief dich bei deinem Namen; du gehörst mir. Wenn du durchs Wasser gehst, ich bin bei dir; wenn du durch Ströme hindurch mußt, sie werden dich nicht fortreißen; wenn es durch Feuer geht, du wirst nicht verbrennen; keine Flamme kann dir schaden. Ich bin der HERR, dein Gott, dein Heiland, der Heilige Israels," (der Prophet Jesaja 43: 1-3).

"Fear not: for I have redeemed thee, I have called thee by thy name; thou art mine. When thou

passest through the waters, I will be with thee; and through the rivers, they shall not overflow thee: when thou walkest through the fire, thou shalt not be burned; neither shall the flame kindle upon thee. I am the Lord thy God, the Holy One of Israel, thy Saviour," (Isaiah 43:1-3, KJV).

As she prayed and thought about this great promise of God to ancient Israel, she knew it was God's promise to her at that very crucial moment in her life. A deep peace suddenly flowed over her entire being; it was like the calmness of the setting of the sun in the western California sky after a day of intense heat. She knew she and her family were in God's watch-care. He would see them through this nightmarish struggle. She soon found her bed and fell into a deep, restful sleep.

From the day John lost his eyesight, Lena knew what she had to do to keep things going on the farm. She and Jacob got up before dawn and milked the six cows, fed the cattle, horses, pigs, and chickens, and gathered the eggs. They finished just in time for Lena to prepare breakfast for the family and pack the children's lunches for school. All the chores needed to be repeated each evening. The sun was setting in the west before the family came in for supper. She did this day after day for nearly two months.

It was not long before the feed they had stored for the winter was exhausted. The fresh feed was still in the field. I quote verbatim from Lena's journal:

What could I do? I got our horses, harnessed 'em, and hitched 'em to the wagon. Then, off to the milo ears with a knife, every morning for a month, chopped the stalks down in piles with a corn knife. After school, my oldest son Jacob and I, we hitched one horse before a sled and picked up those juicy stalks and fed the horses and cows. Alma, the oldest daughter, prepared supper, using baked sweet potatoes which I had prepared to put in the oven. With that we had a salad and some kind of fruit, and homemade bread.

John's eyesight slowly improved after being dismissed from the hospital. But during this time, the Gunther family ate a lot of beans bought in 100-pound sacks. Mama cooked and buttered them. A hundred pounds were gone in no time. Many farmers started growing potatoes in the area. During harvest time, Lena and the children, with the permission of the farmers, gleaned potatoes in the harvested fields. Since most of the Valley in those early years was open, semi-desert land, wood was scarce. So the children were sent to the pastures nearby to gather cow chips for keeping the house warm during the coldest winter months. Lena went to the Salvation Army store in Bakersfield and bought dresses, coats, and shoes for almost nothing. She ripped the dresses and coats apart and redesigned clothes to fit their growing children – dresses, coats, shirts, nightwear and even underwear.

The family continued their struggle with the farm. Would they conquer the stubborn land, or would the land conquer them? After five years John and Lena held up the white flag and conceded defeat. They sold the farm at a loss, and with $1,000 in their pockets rented a neglected house in Shafter, a small town to the north. John went to work as a day-laborer wherever he could find work as a farm hand. His hourly wage was 37 cents: that was ten hours of work a day for a total of $3.70. A number of farmers in the Shafter area grew grapes for raisins. During the grape picking season, John and Jacob picked grapes, which were spread out on trays for drying. They were paid 2 ½ cents a tray. It was hard work, but sometimes they brought home $9 or $10 a day! Unfortunately, the season only lasted about a month.

Thus ended six of the most difficult years in the John Gunthers' sojourn. With ten children to feed and clothe, and no place to call home, it was time to move on.

Things were bound to get better.

Chapter 20
Kerman

On November 2, 1927, at 4:36 in the morning, Lena gave birth to her twelfth child, thus fulfilling John's dream of having a family of twelve children. In anticipation of this long-awaited moment, the doctor had been notified to stand by, and the children had been dispersed to friends and neighbors so the birthing could transpire without distraction in their new home in Kerman, California. It was a long night for John as he waited for Lena to give the signal to call the doctor. He arrived on time and the birth of John Wesley was without incident. They had decided to name him after his father.

When the children came home the next morning, they were curious and excited to see yet another masterpiece of God's creative hand. All ten children were led into the bedroom one by one to see their new-born brother. They peeked into the little basket and saw a tiny baby with a red, wrinkled face, and just a bit of white fuzz on his head. What a disappointment! After each had had a turn viewing the newborn, the father proudly but carefully picked up his twelfth child and carried him over to where little John's mother lay resting. They talked about how each child Lena had given birth to was a miraculous gift of God, and each was special and unique in his or her own way.

Note: Except for Part II, Chapter One of this story, which in its style and approach to writing is a horse of a different color, I have referred to my father and mother as John and Lena. Now that I have made my appearance in this world, and become a bonafide member of the Gunther family, I can legitimately begin referring to John and Lena, not in the formal tradition of some cultures as Father and Mother, or in informal tradition as Papa and Mama. Father was never Pops and Mother was never Maw, and I certainly never referred to my father as "My Old Man" (God forbid!), but respectfully (according to strict German/English ethnic tradition) as Paupi und Mammi (Paupi pronounced Poupa, and Mammi pronounced Mama) in Low German, the language which was spoken almost exclusively in our home at that time. If we spoke English we simply called them Dad and Mom, which I will do in the rest of my story.

John Wesley Gunther,
John and Helena's twelfth child

Kerman is a small town about 100 miles north of where the family had lived in the Rosedale-Shafter area. It was fifteen miles directly west of the thriving city of Fresno in the San Joaquin Valley of California. After five years of trying to keep the farm in Rosedale from going under, the family had sold their 40-acre farm at a loss. With the cash they had stashed away from time to time, and the livestock they had sold, they were able to pay the family's debts and retain a surplus of $1,000 with which to make a new start elsewhere. One thousand dollars was a paltry amount of money during the otherwise prosperous and infla-tionary decade of the 1920s. They chose Kerman, California, because they had heard that a new Mennonite community was developing there.

The years the family had lived in Rosedale were lean years. Dad and Mom had neither the money, nor the inclination, to venture out and buy a farm in the Kerman area without knowing if it would be productive. They had learned their lesson on that score in Rosedale. However, Dad had scouted out the area and found a small house on the south edge of town for rent. This, he decided, would be home for a while. He had also inquired about land he could rent and discovered that the Fresno Land Company had farm land and was looking for renters. He struck a deal with the Land Company and rented 40 acres on the north edge of Kerman.

The move to Kerman was by wagons pulled by teams of horses. All of the family's earthly belongings were loaded onto two wagons. Dad drove one, and fourteen-year-old Jacob, by now known as Jack, the other. The rest of the family had the luxury of boarding the Sante Fe train in Bakersfield that took them straight to Fresno where relatives met and housed them until Dad and Jack caught up three days later.

The rented house in Kerman was painted an obnoxious green. It had two bedrooms, a kitchen, parlor, bathroom, and running water. An eight foot enclosed porch had been built along the entire front of the house. The small house was a tight fit for the large family, but with Mom's ingenuity and the use of the enclosed porch, all members found a spot they could claim as their private space.

Our Kerman home where I was born.

Gunther sisters at home in Kerman, California, about 1927.
Back row, left to right: Caroline, Alma, Martha.
Front row: Marie, Lydia, Eva, Rubena.

Mom and Dad were very much aware of the fact that the $1,000 they had brought with them from Shafter would have to take them through the next winter, summer, and fall before they could harvest the first crop on their rented land. A garden provided an indispensable part of the family's limited budget during that first year in Kerman. The parcel of land on which the house was situated was a small town lot with little room for planting Mom's usual garden. She managed, however, to find space for the most essential vegetables to feed her family.

The area surrounding the town of Kerman was well suited for growing raisin grapes. To help the family budget that first year, Dad and the older children picked grapes. In the three weeks prior to the opening of school in the fall, they had earned enough money to buy the children's school clothing and pay the rent on the house for several months.

By 1925, Jack was old enough to enroll in his first year at Kerman High School, located two miles to the north. Alma, Caroline, Martha, Marie and Ernest were enrolled in the elementary school which was located across the railroad tracks and to the east along Kearney Boulevard. That left Peter, Lydia, Eva and Rubena at home to be cared for under their mother's feet. As noted earlier, I was born two years later, by which time Peter and Lydia were also enrolled in grade school.

The land Dad had rented was open ground, meaning it had not been planted into a vineyard or other perennial crops. He had decided before renting it that the land was suitable for cotton. Since cotton would not be planted until the next spring, he planted a crop of milo. This was a crop that matured during the summer and early fall and was a good cash crop to help tide the family over until the cotton could be harvested the next fall. The same preparations were required for both milo and cotton – plowing with a single-share plow drawn by Dad's team of horses. After being plowed, the land was harrowed and then planted with a two-row, horse-drawn cotton planter. After the crops had sprouted and grown several inches high, they were cultivated and prepared for irrigation. Dad's days started before sunup and did not end until after dark.

Dad's hard work finally paid off. The crops showed a profit during the years the family lived in Kerman. Among other things, he was able to secure five beautiful, strong work horses during those first years. Working with his horses day after day, he gained an attachment to them; they were his pride and joy.

During the winter of 1927, Dad needed only two of his horses, so he found free pasture for the other three on land owned by the Fresno Land Company. One day he went to check on his horses only to find they were not in the pasture. Thinking they might have gotten out of the fence, he asked the neighbors if they had seen them running loose. No one had. He found no break in the fence, so he could only conclude they had been stolen. Some time later a neighbor told Dad that he had seen an advertisement in the local paper indicating someone had found some horses and was going to sell them. The law was that if horses were lost, the owner had one month to find and lay claim to them before they could be sold by the finder. One day Dad saw some horses on a farm along the road between town and Kerman High School – a road Jack took to school every day. "Those are my horses!" Dad exclaimed. He concluded that they had indeed been stolen, then sold to this farmer, and there was nothing he could do about it. (In earlier years in the wild west, horse thieves, when caught, were strung up and hanged.) Dad grieved for months thereafter over the loss of his companions of the field.

The loss of those three horses was not the end of Dad's trouble with horses while living in Kerman. He needed to replace the horses he had lost in order to keep up with spring field work. He finally found two horses that looked good, but after a few days of working with them found them to be high-spirited and hard to handle. At the end of each day's work, he tied them securely with a rope to a heavy wagon. One morning he went out to harness the horses for the day's work. He could not believe what he found. One of the horses had twisted the rope around his neck and hung himself. The scene of that dead horse was almost more than he could bear.

Dad soon found another horse to replace the one he had lost. One day he went out to the fenced pasture to harness his new horse and discovered she had become tangled in the barbed wire of the fence. Her chest was covered with blood. Dad and Mom doctored the horse for months before she was ready to return to work. In the meantime, the Land Company loaned Dad a couple of old mules to help with the spring planting. Mother wrote in her journal, *"This sure was a testing time. We ask why?"*

Dad knew he would have to catch Mom in a rare carefree and generous mood before he broached a new subject. He had been giving it much thought, and had even done a good deal of investigation during one of his many trips taking loads of cotton to the gin in Fresno.

"Lena," he said one day in late 1927, "God has blessed us with good crops of cotton and better than average prices these two years. I have been thinking that we ought to buy a truck."

Mom could not believe what she was hearing. "John," she said in her broken English, "a wagon with a motor and steering wheel, like a car; you not mean that? You had bad dream, it cannot be. We have not money for such a thing. It is not right to think bad thoughts about a modern machine like a truck!"

John said, "Lena, I have been having to haul our crops of milo and cotton fifteen miles by wagon and horses to Fresno for the past two years. Those trips are long and hard. I have to leave early in the morning and do not get back until late at night. The trip alone takes three or four hours. When I haul the cotton to the gin I have to wait for hours before I can get it unloaded. It is dangerous to drive on the busy road with our wagon after dark. You know all this, and have often said how you worry until I get home. With a motor truck I can haul more cotton in one load, get there in half the time, and be home before dark."

By this time Mom had simmered down and began to understand that there might be some advantages to having a motor truck. "How much you pay, and what kind?" she finally asked.

"I have found a used Ford Model–T truck with a flat bed. We can buy it for $300. I can put racks on the flatbed and haul up to two bales of cotton at once – twice as much as with the wagon. It will go up to forty miles an hour."

Dad continued: "This truck is big enough so our children can sit on the flatbed and we can all go to church together." Children riding in the back of a truck was a common practice in those days.

According to Mom, taking the truck to church was Dad's strongest argument for buying the truck. Since moving to Kerman, the nearest Mennonite Brethren church was twenty miles away. Getting there by wagon and horses took up to two hours. In order to go to their own church, they were willing to get up before dawn on Sunday mornings to get everyone ready – then make the two-hour journey by wagon and horses. After thinking it over, Mom was almost convinced the truck might be a good idea.

Dad continued his argument by reminding Mom that Model–T flatbed trucks were a rarity. Those with shorter beds were popular for use as *delivery* trucks and available in a variety of models. When Dad ran across a truck with the larger flatbed he considered it a real find, just what he needed. After finally receiving Mom's blessing, he immediately made the deal in hard cash. It was the beginning of Dad's romance with motorized vehicles, an affair that lasted until the day he died.

Note: Henry Ford began building Model–T cars as early as 1908. After the invention of the "assembly line," Ford was able to lower the cost of a car to where the average American could afford to buy one. It is reported that he coined the slogan "Any customer can have a car painted any color that he wants as long as it is black." Manufacturing the Model–T is said to be one of America's all-time business success stories. At one time, nine out of ten cars sold worldwide were Model–Ts. While other cars were selling for $2,000 to $3,000, the first Model–Ts sold for $850. By the 1920s one could buy a new Ford car for $300 (in 2005 currency, $3,300). Trucks were a bit more expensive. Therefore, the $300 Dad paid for his truck was at a "used truck" price.

As noted earlier, one reason Mom and Dad chose to move to Kerman instead of some other rural California community was that they had been told that a Mennonite Brethren church was being formed in the area. What they had not under-stood was that the church was located twenty miles northeast of Kerman. The church, in fact, was several miles west of the farming community of Fairmead and called the Dixieland church. No Mennonite Brethren Church existed in Fresno at the time. In the Gunther's first visit to the Dixieland church, they discovered that it was made up of a mere handful of families, had no regular preacher or morning worship service, and most of the time offered Sunday school classes only. Twenty miles was a long way to travel by wagon and horses for just an hour of Bible classes. But it was a Mennonite Brethen church, and Dad and Mom were completely loyal to the church in which they had been raised and so were not about to look for a church of another denomination. Being part of a Mennonite Brethren church was important enough that they were willing to make the sacrifice of time and energy to drive the distance every Sunday. Their children were being nurtured in their church, and that was all that mattered. During the years they lived in Kerman, they developed a deep love for the brothers and sisters of the Dixieland church.

It was during those years that Mom and Dad experienced one of the highlights of their family life. It happened on Sunday, February 28, 1926, Mom's thirty-ninth birthday. On the Saturday before, she and the girls had baked a *tub full* of Zwieback plus several batches of cookies and a cake or two. She had also cooked a large kettle of Komst Borscht – a cabbage soup from a recipe borrowed from Russian cooks back in the old country. She had invited the brothers and sisters from their Dixieland church to the Gunther home for the birthday celebration. Mom wrote in her journal that they spent a blessed Sunday afternoon reading God's word, singing, and praying. But she says that the real blessing of the day came later that night.

Mom and Dad were both very tired by the time their guests had left, so they went to bed earlier than usual. They had barely fallen asleep when there was a knock on their bed-room door. Caroline slowly nudged the door open and came to Mom's bedside. She whis-pered in Mother's ear, "I want to be saved. Will you pray with me?" Upon hearing these words from their eleven- year-old daughter, Dad and Mom were immediately wide awake. They had been praying that their older children would come to the place where they would recognize the need for salvation and ask Jesus to come into their hearts. To ask to be saved was something that usually happened at church during evangelistic meetings, not at home in the middle of the night prompted directly by the Holy Spirit. Completely astonished by what they soon realized was happening, they bounced out of bed, knelt one on either side of Caroline and prayed that God would forgive her sins and receive her as His child. They then asked Caroline to pray a similar prayer. As she did, she was immediately overwhelmed by a deep, settled peace. She said later that she did not understand everything that happened to her at the moment she prayed, but she knew she was a Christian and Jesus was her Savior. Caroline left Dad and Mom's bedroom a new person.

Before returning to bed, Dad and Mom knelt to give thanks to God for answering their prayers. They had barely gotten back into bed when there was another knock on the door. To their further astonishment, it was Jack. Without knowing that Caroline had just left, he also wanted to be saved, and was asking for prayer. Thankful and with joyful hearts they knelt with Jack between them and prayed until he found his peace with God. Again, before returning to bed, they knelt to thank God for a second answer to their prayers.

The next morning, with the family seated around the breakfast table, both Caroline and Jack shared what had happened to them the night before, how they found salvation and made peace with God. Upon hearing this, Alma, just a year older than Caroline, broke down and began to weep. Mother could tell she wanted to be saved, but it was time to go to school. Both Dad and Mom breathed silent prayers throughout the day that Alma would soon make peace with God. Their prayers were answered that afternoon. As soon as Alma got home from school, she pulled at Mother's apron and asked if she would talk to her about how she could be saved. Mom was so eager to help her daughter Alma experience salvation, she stopped kneading the dough for the bread she was preparing to bake for supper. She and Alma disappeared into the bedroom where they talked and prayed until Alma found peace.

In the meantime, Mom's batch of dough spoiled, and she had to start a new one; but she was glad to throw out the old and start again. Her daughter had found salvation. A loaf of bread – what a small price to pay for such a great, victorious experience! Within less than twenty-four hours, her three oldest children had given their hearts to Jesus. What more could a godly mother and father want? Years later mother wrote in her journal, "*It was such a rich blessing to kneel with our own children, and lead them to the Giver of eternal life. John and I thank God many times for the blessing of those twenty-four hours.*"

The crowning joy of the salvation of Mom and Dad's three oldest children was completed two years later when Jack asked if he could be baptized. Alma and Caroline soon made the same request. It so happened that Jack had made a friend while living in Shafter. This friend's father had a reservoir for storing irrigation water. The children asked if Dad and Mom would take them to Shafter to be baptized in the reservoir. They were happy to oblige. Making the 100-mile trip was no problem. The family now had a Model-T truck.

The family was out of bed long before dawn that day. They quickly did the chores, and ate a light breakfast. The older children found their places on the truck, with legs dangling over the side of the flatbed. The younger ones were bundled up in the front center of the bed, Rubena at age three being the youngest. (I was less than a year old, so I was privileged to be held on the front seat by my mother.) Thus we made the three-hour journey to Shafter in time for the church's morning service. On May 13, 1928, after giving their testimonies in front of the Shafter Mennonite Brethren church members, Jack, Alma, and Caroline received Believer's Baptism by immersion at the hand of Rev. Schultz, leader of the church.

In early 1928, our family moved to a different house closer to downtown Kerman. We had been living *across the tracks*. This second house was located on the edge of town, on the north side of Kearney Boulevard, east of downtown. The bungalow style house was painted white, and included a small barn and *tank house*.

The tank house was a common part of the landscape in those days. Most were three stories high. The ground level had a room about twelve feet square that could be used as a wash room, a summer kitchen, or for the storage of garden tools. The second level was a room that often served as a spare bedroom. If used for that purpose, it had a stairway built on the outside and leading up to it. The third level housed a water storage tank which provided water for the house and garden. It needed to be as high off the ground as possible in order to provide adequate water pressure in the water pipes in the house.

When our family moved into their newly rented house, it was not large enough to include sleeping quarters for all members of the family, so Jack, Ernest, and Peter were given the second floor of the tankhouse as their bedroom. It is reported that the boys got up one morning and stood on the stair landing outside their bedroom to relieve themselves. As they did, one of the younger of my sisters happened to look out of the window, and not seeing a full view of the boys, but only the *water* coming down, immediately ran to Mom and reported that it was raining outside. It was the last time the boys were allowed to use the stair landing for that purpose!

A typical California tank house.
Photo Courtesy of Roland Bergthold.

Our house on Kearney Boulevard also had a small barn. Dad had bought a milk cow for the family. Of course, his horses were kept in the barn which also had a hayloft. Dad always kept sufficient hay in the barn to feed the livestock. The barn not only had hay in the loft, but also on the ground below. The children, especially Peter, loved to jump from the loft to the hay below. The myth persists to this day that later in life Peter developed a stutter he had to deal with the rest of his life from all his jumping.

Excitement began to mount during the winter of that first year in our *white* house. Not only was Christmas coming with gifts for all good boys and girls, but God was preparing a gift of another kind. Just three days after Christmas, December 28, 1928, my brother Raymond Leonard was born in that white house. He made his appearance into the world with a full head of red hair, and soon displayed a temperament consistent with the color of his hair. Being less than two years younger than me, he and I quickly formed a bond that lasted through the years. We spent many happy hours in our youth playing and working together. Where Mom found one of us, she usually found the other.

Our home had a wood stove for cooking and keeping us warm in winter. Firewood was scarce in those days, so the children went out to the pastures in the area to gather cow chips which were burned in the kitchen stove to supplement the wood. There was always a box of chips behind the stove. Another myth that has never been forgotten is that more than once I crawled to the bin and supplemented my diet with the delicacy.

One day an accident occurred near the elementary school my older siblings attended. It was spring, and a farmer was grazing sheep in the open field next to the school. Dad had made an agreement with the farmer to have some of the children tend the sheep during the day. One afternoon, Rubena, barely six years old, started across busy Kearney Boulevard to help tend the sheep. At the same time, the next door neighbor got into his car, turned on to the Boulevard and, not seeing Rubena, ran into her, knocking her over. It was a wonder she came through the accident with nothing more than a broken collarbone. Had he not been driving slowly he easily could have killed her. Mom and Dad took the matter seriously, but saw no need to take Rubena to the doctor and would not have dreamed of taking action against the neighbor. It was Easter time, and the neighbor, agonizing over his carelessness, brought Rubena an Easter basket filled with both candy and real colored eggs. She was so thrilled to receive such a splendid gift, she immediately forgave the man for causing her suffering and shared the eggs with the rest of the family. The bone eventually healed, but not without a permanent scar on her shoulder.

In 1929, Dad bought his first motor car. It was a brand new 1929 Studebaker President Touring Sedan, a car that was a sign of American prosperity during the Roaring Twenties. It also indicated that, for the first time in their married life, Dad and Mom had spendable cash for such luxuries.

How could they have known that America was on the verge of the worst economic crisis in its history? The Great Depression of the 1930s would cast a pall over the land like the midday darkness of an Alaskan winter.

How would the Gunther family of fourteen be able to survive in such hard times? Part III of my story describes how we managed to subsist during the years of the Depression and the Great World War that followed.

Postscript

I recently came across a newspaper article relating to the time our family left Kerman and moved to another new home. I do not know which paper it was in, whether an article in the Fresno Bee, or a local paper, nor do I know the exact date of the article. It simply bears the headline KERMAN LOCAL NEWS. I think it is worth including in my story.

```
     It is with regret that we chronicle the departure of the J. P.
Gunther family from Kerman.  They left last Saturday for their new
home near Dinuba.  Mr. and Mrs. Gunther and family have lived here
the past five years, and during that time have earned the respect and
love of everyone that learned to know them.  Theirs is a large family,
twelve children, we believe, and many people have often marveled how
Mr. and Mrs. Gunther managed everything so well.  Their children are
all physically and mentally perfect, and every one of them has some
talent or accomplishment that made them welcome in all circles.  The
older ones are splendid singers and musicians, and certainly will be
missed, both in the schools and the churches, where they took active
parts.  We believe we voice the sentiment of the entire community when
we state we regret to see them leave Kerman, but there is none that
does not wish them well in their new home.
```

Part III
The Family

"I have singled him out so that
He will direct his sons and their families
To keep the way of the Lord
And do what is right and just."
–Abraham, Genesis 18:19

Introduction to Part Three

In 1930 our family moved to a small farm south of Dinuba, California. Just months before the move, the New York stock market crashed, sending our nation and the world into a decade of economic depression such as it had never known. That was followed by an even more tragic decade, World War II. Even though our family was living on the edge of what seemed like no-man's-land, minding our own business, we found we could not escape the impact of these historic events.

Part III describes how those turbulent years affected our family. The format will switch from chronological to one of recounting anecdotes.

My parents had fourteen children; seven boys and seven girls. Their oldest, Johanes, and youngest, Roger, died in infancy. Their fifth child, Martha, died at age eighteen, leaving eleven siblings to share our family life. I believe it is noteworthy that during the first twenty-three years of our family life God called home three of our family members. However, God graciously allowed fifty years to pass between the time Martha died in 1934 and the time my younger brother, Raymond, died in 1984. The stories that follow basically revolve around Dad and Mom and the ten brothers and sisters with whom I grew up. They are told primarily as I remember them. I admit that the details may not all be correct. But a serious attempt was made to tell things as they really were. Any inaccuracies, hopefully, will not affect the essence of the narratives.

My parents and each of the siblings had their own unique personalities. I have included, in one or the other of these stories, my perception of each family member's personality. As imperfect as my portrayals may be, I have nevertheless tried to characterize them as I saw them.

I have added a new feature to this part of the book. At the end of most chapters I have written *A Reflection* related to the story – something that may provide the reader with food for thought. Most of the Reflections include verses from the Bible. Where the acronym NLT is used, it refers to the New Living Translation. The acronym for the King James Version is KJV.

A serious attempt has been made to arrange these stories by subject matter. This was not entirely possible. Some appear to be completely misplaced. Please let your mind wander back and forth as I try to give you a glimpse of what family life was like during the most impressionable and formative years of my life.

–J. Wesley Gunther

Chapter 21
Farm House

The first time I saw the farm house, it was surrounded by dry weeds taller than me and had never felt the soft bristles of a paint brush against its weathered siding. I was less than three years old at the time, but the scene burned itself on my memory and is still there. This was to be home for me from that day to the day Dad and Mom sold the farm and house and retired to a home in Reedley, some twenty-five years later.

Dad had agreed to purchase the forty acres on which the house stood for a total price of $6,250. In one of the files handed down to me I found the purchase receipt for the farm. It was dated July 30, 1930. Thirty-one days after the sale had been finalized, our family moved from our house in Kerman to the new farm located four miles south of the town of Dinuba, California. The address on the mailbox at the road read: Rt. 1 Box 349.

The Purchase Agreement was signed with only Dad's name. Mom apparently had not seen the house and farm until we turned into the dusty, dirt driveway on that August morning. Mom got out of the car, stared at what appeared to be a rundown shack, and decided that her husband, whom she had always trusted to use his head, must have lost it when he bought this place. She was about to tell him so, but this time she bit her tongue.

As the family gathered in the shade of an old cottonwood tree to cool off after the hot August sun had beaten down on us en route, a canteen of water was passed around the circle as each of us took a sip to wet our parched lips. At the same time, we drank in the broad view of what was to be our new home. The family was not even a little excited. Dad began to worry that perhaps he had made a big mistake in buying the place.

Finally he said, "Let's take a look." We lined up one behind the other as if we were going to play 'Follow the Leader.' With Dad taking the lead and Mom following close behind, we began the tour of our new home. We started on the northeast corner, trampling down the tall, dry weeds as we went. The first thing we noticed was a flimsy screened–in lean-to set on a foundation of wood pilings and attached to the back of the house.

As we continued, Mom noticed that the windows were so dirty she could not see through them to the inside of the house. The heat of many summers had turned the wood siding and roof shingles of the house into what looked like dry kindling. Dad kept an eye on Mom's face, hoping to see a sign of approval, but up to this point she showed no emotion.

The inspection of the north side of the house had barely begun when Dad, wanting to impress Mom, called us to a halt and pointed to a small box attached to the house. Wires from an electric power pole were attached to it. "This," he explained as he pushed cobwebs aside, "is what is known as the electric box." As he lifted the lid which was hinged at the top, we could see a maze of wires that, Dad explained, would light up the house in the dark of night, making the use of kerosene lamps obsolete. At that time, many houses in rural parts of the country did not have electricity. He pointed to the bank of switches and fuses called circuits, explaining that if any one of the eight circuits was overloaded, a fuse would blow, leaving at least a part of the house in the dark. "It is a safety feature," he said, "that could prevent a possible fire. But see these copper pennies at the bottom of the box. The previous tenant of this house inserted a penny behind a fuse and the overloaded circuit would continue to provide electricity to the house. To do that is a very dangerous solution to an overload." He cautioned the older family members never to use pennies for that purpose. But in the years that followed, they often did anyway.

When we got to the front of the house, things looked more promising. A spacious, airy porch had been built across the front. The roof of the porch was supported by columns that looked like architectural masterpieces compared to the rest of the house. Mom noted that at one time a lawn had been planted in the front yard, but it now was as brown and dry as an Oklahoma farm after seven years of drought.

Continuing around the south side of the building, the tour group returned to the backyard, where they took note of several huge cottonwood trees that provided shade from the summer sun which, by this time of day, was mercilessly beating down upon us. The trees had begun to shed dry leaves, creating an unsightly mess across the yard. Dad pointed out to our tour group that a well with a pressure system would provide water for the kitchen and bathroom inside the house. There would be plenty of water to irrigate a garden and the now dry lawn. A steel pipe leading from the system's tank had a faucet which Dad turned open. To our amazement, a stream of fresh water gushed out. Each of us, in turn, put our mouth to the spigot and had a good long drink.

Dad kept his eyes on Mom to see if he could read her reaction to what she had seen so far. He could tell that Mom was visibly impressed with the water system.

After the respite in the shade of the trees, the family filed into the lean-to through its dilapidated screen door. Jack judged that the lean-to was about twenty feet in depth and extended across the back of the house – perhaps thirty feet. The wooden floor creaked as we walked across it.

As we stepped into the house itself it was obvious that it had not been lived in for a long time even though someone had been tending the livestock left there after the sale. Everything from the doorknobs to the windowsills was covered with a thick layer of dust. The backdoor of the actual house opened to a good sized kitchen. The previous occupants had left behind a wood cook stove connected to a chimney by way of a stovepipe. A sink, with faucets for cold and hot running water, was set under a small window which faced to the south. A single, bare lightbulb at the end of an electric wire hung from the ceiling. Dad could tell it pleased Mom to see shelving for dishes lined the walls. It didn't seem to matter that the shelves had no doors. Off to the side of the kitchen was a bathroom, a pleasant surprise to Mom and the girls. Our first house with an inside bathtub and toilet!

A doorway led from the kitchen to a dining room large enough for a table that would seat the whole family in one sitting. A set of double windows on the south wall filled the room with sunlight. Off to the side was a bedroom which Mom and Dad immediately claimed as their own. A doorway led from the diningroom into a parlor that would accommodate the whole family for singing around a piano, or visiting with friends. A heavy, ornate door, with three inset beveled glass panels, opened to the front porch.

There was a second bedroom off to the side of the parlor. It was small, but had a window facing westward, and a set of double windows facing north. The north windows were set over a unique window-seat. The window-seat opened to storage for linens and quilts. Obviously, it also was intended to be kind of a lounging area.

After viewing the entire house, Mom finally turned and looked at Dad with a smile. Dad concluded that she apparently was quite pleased. We all thought it would have been nice if Mom had stepped over to where Dad was standing and embraced him with a kiss, but she had never kissed him in front of us before, so we were not surprised that she made no move in his direction. Instead, her first response was, "A house with two bedrooms. But where will all fourteen of us sleep?" Dad, as usual, didn't say a word.

The girls didn't really care, but Mom and the boys wanted to see the rest of the farm. So the tour group made its way to an old weatherbeaten barn located 100 yards from the back of the house. It was a typical California style barn – a hayloft in the center and a lean-to on either side. The lean-to on the south housed a tool bench and storage for tools, plus stables for two mules. The one on the north was used for milking and feeding cows. As our group entered the barn, Dad quickly pointed out that something would need to be done with the roof – we could see sunlight through the shingles.

A corral behind the barn was large enough for several cows. From there, Dad pointed to an old windmill standing halfway between the barn and the far end of the farm. We could see that several blades of the windmill's wheel were missing and lying on the ground. Obviously, it would not be pumping water into the stock-tank that stood empty at its base. Dad said, "We really don't need the windmill anymore. Water has been piped from the pressure system at the house to a water tank in the corral."

Our tour group began walking back to the house. As we did, Dad directed us to a dilapidated shack halfway between the house and the barn. Mom asked why the little shack was so important. He explained, "Inside that little shack is a water pump which is the lifeline of this farm." Our group soon gathered around the old pump house.

The Old Barn. Note the Milk House on the left.

The Old Pump House on the right. A new well and pump replaced the original by the time this picture was taken.

Dad excitedly told the family to stand back and watch while he pushed a button in the pump house. An electric motor instantly spun to life and produced a stream of water that filled an eight-inch steel discharge pipe. We could hardly believe what we were seeing. Mom was so amazed, she forgot, for the moment, all the work that would need to be done to make her house livable. "That's wonderful!" she exclaimed.

Dad proudly explained, "This well is less than a hundred feet deep. The wells in Rosedale were eight-hundred feet deep. If I had a shovel and if I would dig a hole four feet deep right where we are standing, I would hit the water level beneath the ground! We'll never run out of water on this farm!" Mom remembered the nightmares they lived through on the Rosedale farm – three wells, and still not enough water to irrigate that forty acres. She thought to herself, "What a relief to know that we will not have to deal with water problems on this farm." That ramshackle pump house was indeed the farm's most important feature.

The move from Kerman to our new farm home was a huge undertaking. Dad and Mom had prepared every detail they could anticipate, but they were both a bit jittery when moving day actually came. Dad worried about the possibility of the old truck breaking down en route.

It took two days to carefully load their furnishings onto the Model-T truck. Before beginning the trip to their new home, Mom took a final look around the inside of the house to see if anything had been left behind. The truck, with its six foot high cotton racks in place, was a sight to behold. The last thing to be put on top of the load was a mattress tied down securely. Alma, Caroline, and Martha were told they would have to find their places for the trip to our new home lying on the mattress. Fortunately, the truck's racks were high enough to keep the mattress from sliding off as the truck turned corners. Dad in the driver's seat, with Ernie and Peter beside him, led the sixty mile procession from Kerman. The Studebaker, with the rest of the family and Jack at the wheel, followed close behind. The trip took longer than expected, but was otherwise uneventful.

By the time our family had driven from Kerman on that moving day and had completed its tour of our new farm it was past lunch time and we were all hungry. As usual, Mom had had the foresight to pack a lunch before leaving our house in Kerman – a stack of ham sandwiches made with homemade bread, freshly cured dill pickles, cookies Caroline had baked, and a sack of fresh peaches. A canvas was spread on the ground under the nearest cottonwood tree. Each of us soon found a place to sit before Dad raised his voice in thanksgiving for the safe trip and for the abundance of food – the mound of sandwiches for fourteen (Dad and the boys each had two) and the rest of the meal. The faucet near the pressure system provided sparkling, cool water.

Even though everyone felt that a nap was in order, they knew there was too much work to be done. Immediately after lunch, Mom and the girls found buckets, rags and brooms to start cleaning up the dust and grime that had accumulated in the house. In the meantime, Dad and the boys unloaded the truck, carried each box and piece of furniture into the house and placed it as Mom directed. Mom's biggest concern, the sleeping arrangements, were worked out. Three of the seven girls would sleep crossways on the bed in the front bedroom. The other four would have to sleep on mats on the parlor floor. The five boys would sleep on cots in the screened-in porch. That was okay during the hot summer months, but not so good when the cold of winter approached. Mom and Dad, of course, had their own bedroom.

After a supper of bacon and beans, the family was ready for its first night in their new home. As each of us found our place to stretch out, contentment and peace settled over us like a sunset on the desert.

Dad and the older boys returned to Kerman in the Model-T truck the next day to move several pieces of farm equipment and anything else left behind.

In addition to the purchase price of the house and farm, the terms of the sales agreement Dad had made with the sellers of the farm, G.W. and Tazzie Merriot, included the following; all for just ten (10) dollars:

1 black mare mule, weighing about 1200 pounds, aged about 7 years, answering to the name of "Beck"; 1 brown mare mule, weighing about 1200 pounds, aged about 7 years, answering to name of "Kate"; 4 black and white cows of Holstein stock; 1 black cow of mixed Jersey stock; 1 yellowish heifer, 3 red and white spotted heifers; 1 black and white spotted heifer, 1 white heifer, said heifers being of mixed Holstein and Guernsey stock; one half interest in bull; 1 "royal Blue Sattley" cream separator; 31 head hogs; one mowing machine; 1 hay rake; 1 two-horse wagon; 1 vineyard truck; 1 drag harrow; 1 single plow; 1 double plow; 1 disc harrow; miscellaneous tools and farming implements on the place belonging to the parties of the first part; all hay in barn or stack; (Copied exactly as it appears on the original Bill of Sale)

Since no one had actually been living in the house for quite some time, a neighbor had been hired to take care of the livestock until the sale of the farm was final. This meant, of course, that the day our family took possession of the farm, and before we could sit down for supper, the men had to take care of the livestock that had been left by the sellers. The cows had to be milked, the hogs slopped, the mules and cattle fed, etcetera. Such chores continued morning and evening, seven days a week, from that day until Dad ultimately sold the farm twenty-five years later. We could not skip a day here or there. Whether we were actually involved in doing them or not, it became a way of life that affected all of us. No matter what other activities were planned for the day, we had to plan them around the chores that needed to be done. For my part, I started helping with the chores when I was seven years old and continued until I was twenty. They demanded diligence, commitment and promptness. There were times in the course of those years that we boys would have chosen to do other things, but the discipline of milking the cows twice a day, gathering the chicken eggs, and feeding all the livestock taught us valuable lessons that stayed with us for the rest of our lives.

The farm itself came with mixed blessings. The water well and pump were the farm's greatest assets. The water was splashed into what we called a cement "stand" (a 24 inch cement pipe that stood about six feet high). A cement pipeline was buried about three feet below the surface of the ground and extended from the stand in two directions, one to the east and one to the south. Each of these was 300 feet in length, and the water could be directed into either line with valves that had been installed in the stand. The one line watered the east half of the Forty, the other the west half. From the place where the lines ended, Dad had to plow an irrigation ditch in order to actually irrigate the farm.

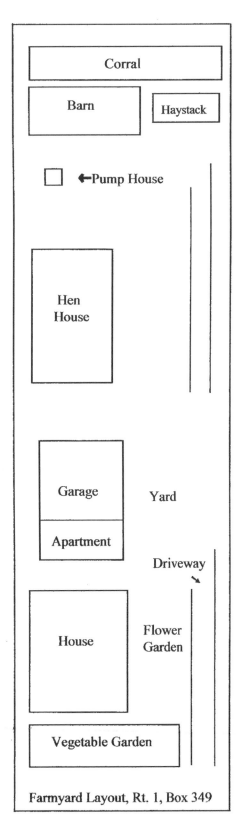

Farmyard Layout, Rt. 1, Box 349

One negative aspect of the farm was that about half of it was alkaline soil. Even weeds would not grow on this dirt. Because of this, the east twenty was practically worthless, except for a few acres here and there where grass would grow. So it was irrigated and used for pasture. Through the years, Dad poured tons of gypsum and fertilizers on it. He even bought Jack a big, new dump truck so he could haul gypsum from the Lost Hills area west of Bakersfield (a 140 mile trip one way) and spread it on the alkaline soil. Jack made the trip back and forth for weeks. Dad finally realized that it made no difference. He was once told that castor beans would grow in any kind of soil, even alkaline. So he planted two rows of castor beans. The experiment was a failure, something I considered a blessing. Mom would likely have crushed the beans and insisted that each of us take a teaspoon full of castor oil once a day for our health.

The farm actually had only twenty acres of good soil, black and heavy, but productive. It produced enough feed for our small dairy, but that was about all; not enough to feed and clothe the family, pay off a mortgage and taxes, or pay for needed improvements.

When Dad signed the papers for buying this farm, he had no idea of the tumultuous years ahead, plunging our entire nation into a financial crisis that would ultimately also effect us.

Would we survive?

Chapter 22
Surviving the Great Depression
1929 to 1931

Almost no one in America was exempt from the effects of the Great Depression of the 1930s, including our family. I was too young to remember the early years of that chaotic time. Years later, while farming with my father, I asked about those early Depression years. He and I were milking our fifteen cows one evening when those memories came flooding back to his mind.

Dad started rehearsing this story by saying, "We did quite well during the years we lived in Kerman in the 1920s. Although we only rented land, I was able to buy a truck and car, and save up enough money to make a down payment on this farm. I bought the farm on July 30th, 1930, for a total cash price of $6,250 which, one year into the Depression, was a lot less than it would have sold for a few years earlier. I made a down payment of $2,000. I then drew up an agreement with the seller, G.W. Merriott, to make interest free payments of another $250 on December 1 of that year and $1,000 on December 1 of each following year until the farm would be paid for in 1934.

"When we bought this farm, it came with eleven cows – some were still heifers (cows that were not old enough to give milk). The only "cash crop" we had that first year was the milk and cream we could sell to the Danish Creamery in Tulare. During the first year of the 1930s our family subsisted on the money realized from the sale of milk and hay.

"The price of almost everything was deflated during those years. A loaf of bread cost nine cent, two pounds of peanut butter was 25 cents, and a dozen eggs sold for eleven cents. Gasoline was delivered to the farm for twelve cents a gallon. But milk was expensive – 58 cents a gallon in the stores.

"If I had been a day laborer, and could have found work," Dad said, "I would have been paid ten to fifteen cents an hour. I would have had to work almost an hour to buy a loaf of bread, or work half a day to buy a gallon of milk. If I had been the only wage earner in the family, we would never have made it.

"Since we had the farm and our own cows, we had enough milk to feed the family, and some milk left to sell. The farm put all of you children to work milking cows, putting up hay, harvesting the milo, and a dozen other jobs that needed to be done. The milk and cream we sold were enough to buy the staples we needed – flour, beans, sugar, cereal, etcetera."

By the time Dad had explained all this, I had moved my milking machine to my fourth cow and broke in to ask, "But how did you have money for all the clothes we needed, gas for the car and truck, and to pay the electric bill? I don't see how you managed to pay for all these things."

He continued, "As you know, this Forty on which we live is not very productive since almost half of it is alkaline soil. The back twenty didn't have enough good land for pasturing our cows and mules without additional feed. I planted what good land there was into alfalfa and milo. The alfalfa produced enough hay for the livestock. The hogs were fed from a barrel into which we put all the table scraps plus a bit of grain.

"We also started raising our own chickens and ducks. The first few years they ran freely on the farm, so they needed very little of the grain I had planted. The chickens laid enough eggs to help feed the family and, after a while, reproduced fast enough so we could occasionally have a chicken dinner. Mom, of course, planted a large garden. It produced enough to feed the family all of the vegetables we needed."

While I finished milking the last cow that evening, I stuffed my memory box with what Dad had reviewed for me about how our family survived on the food the farm produced: milk and butter from the cows, eggs from the chickens and vegetables from the garden. One major food item was the hogs that came with the farm – 31 of them. When we needed meat we butchered a hog. One hog gave us ham, bacon, and a variety of other meats.

While these stories of the early years on our farm were still lingering in my mind, I brought up the subject again the next evening while we were milking. I kept prodding my father for more details. "Dad, you still haven't said how you managed to buy shoes, pants and dresses, underwear, nightwear and hats, which were essential for working under the hot summer sun in the valley. Where did the money come from for these things?"

"This Forty sustained us for the first year of the Depression, but ultimately, we had to borrow money and rent additional land to pay off our debts. You have to remember that your mother was very creative when it came to meeting the needs of the family. She often visited the Salvation Army store and bought clothes for almost nothing, came home, ripped them apart, and made beautiful dresses for the girls and shirts for you boys. She even made your underwear. We bought most of your shoes at the Salvation Army store. You will also remember that you often went barefooted during the long summer months."

"Yes," I said, "I remember that – and how sore my feet got from walking across a field of clods – and how it hurt when I accidentally stepped on a puncture vine; the blisters when I stepped on the hot pavement. All the country roads, even then already, were paved with asphalt – actually it was oil mixed with dirt but served as well as asphalt."

When I now think back to 1930 and 1931, there are things that stand out vividly in my mind's eye. By the time I was five years old (1932), life as we lived it began to make an impression on my memory. As I have reflected on those early years, it has occurred to me that, although we were poor, I never thought of our family as being poor – everyone around us was poor. No, I didn't have any fine store-bought toys to play with. I had to wear hand-me-down shoes and underwear. I seldom enjoyed a piece of penny candy. A slice of bread bought from the bakery was a special treat. The only time we left the house was to go to church on Sundays. We didn't have money for gas to go to church for Wednesday night prayer meeting during those early years. But we always had plenty of food on the table at least three times a day. I was well-dressed with clean clothes.

Life was good!

Postscript to Surviving the Depression

During the years of the Great Depression, the great majority of Americans were not as fortunate as our family. Industry came to a standstill. Millions of men and women lost their jobs and had no source of income. Soup lines sponsored by churches, charitable organizations and the government were common in every large city. People formed lines that were blocks long and waited half the day for just a bowl of soup to keep from starvation.

If a business owner was fortunate enough to survive the crash of the market and needed to find an employee, men lined up for blocks just for the chance of getting a job. Other men left home and hitched rides on the cars of railroad trains to get to more prosperous cities, thus giving rise to the "hobo" era. When a hobo came to what appeared to be a wealthy neighborhood, he went from house to house and asked if he could do odd jobs in exchange for a meal.

The Dust Bowl era began at about the same time that the Stock Market crashed. Share-croppers lost their farms and moved to California with the hope of landing a job picking fruit or cotton in the great Central Valley. Most of these migrant workers lived out of their dilapidated old trucks or cars while going from farm to farm to pick fruit. There were so many of these migrant workers that they had to compete with each other to get a job, thus driving down the wage they were willing to work for.

All this is to say that we as a family were exceedingly blessed to be living on a farm we could call home. It didn't matter that our house was small and dilapidated, and had never seen a coat of paint. It didn't matter that we boys had to sleep in cots in a screened-in lean-to that got cold as the North Pole in winter and hot as the jungles of Peru in summer. It didn't matter that my sisters had to crowd together in a tiny bedroom or sleep on the floor in the living room.

We had a place we could call home. We didn't have to stand in soup lines. We didn't have to split up to go out and look for jobs that might pay a dollar a day. We were a family. We lived under the same roof. We could:

work and eat together,

gather after a hard day's work and pray and sing together,

go to church together.

God marvelously provided for this big family in spite of the poverty that surrounded us. The cattle on a thousand hills were His, and He allowed us to take care of some of them.

Chapter 23
Surviving the Great Depression
1932 to 1941

The Great Depression of the 1930s hit rock bottom in 1932, and so did Dad's pocketbook. In order to provide the cash flow needed to keep the farming operation afloat and pay their debts, Dad and Mom had to refinance the farm with one loan of $2,455.75 and another one in the amount of $1,500. Annual repayment plans were agreed upon whereby these loans were to be repaid by December 1, 1934.

Our family's economic situation continued to deteriorate even after these two loans were paid off. Documents show that in 1934 Dad and Mom had to take out another loan for $2,200. As an indication of the severity of our economic plight, the loan was to be paid off over a period of seven years with annual payments of $300, plus 8% interest. The interest alone was $176 a year, more than half the amount of the principal due, a huge amount to add to Dad's already heavy burden of debt. The interest for one year would have bought 1,955 loaves of bread (enough bread for our family of 14 for five years), or 303 gallons of milk, or 1,466 gallons of gasoline, or 17,600 pieces of penny candy. Documents indicate that all debts against the farm were paid on time by 1939 and the forty-acre farm south of Dinuba finally belonged to Dad and Mom free and clear.

The reason I am giving some of the above details on borrowing money is to illustrate the economic straits we were in during the depths of the Depression. My parents had expected that the original mortgage against the farm would be paid by 1934. They could not have anticipated either the severity nor the length of the economically difficult years.

Soon after America's plunge into the Depression, Dad became aware that the Dinuba farm would not produce enough to sustain the family and pay all the bills. Farm products were almost worthless. He knew he needed more produce to bring to the market and would need to rent additional land. In 1932 he found a farm on the corner of what is now Road 56 coming south out of Reedley and Avenue 416 coming west out of Dinuba. He noted that a main canal ran along the south side of Avenue 416 and that the farm had been planted in alfalfa. Upon further inquiry, he found that it was an eighty acre farm with a good water well and pump. Since it was seven miles from home it was not an ideal location for a rental, but otherwise appeared to be an excellent piece of land.

The decision was made in 1932 to rent the farm, but the rental agreement called for $1,500 up front. Unfortunately, Dad did not have that kind of money, so he went to the Bank of America in Dinuba and through the Bank found an individual who was willing to put up the money that was secured by a deed of trust.

During the years that Dad continued as a farmer, he rented land in various locations including an eighty acre farm on the east side of Smith Mountain northeast of Dinuba, the Anderson eighty just a mile north of our home place, and Jack's eighty, two miles to the west. When our family's economic condition had improved during the 1940s, he bought forty acres just a half mile north of our home Forty. He later sold this place to brother Ernie.

Dad often struggled with the family's economic plight. Of course, he did not dare share his concerns with Mom. He did not want to burden her further with his cares. But he often got up early in the morning, went behind the barn where only God could see and hear him, and poured out his heart in prayer. He once made the observation, "Those that had money, made money during those difficult years. Those that owed money simply went further into debt." The good news was that God heard and answered Dad's prayers; not immediately, or through some great miracle, but through hard work and perseverance. The 1930s were lean years for our family, as they were for just about every family.

Even though Dad and Mom had to borrow money from time to time, the Depression years were not as bleak for our family as they might have been. During this decade, we were able to buy our first tractor, another truck, trade our well-used old cars for new ones, build a very large chicken barn, make improvements on our house and farm, make a significant addition to the original house, and pay our debts. I believe we were able to do these things because we were good stewards of the little God had entrusted into our hands. Even when it seemed there would not be money to pay the bills, my parents faithfully paid a tithe on the little they had. And God graciously provided every need *from his glorious riches, which have been given to us in Christ Jesus,* (Philippians 4:19 NLT). Beyond that, they planned carefully and scrimped wherever they could. As it turned out, having a large family was an asset and not a liability, because each of us worked hard, and all contributed to the family's well-being.

A Reflection

"HE WALKS WITH US: The road of life may take us where we do not care to go – up rocky paths, down darkened trails, our steps unsure and slow. But our dear Lord extends His hand to hold, to help, to guide us. We never have to feel alone, for He walks close beside us."   –Dayspring Cards, Siloam Springs, Ark.

Chapter 24
Dad

Dad was a tall man of slender build. His unusually big ears provided the perfect frame for his lean cheeks fixed above his angular jawbone. He was strong and muscular from having walked behind a team of horses and plow from the time he was a boy. On Sundays, Dad wore a suit and tie to church but on weekdays he typically dressed in blue striped overalls, a blue work shirt and a straw hat – clothes ordered from the Sears Roebuck catalog. Whether he followed the plow on the dry dusty farmland or changed the oil in a piece of machinery, his clothes were clean when he began each day's work.

My father was a man of few words, but the twinkle in his blue eyes bespoke his warm, personable disposition. Everyone seemed to like him and there were few people he didn't like. New neighbors and strangers were soon his friends as he extended a cordial greeting to each one he met.

I do not remember Dad ever raising his voice in anger, nor do I remember ever getting spanked. That does not mean that he didn't discipline us kids. When we did something that displeased him it took just a word or two to set us straight. We knew we had better not cross the line he had drawn in the moral sand. I soon learned the rules by which I needed to live my life – the same rules he followed in living his. Some of the more basic ones were:

never forget what it means to live the Christian life,
always keep your word and pay your debts,
don't ever talk back to your parents,
never utter a bad word.

Dad enjoyed teasing his children and people wherever he met them. For example, no matter how much work there was to be done on the farm, he shaved his face every morning. Usually he stood in front of the mirror hung over the sink and used a cup of shaving cream and brush to lather his face. He then sharpened his straight edge razor on a leather strap and started shaving. If any one of us children happened to walk by, he invariably dipped his finger into the cup of soap and smeared it on our faces.

Another of his tricks occurred when we were all seated around the supper table after a big meal. He drank the water out of his glass until there were just a few drops left. He then scrutinized each of us children, looking for the most unsuspecting one. Having made his choice, he lifted his glass and quickly flipped it over. As he did, the few drops of water left in his glass went flying across the table into the targeted face. He seldom missed his mark.

If Dad met people going to their cars after church, he often teased them by making a remark like, "I saw you nodding your head during the sermon today," something he himself did quite frequently. His unassuming wit, rather than turning people off, endeared them as friends.

Although Dad liked a good laugh, he also had a serious side. One was his prayer life. He always got up before daylight to go to the barn and start the chores. He didn't expect us boys to get up when he did. We usually straggled to the barn an hour later, still half asleep. When we finally got there we often heard a voice behind the barn. Dad was kneeling, whether in the cool of a summer morning or in the cold of winter mornings, praying to his heavenly Father, interceding for his family, the pastor, missionaries, and those who were sick.

There were times when what another person said or did hurt Dad deeply. At such times he became very quiet and hardly said a word for two and three days straight. We all knew something was bothering him, but usually didn't know what it was, nor dared we ask. His silence was hard on the whole family as we waited for his *balloon* to burst. It never did. He gradually worked his way through his hurt until he was his old self again.

Dad, John P. Gunther

In my estimation, Dad was the epitome of a godly man. In order to provide for his family, he worked harder than any man I ever knew. He loved Mom and his children. Although he expected us to toe the line when it came to matters of right and wrong, he never expected us to live on a plane higher than the one on which he lived. Church, the Bible, and prayer were at the core of his life. In his lifetime, he memorized hundreds of Bible verses, both in German and English. The one he quoted most frequently was, "*But they that wait upon the Lord shall renew their strength; they shall mount up with wings as eagles; they shall run and not be weary; and they shall walk, and not faint.*" (Isaiah 41:31 KJV).

Dad was a deacon whom the Reedley Mennonite Brethren Church ordained for life, and Mom was a constant companion in this ministry. They did not see the deaconate as a position of honor, but as a service responsibility to be taken seriously. In spite of all the work that needed to be done on the farm, they found time to visit the sick and shut-ins, often taking food to share with them.

Dad's big ears were an asset in that he was a good listener. There wasn't a thing I could not share with him – and often did. Although he had all the qualities of a friend, I would never have thought of him as a friend. He was my father!

What more could a son ever expect of his Dad?

A Reflection

While still a young man, my father memorized a ten-verse German poem entitled "Das Leben Unter Dem Bilde Erner Schiffahrt." It asks the question, "What is your goal?" and tells the story of four ships. Three of them disregarded the warnings of the beacon lights along the shore and crashed against the rugged shoreline. One was careful in heeding the warnings and managed to safely sail into the harbor. Dad once said, "That poem was like a beacon light keeping my tiny ship from the treacherous rocky shoal. I knew that one day it would bring me into the safe harbor where I would finally be welcomed by my Lord and Master, Jesus Christ." He reviewed this poem so frequently that he was able to quote it word-perfect until the day he died. The poem together with the many Bible verses he had memorized, became the compass which guided his daily life. All of us children knew that if we followed his ship, we would have no problem reaching that safe harbor.

Dad, about 1939. The car is a 1938 Studebaker.
The dog is named Rover.

Chapter 25
Mom

My Mother had a beautiful round face with delicate features. She was a bit bigger around the middle than my father. (At least from the time I was born and through all the years that I knew her. After all, she had carried 14 children to birth.) Her long brunette hair was usually tied in a bun so as not to get in the way of her hands that were busily at work. I do not recall that her hair ever turned gray in the later years of her life – probably because she didn't have time to get old.

Mom's temperament was very different from Dad's; a psychologist would have described hers as *Type A*. From sunup to sundown, she literally ran from one task to the next. No job was too hard or too menial for her to tackle. As mentioned earlier, she got more done in a day than most housewives could do in two. It seemed that she could do two jobs at once – like mixing dough for bread while making sandwiches for our school lunch boxes.

It was fortunate that Mom was blessed with a patient and loving spirit. She did not easily or often become angry, but when she did, her temper flared as quickly as her words were harsh. I learned early in life that it was best not to test her patience. I also discovered that after she had vented her anger, she recovered quickly and was once again her usual pleasant self.

Mom was the one who kept us children on the straight and narrow. More than once, she asked for a switch from a nearby tree to discipline a wayward son, but only after it was apparent that he deserved a little paddling. After all, she was only following the advice of the Bible, "*Foolishness is bound in the heart of a child; but the rod of correction shall drive it far from him,*" (Proverbs 22:15, NLT). Brother Ernie was often the brunt of such discipline. The image is still vividly and indelibly impressed upon my memory: Mother, with a switch in hand, running after Ernie. On one occasion they encircled our entire Forty before Mom finally caught up with him and gave him the switching she thought he deserved.

As Ernie got older and began dating, he sometimes broke the rule that all family members were to be home from such activity before midnight. Being the worrier that Mom was, she always left a light on and never fell asleep before all the children were safely home and in bed. On those nights when Ernie didn't get home on time, he usually felt the sting of the switch Mom had hidden behind the door.

Although Mom was always ready to do any work that needed to be done, she knew how to delegate responsibility. Each one of the girls knew what was expected of her and she didn't have to tell them twice. We boys also knew we could not get by with our clothes strewn on the bedroom floor. The room had to be neat and tidy before we left for school or work.

As noted earlier, Mom was a worrier. Next to our spiritual well-being, her biggest concern was the health of each family member. She took great pains to feed us well-balanced meals and see that we were kept clean and well cared for. She had good reason to be concerned about health problems. Health insurance was not something my folks knew anything about. Dad and Mom had, after all, lost three children to health problems. But if any one of us was not feeling well, she usually assumed the worst. If I complained about a pain in my gut Mom would say, "I wonder if it isn't cancer." If I had a fever she would say, "I hope it isn't polio," a disease that was rampant during those years and for which a vaccine had not yet been discovered.

From time to time, Mom had her own health problems to deal with. In the early 1940s she was diagnosed with her first hernia, a condition, no doubt, the result of her many years of hard work. She suffered severe pain for months. At times she would lie on her bed crying out in agony before she finally submitted to having it taken care of surgically in the Kingsburg hospital. Complications set in after the operation, and we all thought she would not recover. It was a nerve-racking time for all of us; how could we possibly manage without our mother? Many prayers were sent up to God for her during that time. It was several weeks before she could be on her feet, and nearly a year before she was her old self again. She vowed never to allow herself to undergo such an operation again. It wasn't long before another hernia appeared, then another and another. She had to have five such surgeries in her lifetime, each one more life-threatening than the other.

Prayer was at the core of Mom's life. No matter how much work needed to be done, she always took time to pray

Mom, about 1936, so beautiful and stylish in her new winter coat.

for her family. It was as important as feeding and clothing them. Even as Dad had his place of private prayer behind the barn, Mom's was her bedroom. I often came home from school at about 4 o'clock. As I walked past Mom's closed bedroom door, I heard her interceding for her children, many times with weeping.

Mom also encouraged each of us to develop a time of private prayer. How many times did she ask me, "Vesley, did you pray today?" Did her reminders pay off? They certainly did. During my growing up years, I hardly ever left for school without spending a few minutes praying in the privacy of our one bathroom. And the habit has stayed with me throughout my life. Prayer became important to me because I saw it exemplified in both my father and mother.

A Reflection

I recently found the following prayer in one of Mom's scrapbooks, carefully typed out in English:

Our loving children: are you walking in our footsteps?

Father, help them to have so much faith that they not wither away from your ways as did the seed wither because there was no depth to its roots. Father, help them not to hide away in the ways of the world, so they may stand. Give them the power that [they] might overcome the temptations that are set before [them] by worldly things. May [they] realize that the only way to sink roots deep within Him [God] is to be in constant fellowship with you by praying and reading your word.

Chapter 26
My Faith Journey

The old Mennonite Brethren meeting house, with its turrets, colonnades and stained glass windows was quite a stately edifice. It was easily the most impressive structure in the town of Reedley with its population of 3,000 at the time. The building accommodated 1,200 people, including the balcony. Pews of solid oak were slightly curved and placed on the main floor in amphitheater style. Each pew end was embellished with a carved design that was appropriate to a worship setting. An ornate clock, with pendulum, was a permanent fixture fastened to the north wall. A full basement formed the lower level of the building. The basement was used for Sunday school classes, social events, wedding receptions, and young people's meetings. In former days, all Mennonite church buildings were simply referred to as meeting houses, so in the stories that follow I will randomly refer to a house of worship as a *church* or *meeting house*.

The elegant Reedley Mennonite Brethren Meeting House.
Photo courtesy of Norman Huebert

At the front of the main floor was a platform about five feet high and included a loft from which a choir of sixty members provided glorious music each Sunday. An ornately designed pulpit built of rare solid walnut was given a prominent place in center front. Four imposing pulpit chairs completed its furnishings. An eighteen inch high green velvet curtain hung from a steel railing at its edge. A grand piano was conspicuously placed at a lower level to the right.

The church was filled to capacity on Sunday mornings. Usually, the men and boys sat on the north side of the main floor. The women and girls were assigned pews on the south side and young married couples in the center section. The young people were allowed to sit in the balcony.

Besides the regular Sunday services and Wednesday night prayer meetings, the leadership scheduled evangelistic meetings, sometimes called revival meetings, once or twice a year. These were usually in the form of a two-week series, with meetings every week night and two services on Sundays. A guest evangelist was invited to preach at each of the meetings. During the first week the sermons focused on encouraging those members of the church who had become backsliders to rededicate their lives to the Lord. The second week was given to extending an urgent call to wayward family members and people in the community to give their lives to Christ.

I was twelve years old when in the fall of 1939, the church held such a series of meetings. Reverend A.J. Harms had been invited to be the evangelist. Each meeting began with a rousing song service led by Henry Martens. My sister Lydia or Anna Marie Nachtigall were at the piano. The church choir sang a special gospel song or two, after which Brother Harms preached a powerful sermon and concluded with an altar call. While the congregation sang an invitation hymn like *Softly and Tenderly Jesus is Calling* or *Just as I Am*, the evangelist earnestly pleaded with those who were not saved to get up from where they were sitting and come to the front. As the altar call came to a conclusion, those who had come forward were asked to proceed to the basement where they would be met by personal workers who were prepared to explain the way of salvation to each one, answer questions, and pray with them.

I had gone to each of the meetings during this particular series, sitting in the balcony with my friends. As the week progressed I began to experience some strange feelings deep within my soul. It was as if someone was pounding on my chest – like an urgent knock on a door. I was eager to answer the door but at the same time, afraid. By the end of the second week, I didn't want to attend the meetings because I knew that familiar beating in my breast would return. I even felt it during the day while in school or at home doing the chores. I tried to dismiss it, but it wouldn't go away.

It was the final night of the meetings and I was sitting as far back in the balcony as I could, surrounded by my best friends. Brother Harms had preached his last sermon and was giving the altar call. The congregation began to sing *Why Do You Wait? (by George Frederick Root)*:

> *Why do you wait, dear brother, Oh why do you tarry so long?*
> *Your Savior is waiting to give you, A place in His sanctified throng.*
>
> *What do you hope, dear brother, To gain by a further delay?*
> *There's no one to save you but Jesus, There's no other way but His way.*
>
> *Do you not feel, dear brother, His Spirit now striving within?*
> *Oh, why not accept His salvation, And throw off your burden of sin?*
>
> *Why do you wait, dear brother, the harvest is passing away;*
> *Your Savior is longing to bless you, There's danger and death in delay.*

I could not join with the congregation in singing that invitation hymn. Its every word felt like an arrow piercing my tender, young heart. I knew my time had come. With sweat on my brow, my heart pounding and my knees knocking, I slowly pushed my way from the center of the pew on which I had been sitting and made my way down the steps and aisle, which seemed a mile long. Although the congregation had been asked to keep their heads bowed and their eyes closed, I knew that 1,199 people were craning their necks to get a peek at this wayward soul that was making his way to the altar.

Yes, it was the son of deacon John Gunther going forward to be saved. The evangelist and pastor G.B. Huebert met me at the front and sent me down to the basement. By the time I got there my mother was already waiting for me. She put her loving arm around me as we wept and talked. We then knelt at a bench while I prayed, confessed my sins, and asked Jesus to forgive me and receive me as His child. My mother then prayed a special prayer for me and gave me a Bible verse upon which to rest my new-found faith, *"Believe on the Lord Jesus Christ, and thou shalt be saved,"* (Acts 16:31 KJV).

I left the church basement that evening knowing that I was a child of God. I had been born anew. Suddenly, the burden I had carried for two weeks was lifted. I felt light-hearted and free. Although my faith was tested in the weeks and months that followed, I knew that what had happened to me was real; it was grounded in the promise of God. And through the years that have followed, I have had a peaceful assurance as to my eternal destiny.

The night was pitch black as Mom and I emerged from the church building after that meeting. When we got to our car to go home, the rest of the family was there, waiting for the moment they could hug me and affirm the decision I had made.

I knew that the next step in my pilgrimage of faith was baptism. I also knew that, according to the strong convictions of our church, I could not be baptized until I had proved to my family and the church that my salvation was genuine; I would have to show it by the way I lived my life on a daily basis. So it wasn't until I was fourteen years old that I was ready to take the step of baptism.

Let me give an example of the policy of the church about proving myself. The Sunday afternoon before I was to be baptized, my brother Ray and I sneaked away from home, walked to the little country store a mile away and bought some penny candy. It was so sweet and delectable as we ate it while walking back home. Its sweetness, however, turned to gall as we were met at the door by our mother who had already guessed what we had done. Her words struck like a bolt of lightning as she told us that because we had disobeyed one of Mom and Dad's rules by going to the store on Sunday, we would probably not be ready for baptism the following Sunday. We immediately confessed that we had done wrong and asked forgiveness. Mom relented.

The procedure for taking the step of baptism was not an easy one. In fact, I felt the church made the process as difficult as possible to weed out those who had simply gone through the motions of becoming Christians and were not genuinely saved. This was the process: after a period of instruction, I was asked to give my testimony in front of the whole church as to what happened to me that night when I knelt in the basement with my mother. Giving this testimony was even more scary than when I took that walk from the balcony to the altar! I was a shy little fellow. I was expected to stand on that big platform in front of a church filled with these old men and women who knew what a troublemaker I had been in spite of being the son of a deacon!

I had my whole speech written out. Once again, with my knees knocking and heart pounding, I stood behind that ornate pulpit from which my pastor preached every Sunday in the big Reedley meeting house. While Pastor Huebert stood beside me and lovingly placed his hand on my twitching arm, I opened my mouth to speak, but no sound came out. It was only after an embarrassing moment of complete silence that I finally tried again, and somehow managed to make my little speech. When I finished, the pastor asked the members of the congregation if they had any questions. Boy, did the ensuing silence freeze me in my tracks! The whole church was quiet. No one stood up to speak or ask a question. I thought I was a goner.

I was then asked to step into a small waiting room while the church discussed my testimony. My father and mother and Sunday School teacher, I was told later, bore witness to what kind of life I had lived since my conversion. Mom was true to her word and didn't mention the incident about sneaking off to the store the Sunday before. But those minutes in the waiting room seemed like an eternity. Believe you me, I could see my whole future hanging in the balance. The church could vote to tell me I was not ready for baptism, in which case I would have to go through the whole procedure again a year later.

Ultimately, I was called back before the church as the pastor announced that the congregation had voted to approve me for baptism. I had passed the test and was baptized at the Reedley beach in the Kings River as an adult believer by Pastor Huebert on Sunday afternoon, April 21, 1940. My brother Raymond and about fifty other new converts were baptized the same day.

That evening the church had a special Communion Service. All of us who had been baptized were called to the front where we knelt as Pastor Huebert read the rules of conduct for church members, laid his hands on each of us, and prayed a benediction prayer: *"And the*

A Mennonite Brethren baptism in Kings River
at Reedley Beach, where I was baptized.

very God of peace sanctify you wholly, and I pray God your whole spirit and soul and body be preserved blameless unto the coming of our Lord Jesus Christ," (I Thessalonians 5:23, NLT). He then asked us to rise as he extended the hand of fellowship to us, welcoming us into the membership of the Reedley Mennonite Brethren Church.

Thus, my conversion and baptism were the beginning of my faith journey with Jesus Christ.

A Reflection

During my growing up years I learned five key Bible verses:

- Romans 3:23 "*For all have sinned,* and come short of the glory of God."
- Romans 6:23 "For the wages of sin is death; but the *gift of God is eternal life* through Jesus Christ our Lord."
- John 3:16 "For God so loved the world, that he gave his only begotten Son, that *whosoever believeth in him* should not perish, but have everlasting life."
- John 1:12 "But *as many as received him,* to them gave he power to become the sons of God, even to them that believe on his name."
- Revelation 3:20 "Behold, I stand at the door, and knock: if any man hear my voice, and *open the door,* I will come in to him and will sup with him and he with me."

I have used this outline of verses many time to lead a seeker to faith in Christ. There is a key phrase (in italics) in each verse. The last verse leads to a most glorious climax: God's promise, "*I will come in.*" (All verses from the King James Version.)

Chapter 27
Family Life

Life on the farm in the 1930s was not all work; somehow we found time for being together and doing things all of us enjoyed. Breakfast and supper times were a big part of our family life because we never ate a meal until all were present and accounted for. The noon meal on week days was an exception, since the men often worked on farms away from home, and the kids were in school. Before we began breakfast, one of the family members read a chapter from the Bible and a prayer was offered by either Dad or Mom.

With few exceptions, there was plenty of good food on the table for every meal. Breakfast was often a bowl of corn flakes and homemade bread. Meat and potatoes with gravy was standard fare for supper. The evening meal among us common farm folk was referred to as supper rather than dinner. Once in a while Lydia decided to make soup for supper. It was a menu item that was not acceptable for working farm boys like us, unless of course it was topped off with apple pie or chocolate cake, or both.

Some of the supper foods that were acceptable, besides meat and potatoes, were Mom's freshly butchered chicken deep fried in lard, watermelon and crullers, fresh corn on the cob, ham and pluma mousse (a kind of plum pudding), and verenika with sweet cream gravy and sausage. Zwiebacks with butter and jam, fresh peaches and homemade ice cream were also acceptable menu items for Saturday night suppers.

Meals with all these good foods drew us together like flies to honey. During these meal times we told stories, argued, laughed and teased each other. *"Blest be the tie that binds!"*

Recipe For Verenika	
Dough: Mix...	
4 c. flour	1 tsp salt
4 egg whites	½ c. sour cream
Filling: Mix...	
2 c. dry cottage cheese	1 tsp salt
4 egg yolk	dash of pepper

Roll out dough and cut into 4 inch rounds. Moisten edges of rounds and put 1 heaping tsp. of cottage cheese mixture in center and fold dough over and squeeze edges together making half round shapes. Put into boiling water and cook until the verenika rise from the bottom. Carefully lift out of water and put in a skillet half full of hot fat and deep fry until brown. Serve immediately. Sweet cream and ham gravy, or corn syrup make a delectable topping. Other fillings could include potatoes or fruit like plums or apples.

Although I think most of us had inherited a good sense of humor, none of us were comedians. The only one who knew how to tell a joke was Peter. Mom liked to tell stories. Lydia found most events and happenings among us to be hilarious and laughed about almost anything – and we all laughed with her. If any one of us broke one of the house rules, like dawdling on the way to school and getting there late, Mom and Dad eventually found out about it. None of us had many secrets. When one of the girls dated a young man, she was teased unmercifully.

Ray and I liked to tease Rubena who was the sibling just older than me. She had several suitors who came to our front door during her high school years. If she invited them to visit in our parlor, we sneaked behind the chesterfield (a sofa in more recent parlance) and listened to their conversations. When they left, we repeated to her some of the more romantic words they spoke to each other. She had not realized we were there and, boy-oh-boy, did she explode! Rubena had a temperament much like Mom's – something like a hot electrical wire touching a piece of metal. Sparks flew in every direction when she got mad. That, of course, is why we liked to tease her.

Everybody liked Rubena. She made friends easily, which is why so many boys came to call on her. But she was rather picky about whom she would actually date. It seemed that after learning to know them, none of them were just right for her. Perhaps that explains why she didn't marry until she was fifty years old.

Like Mom, Rubena preferred being in charge of things and enjoyed telling us boys what to do. Most of the time Ray and I ignored her, which of course irked her to no end. It was generally agreed that she had a stubborn streak in her. After she made up her mind to do something, not even Dad could persuade her otherwise. On the contrary, if there was something she was not interested in doing, neither heaven nor angels could convince her to get involved.

One of the many things our whole family liked about Rubena was that she was always doing things for us. Without me asking her, she often helped me with the chores: gathering the eggs in the hen house and cleaning them, or raking the yard. She often had an encouraging word when I needed one, like when my report card was not as good as it could have been. What a unique personality God gave her! More than any of my siblings, she was the one who added luster and spirit to our family life. But back to my story.

During the long winter evenings we had little to do. I don't remember ever taking a book home from grade school and doing homework. Being in a school with three grades in one classroom, we could do our homework while the teacher was working with one of the other grades in the room. We often stood around the piano in the parlor and sang, or after we got a radio, gathered around to listen to *Amos and Andy*, *Edgar Bergen and Charlie McCarthy*, or *Fibber McGee and Molly*. Some evenings we sat around the table and picked the meat out of black walnuts Mom had cracked during the day. We also had a few table games we liked to play: Dominoes, Bible Lotto, and Pick Up Sticks.

I vividly recall the night we were at Jack and Helen's house, just down the road from our house, playing Pick Up Sticks. Mom and Dad had stayed home to take their baths and get an early start on a night's rest. We were having a hilarious time playing our game when Mom came running over to tell us that Dad had fainted while in the bath tub and there seemed to be no reason for it. Our fun came to an abrupt end as we quickly ran home to see how Dad was doing. I cried the whole way home as I thought about what life might be like if Dad were to suddenly die. The incident frightened me so, it took several years before I could get the terrible scare out of my system or play Pick Up Sticks again.

In summertime we played games outside, games like Kick the Can, Ante-Over, or Hide and Seek. We boys played marbles and *knife* while the girls played hopscotch, jump the rope, and Mother-May-I. Or we often invented our own games. Even after a hard day's work, Dad often joined in playing these games, while Mom stood on the sideline as our sole spectator.

We didn't have money to buy toys, so we made our own. Ernie was good at making toy tractors, plows and other farm implements. We boys spent many hours under the walnut tree playing *farm*. Mom made rag dolls for the girls, then taught them how to make doll clothes.

Certain relatives came to visit us from time to time. Uncle Pete and Aunt Tina Reimer and their family lived near us, so they often came over for an evening. Those were the evenings we played dodge ball late into the night, and capped the evening off with a freezer of homemade ice cream and soda crackers.

Church played an important role in our family life. We went to church every Sunday. When farm work was not too pressing we went to Wednesday night prayer meetings. Once or twice a year the church had revival meetings, which we attended without fail. Jack, Alma and Caroline became Christians at home during the time we were living in Kerman. As best as I can recall, the rest of us accepted Christ as Savior by responding to an altar call at one of the church's revival meetings.

Although our family went through some tough times during my boyhood years, it was our faith, exemplified by Mom and Dad, that kept us together and helped us weather the storms of life. We didn't have much money but we:

worked and played together,

ate our meals together,

read the Bible, prayed and went to church together.

Family life was good!

Left to right, back row: Dick Reimer, Elsie (Regier) and her husband Ralph Reimer, Irene Reimer, Irvin Reimer. Front row: Peter Reimer, Jimmie Reimer, and Kate (Tina) Johnson Reimer.

Chapter 28
Mom's Garden

Without a doubt the thing that brought Mom the greatest pleasure in life was working in her garden. It apparently was her means of escape from the routine of changing diapers, washing and ironing, cleaning up after us, packing our lunches and a hundred other chores required in raising her family. The worry about Martha's health, the concern that one of us might stray from the straight and narrow, and all the burdens of motherhood could be buried beneath the layers of her consciousness for a few hours as she worked in her garden. While she planted the seeds for her carrots and radishes, or tied the string beans to the trellis Ernie had built for them, she was lost in another world.

Keeping the garden irrigated during the hot summer months was a continuous job. If all of us kids were out working in the fields, Mom tried to keep it irrigated. This meant interrupting whatever she was doing, going out to the garden every hour or so and changing the watering hose from one place to another. There were times when she put a pot of water on the electric stove, turned the burner on *high* then proceeded to her garden quickly to change the water. But rather than doing just that, she stayed for an hour or more, forgetting about the pot of water on the stove. When she finally came in, she was surprised to find the water boiled away and the pot a molten mass.

Mom knew how to grow a garden! She could raise almost any kind of vegetable, flower, or fruit tree. Flowers were actually her first love: roses, lilies, cockscomb, sunflowers, zinnias, and a dozen other varieties. She grew them the old-fashioned way, in rows, or in color spots wherever there was a tiny, empty space among the vegetables. Her colorful flowers literally surrounded our house.

The vegetable garden, of course, was her priority. She knew her family depended on the lettuce, cabbage, turnips, radishes, cucumbers, beans, carrots, beets, corn and tomatoes. So she planted row after row of them, knowing that many of them could be canned and used to feed her family during the long winter months.

Mom knew that her family's diet was not complete unless it included a variety of fruit. We had not lived on the Forty long before she convinced Dad that we needed some fruit trees. One day she announced that she wanted an acre of land directly across from our driveway dedicated to an orchard. Dad had no option but to lay out a piece of his most prized farm land for a variety of fruit trees: peach, apricot, pear, cherry, plum, and apple. Besides that, Mom suggested that part of the land be planted into blackberries, boysenberries and strawberries.

Dad finally complained, "Do you want the whole Forty for your garden? It's getting bigger all the time. Who is going to take care of it all?" Then he picked up a hoe or shovel and worked beside her.

"It's why we have big family," she reminded Dad in her broken English. "It keeps the children busy and they not get in trouble." So she conscripted us kids to do the digging, hoeing, weeding, and irrigating. Most of us spent many Saturday afternoons in the hot sun, dealing with the invasive scourge of weeds that never stopped growing – and growing again. But that was another job farm kids took for granted during the Depression years. It didn't take long for us to figure out that our own well-being depended on the produce from Mom's garden.

In the early years, the orchard was watered by a ditch along the driveway. As the years passed, and Dad had money to install a pipeline along the north end of the Forty, the line also included the orchard, making it much easier to irrigate. Weeds, of course, spread across the entire orchard. So as I got older it became my job to hitch the disc to the 22 Caterpillar tractor, work down the weeds and then draw furrows for irrigating. Mom was so pleased when I did that she usually had a special piece of pie waiting for me when I had finished the job.

The abundant harvest kept Mom and the girls busy all summer long canning quarts upon quarts of the precious fruits and vegetables. The hard work was finally rewarded as we opened jars of pickles, corn, peaches and all the other produce from Mom's garden.

Dad and Mom in their garden.

Besides Mom's orchard and vegetable garden, Dad decided to plant a row of nine black walnut trees along the driveway leading from the house to the barn. Mom insisted that after the trees began to bear nuts, they could not be wasted. So during the long winter evenings she stood at the kitchen counter and with a hammer in hand, went to work. With the precision of a robot, she cracked the precious nuts one at a time. Then she gathered us kids around the dining room table and put us to work picking the meat out of each nut, one small piece at a time. As anyone knows who has ever grown a black walnut tree, getting the meat from the nut is like taking a banana out of the mouth of a monkey. The meat of black walnuts was delicious when added to homemade ice cream, or baked into cookies. But we sometimes wondered if it was worth the effort.

The day came when, on a fall morning, a stranger showed up at our door and told Dad he had come to graft our walnut trees. It was then that the younger kids in the family learned that black walnut trees could be changed into English walnut trees. "What kind of a mysterious miracle will that take?" we asked. The stranger had come with a bundle of twigs, a saw, a sharp knife and chisel, and a bucket of tar. Our curiosity got the best of us as we followed him out to the row of trees.

Realizing how interested we were in what he was about to do, Mr. Grafter told us he would allow us to watch while he grafted the first tree, but after that we would have to vamoose. He explained the process as he worked. "First," he said, "I am going to cut every main branch of the tree except one." We watched as he took his saw and cut each of the limbs near the trunk of the first tree. He then said, "Now I will take my chisel and make a slit on the end of each of these limbs where they have been cut." He then pulled a couple of twigs from his bundle and whittled one end of each twig into a wedge. "The next step," he said as he worked, "is to widen the slit I made in the limb so I can push the sharp wedge of these twigs into the opening." After he had done that, he took the bucket of tar he had heated on a gas burner. "This hot tar," he explained, "is very important. It will seal any open spaces left after the slit was made and the twig pushed into it." When he had finished applying the tar, he said, "Okay kids, that's how we do it. Now go back to the house and don't come back until I have finished the rest of the trees."

We reluctantly went back to the house and sat in the shade of one of the cottonwood trees. As we watched, we suddenly noticed Mr. Grafter trip on a big dirt clod while carrying his bucket of hot tar. We heard him cry out as the tar spilled over his hand and body. We ran to call Dad who was in the barn chopping feed for the cows. When Dad got to the scene of the accident, he found our tree grafter badly burned. Dad immediately put him in his truck and rushed him to the hospital in Dinuba where he was treated. The pain was so severe he groaned the whole time. It was a month before he was back to finish his job. Two years later these trees began to bear the most delicious English walnuts that could be shelled in seconds and enjoyed on the spot. No need to spend whole evenings picking the fruit out of the old black walnuts.

A Reflection

As I grew older, I often marveled at the great variety of fruits and vegetables, not to mention flowers, God created for our enjoyment. Additionally, I was thankful for the brilliant colors He had painted them: the orange in carrots, cantaloupes and oranges; the red of beets, radishes and watermelons; the yellow of squash and corn; the blush of peaches; the saffron of apricots and the yellow of lemons. I thought: what if all fruits had been painted a dull grey? Apparently God knew how much more we would enjoy His handiwork if He colored them with radiance.

Thinking about all the flowers God created, Jesus said, "*And why worry about your clothes! Look at the lilies and how they grow. They don't work or make their clothing, yet Solomon in all his glory was not dressed as beautifully as they are*", (Matthew 6:28,29, NLT).

Chapter 29
House Paint

Mr. Weaver drove up to the back yard of our house one day and knocked on the rickety door which gave entrance to the screened-in porch that served as the boys' bedroom. Dad got up from the breakfast table to answer the door.

"I am here to start painting the outside of your house," Mr. Weaver announced.

Dad responded, "Good! We have been waiting for you. It really needs it. I don't know how old the house is, but as you can see, it has never been painted."

"Well then, its time we get started."

Dad walked with Mr. Weaver to his pickup truck where he found a half dozen five-gallon cans of paint, brushes, drop-cloths, rags, and all the other paraphernalia any good painter would take to his job. Electric sanders, paint rollers and airless spray guns had never been heard of in those days. Mr. Weaver was dressed, as every good painter should be, in a pair of white overalls and shirt, both splattered with smudges of paint from previous jobs.

Dad looked at the back of Mr. Weaver's truck and said, "That's a lot of paint."

"Yes, and by the looks of the condition of this house, I will need every bit of it."

By this time, curiosity had gotten to us kids, and we were all outside, swarming around the paint truck. Mr. Weaver said, "It looks like you have quite a family here, Mr. Gunther." He then turned to each of us, shook our hands and asked us to tell him our names and how old we were. As it turned out, Mr. Weaver was a family man and enjoyed children.

It took the painter three days to prepare the house for its first coat of paint; scraping, brushing, and sanding until he had a smooth, clean surface with which work. On the fourth morning, he opened his first can of paint, stirred it thoroughly, and started painting, but not before he had spent some time teasing those of us who had come out to greet him. "You boys look like you are old enough to help paint; here's a brush for you, Peter." We all backed away, not wanting even to try it. As Mr. Weaver began applying one brush full after the other the old, dry wood soaked up the paint like a sponge. In the days that followed, he gave the whole house two coats of white undercoat. And every day, when Dad came in from the field for lunch, he went to see what progress the painter was making. He would ask, "How is it going, Mr. Weaver?"

And every day Mr. Weaver would reply, "Just fine, Mr. Gunther."

On the morning of Mr. Weaver's second week on the job, he opened a new can of paint. The whole family again surrounded his truck. This was to be the day we would find out what color Mom and Dad had chosen for the house. Wanting to surprise us, they had kept it a secret. We crowded around as the can was being opened. The color came to the surface while the paint was being stirred. What was it? Yellow. Bright yellow!

Using his widest brush, Mr. Weaver deftly applied the paint in bold strokes. We all thought it was the most beautiful color a house could be painted. What we did not know was that, in addition to the basic yellow, the house would be trimmed in a different color including the six-inch wide frames around the windows, the doors and other trimming on the house.

On the day the painter was to begin painting the trimming, we again gathered around his truck and waited with bated breath to see what color that would be.

"Open the can!" Martha exclaimed.

We all chimed in, "Yeah, Mr. Weaver, open the can!"

Mr. Weaver picked up the can, teasingly held it in midair for a while, set it down on the bed of his truck, and slowly and suspensefully pried open the lid. He dramatically picked up a stick and began stirring; the color rose to the surface. Green. Bright green!

We all clapped our hands. Our house would be yellow and green. People driving by would not be able to miss it if they wanted to. It would be seen from a mile away. The only house in the county like it. But painting the trim was not the end of Mr. Weaver's job.

The next Monday morning our painter arrived on our yard with a big fifty-gallon barrel on the back of his truck. We were all out to greet him again. "What's that for?" we asked.

Dad and Mom in our front yard, about 1935. Note the dark green trim on our yellow house.

"Well, look at your house. Does it look like it's covered with paint?"

"It looks painted to us," we all agreed.

"No it doesn't," he said. "Look at the roof. The shingles are brown and dirty. Don't you think they should be painted too?"

"We guess so."

By this time, summer had arrived and by midday the roof was hot as a pistol. In spite of the heat, Mr. Weaver got on top of our roof and started sweeping and cleaning its deteriorating shingles. He then pulled his truck up as close to the house as possible, and with a hose attached to a pump, began spraying the roof with aluminum paint. It was the latest thing in house paint. Everybody for miles around was spraying the roof of their house with aluminum paint. The oil in the paint would help preserve the wood. The aluminum color would deflect the hot summer sun. We were assured by the manufacturer that it was guaranteed to keep our house ten degrees cooler, but it didn't.

Through the years that followed, the house needed to be repainted from time to time. Once the yellow and green had faded, it was painted white with blue trim; the next time, with black trim, but never again was it painted yellow and green.

During the month-long job, Mr. Weaver had become our welcomed friend.

A Reflection

My friend Don always seems to notice children when they are around. He has such a unique and gracious way of talking to them. That's the kind of man Mr. Weaver was. What a beautiful gift God has given people like this. *"Jesus said, 'Let the children come to me. Don't stop them! For the Kingdom of Heaven belongs to such as these.' And he put his hands on their heads and blessed them before he left,"* (Matthew 19:14,15, NLT).

Chapter 30
The Fatted Pig

As far as our family was concerned, hog butchering day was a national holiday. Uncle Pete and Aunt Tina Reimer and their family (Ralph, Irene, Irvin, Marvin and Jim) always joined us for this occasion, coming early and staying late. They lived on a farm about three miles to the southwest of us.

We needed Uncle Pete there because he had served in the Army during World War I and not only owned a gun, but knew how to use it. Dad never owned a gun, and you would not have found one on our farm. Uncle Pete was given the wicked job of killing the pig on butchering day. We children were kept in the house behind closed doors while all this was happening out in the barnyard.

Uncle Pete was completely in charge of the butchering operation. In preparation for the big day he told Dad that he would need to be up before dawn that day, fill a 50 gallon metal drum with water and build a fire under it.

He explained, "That water needs to be boiling hot before I go out and kill the pig. You will need to build a tripod with a block and tackle so the whole thing can be placed over the drum of boiling water. After the hog has been killed and bled, we will haul it over to where the drum of water is waiting, tie a rope to the hog's hind legs, and thread the rope through the block and tackle. The hog will then be hoisted up and dunked into the hot water so its bristles will soften. When I give the signal, you can pull the pig out of the drum, and I will start scraping the bristles off the skin with this special tool made for that purpose. When that job is complete, the hog will be ready to cut up for processing."

Dad, of course, knew the exact procedure, but indulged Uncle Pete as he explained it while we little kids were listening.

Uncle Pete knew just how to cut the pig's carcass so no part of it would be wasted. First the head, legs, and feet were removed and set aside to be processed later. The innards were then removed, saving the heart, liver and intestines. The carcass of the pig was now sawed in half down its backbone, placed on a sturdy table and the shanks, sides and ribs cut off to be cured. Scraps were thrown into a tub to be ground up for sausage.

While all this was going on, Dad told us kids about a few more things made from the butchered pig. He said, "We don't waste anything. The head is cut apart and the brains, tongue, snout and ears are ground up for headcheese. The liver is made into liverwurst." While the men did the heavier work, the pig's intestines were thoroughly cleaned, inside and out, by the women. These provided perfect casings for the liverwurst and sausages.

The fat, trimmed from the meat, was chopped up and thrown into a large kettle which in Low German was called a *meagropa*. A fire was built under the kettle, the fat brought to a boil and cooked until it was just the right consistency. Only Mom knew how to do this, so she stood for hours stirring the kettle with a large wooden paddle. While the fat was still boiling Mom added the pig's ribs which, when cooked, were laid out and generously spread with salt for preserving. It was a well known fact that if even a spot the size of a nickel was not covered with salt, the whole rack of ribs would spoil. The rendered fat, when cooled, turned into lard and was used for baking.

The only means of keeping things cold in the early 1930s was our ice box which was kept in the lean-to part of our house. The ice box held a 50 pound block of ice which the ice man brought to our door two or three times a week from the Ice House in Dinuba. The ice box was neither large enough for all the meat, nor cold enough to keep fresh meat from spoiling. So the hams, bacon and sausages had to be cured in various ways to preserve them. It had been proven that salting and smoking these portions of the pig was a successful method of keeping them from spoiling. Jack and Dad had built a smokehouse from scraps of lumber found on the farm. For the next several days, Dad, who had become an expert in the art of smoking pork, was kept busy curing these most precious portions of the pig.

Not long ago, Rubena and I were talking about those good ole days. "Yes," I said, "I remember that as a kid I would come home from school hungry as a coyote in a snowstorm. I would cut a piece of Mom's homemade rye bread and smear *Jreeweschmolt* (the residue left after rendering the lard) on it like it was butter, generously sprinkle sugar over it, and eat it with relish. But," I said, "weren't there bits of crisp morsels left at the bottom of the kettle after the lard had been rendered?"

"These were the *Jreewe* or cracklings," Rubena said. "They were scraped together and stored in large stoneware crocks which kept them from spoiling. I remember Mom stirring eggs or potatoes into them (to make them go further) and frying them for breakfast. Boy, were they good! Better yet, sometimes she fixed them without eggs. We smothered them in Karo syrup and ate them like candy. I can still taste them – best part of the pig. That's not to take anything away from the delicious hams, bacon and sausage Dad cured."

"The best way to eat the sausage," Rubena continued, "was with the verenika Mom and Caroline made for Saturday suppers. They made a sour cream gravy after frying the sausage. We covered the verenika with the gravy! You couldn't find a better meal than verenika and sausage."

"Didn't Mom make something with the pigs feet?" I asked.

"Yes," Rubena remembered. "Mom had a special recipe for pickling the feet and knee joints. They were then stuffed into large jars and canned for preserving. None of us, not even Dad, liked them, but Mom ate them with relish – or so she said because she couldn't get herself to just throw them away. So if no one else would eat them, she did."

The head of the pig was made into headcheese. Even though it turns my stomach when I read how it was made, it was a common item on our supper table.

How to Make Headcheese:

The head of the pig was cooked together with the heart and a few strips of rind. The ears, brains, tongue and other parts of the head were then picked off the bone and the rind discarded. While the meat was still hot it was put through a meat grinder and seasoned with salt and pepper. The ground meat was then placed in a cloth sack and weighed down in a pan to squeeze out the fat. After draining, it was covered with the broth in which the meat had been cooked and allowed to cool. Meanwhile, a solution was made of 1 part boiled vinegar and 2 parts water. The meat was placed in the pickling solution and allowed to stand 2 to 3 days. When the head cheese had solidified, it was sliced and served with vinegar, sliced raw onions, fried potatoes and rye bread.

–Mennonite Foods & Folkways from South Russia, Vol. 1, Norma Jost Voth

The liver was saved for making liverwurst, stuffed into casings and stored in the bottom of a stone crock filled with lard. It is said that it stayed fresh for a month when stored this way. Most of our liverwurst was sent home with Uncle Pete and Aunt Tina. Not that none of us liked it as it was actually quite tasty. It was, however, a custom to give the treat to those who helped in the butchering process.

Butchering day did not end until after dark. By this time everyone was almost too tired to move. It was tradition, however, that anyone who helped butcher the pig would be given some of the fruit of their labors. Uncle Pete and family were invited to stay and eat supper with us. So Mom brought out some of the ribs she had cooked in the meagropa and served them together with heaping mounds of mashed potatoes, green beans from the garden, and the apple pies Caroline and Marie had baked that day.

The rest of the ribs and the liverwurst were sent home with Aunt Tina as payment in full for all the work she and Uncle Pete had done for us that day.

It was the charming, loveable pig fattened from the scraps of our table that in lean times and good provided the much needed protein for our hard work on the farm. Bless the pig.

A Reflection

It was a common practice for members of an extended family to come together to help each other when needed. It was a great way for relatives to bond with each other. While working together they told stories of happenings in their families and laughed about many of them. Sometimes they sang old familiar hymns. There is a song we sang as children: *"The more we get together, together, together; the more we get together, the happier we'll be."* This was also a time for sharing concerns and problems as we are exhorted to do in Galatians 6:2, *"Share each other's troubles and problems, and in this way obey the law of Christ,"* (NLT).

Chapter 31
The Family Wash

I don't know when Mom got her first electric washing machine with a wringer, but she apparently had one when we moved to our Forty in 1930. It was a good thing my parents bought it before the Depression hit in 1929, or they might not have been able to afford it during those lean years. The machine was quite an improvement over the hand operated one she had before that. The old scrub board was invented in the late 1700s and used for years by my mother and millions of housewives around the world.

In 1861, a wringer appeared on the market for the first time. Its intended purpose was to wring the excess water out of a garment after being washed. The first wringers had two rollers operated by a hand crank. In 1907, Maytag came out with an electric washing machine which had a wringer attached.

When Mom got her first electric machine it was much improved over the earlier models. Washday for our family was still a long and hard ordeal even with the latest machine. One day while Alma was doing the wash she took me into our garage and showed me the whole process, step by step.

Alma was my oldest sister. Mom depended on her to do a lot of the household work like doing the family wash and taking care of us kids. She had Mom's temperament – quick to let her temper flare up. When she was put in charge of caring for the rest of us she let us know she was boss – a dominant characteristic she exercised throughout her life – even after we had all grown up and left home. She was a very determined person – a determination compared to a mother protecting her child from the dangers of a tornado that was threatening to destroy her home and family. When she set her mind to do a job, whether large or small, she stuck with it until it was finished regardless of the obstacles involved.

As my readers may recall, Mom played an old reed pump organ during our family sing-alongs. Alma inherited Mom's musical ability and had learned to play the piano. She also had Mom's talent and enthusiasm for telling stories. So her mouth and hands were always busy. When she had nothing else to do, she was telling stories while sewing or knitting, or singing while playing the piano. Like Mom, she could do more work in a few hours than most could do in a day.

In explaining to me how she did the washing, she said, "First we sort the wash: whites here, light coloreds there, dark colored things in that pile." She threw the mens' jeans and overalls into another pile with the rugs and rags.

I interrupted her to ask if the order of color was important. "Of course," she said. "Any dummy," one of her favorite words, "would know that. We use just one tub of water to do the whole wash. If we put the dark clothes in before the white, the white clothes would take on the colors of the dark and look dingy. The work clothes and rags are washed last because they are the dirtiest."

"Yes," I said, "but that also means that my work pants are washed in that dirty water. No wonder they come out looking like something you would put on a scarecrow." She ignored my observation.

"Once the clothes are sorted, the machine is filled with hot water. The only soap we have is homemade by Mom and has to be shaved off a bar with a sharp knife and allowed to dissolve before we put the wash in the machine. With the lid in place, to keep the water from splashing all over the floor, I'll turn on the dasher to dissolve the soap. Do you know what the dasher is, Wes?"

"Of course I do, I'm not as dumb as you think. It's that thingamajig inside the washer that moves the clothes back and forth."

The first load of clothes was put into the machine and washed for fifteen minutes. When the washing was finished, I helped her as we took each piece of clothing out of the water and put it through the wringer to squeeze out as much water as possible. Boy-oh-boy, the water was so hot we had to use a stick to do the job. Each piece fell from the wringer into one of the double tubs attached to the wall of our garage.

Alma warned me to watch out for my fingers because those rollers could easily pull my whole hand through before the machine would automatically release the pressure. Before we were through, sure enough, I caught my finger in the wringer. My carelessness really upset Alma. "Wes," she shouted, " Can't you do anything right? At this rate, you are never going to amount to anything." I had heard that evaluation of me before, and it bothered me that various members of my family actually thought I would never make much of myself in life.

After the crisis of my wounded finger was resolved, Alma calmed down rather quickly, which she usually did after losing her temper, and I recovered from my hurt feelings. So we continued taking care of the wash. The tubs into which the clothes fell after being put through the wringer had been filled with cold water to which Alma added a few drops of blueing.

"What is that for? Won't that make the clothes turn blue?"

"No, you dummy. It's something that makes white clothes whiter." (I was used to being called a dummy by now. She didn't mean to make me feel stupid.)

"Are you pulling my leg? How can something that dark blue make anything white? Are you sure you know what you are doing?" Alma just ignored my ridiculous questions.

I noted that the wash in the first tub was then agitated by hand and put through the wringer and into the second tub. It was then put through the wringer again and into a wash basket.

"There is one more important step in the washing process," Alma said. "The mens' shirt collars and cuffs have to be dipped in starch, so when ironed, they will be stiff and smooth."

"What do you do with the wash in the basket now?" I asked

Alma grabbed hold of the basket of clothes and carried it to the lines located behind the garage, but not before she had started her second load of wash.

I followed her out the back door of the garage where Dad had put up eight long wires stretched between posts. Each piece of clothing, including sheets and towels, had to be hung on those lines to dry. I watched as she took sheet after sheet and towel after towel out of the basket and attached them to the lines with one or more clothes-pins. And I thought to myself; there are fourteen of us in this family. With two of us to a bed, and two sheets to a bed, that's fourteen sheets! That takes a lot of line space just to get the sheets dry, never mind all the towels we use each week! Then I remembered the mound of socks waiting to be washed. Every one had to be hung separately with a clothes pin. When she got to that part of the wash, I counted the total number of individual socks Alma hung out to dry -- 196 in all.

"So what happens when the wash is dry?" I asked

"Then, as any dummy would know, it has to be removed from the lines piece by piece, folded into the laundry basket, taken inside, sorted and gotten ready for ironing." Alma had washed seven loads that day – a whole day's work.

Dad had finally bought Mom her first electric iron, a vast improvement over the former iron that had to be heated on the stove top. But before the clothes could be ironed they had to be sprinkled to dampen them. This was before *wash and wear* had been invented or steam irons had even been thought of. Ironing all those clothes was another long day's work. That was Caroline and Martha's job.

Having survived a washday demonstration for dummies, I had a new appreciation for a clean shirt.

A Reflection

David, the greatest king of Israel, had committed a grievous sin. One day, Nathan the prophet came before the king to confront him with his terrible transgression. Some time later, David wrote Psalm 51 in which he confesses his sin. He prayed, "*Wash me, and I shall be whiter than snow.*" That's clean! Wearing clean clothes after they have been washed is a great feeling. But how much greater it is to know that "*When we confess our sins, he [God] is faithful and just to forgive us our sins, and to cleanse us from all unrighteousness,*" (I John 1:9, KJV).

Chapter 32
Going to Town

It was a hot Friday morning in the middle of the summer of 1934, and Dad had promised Ray and me that we could go to town with him. Town, of course, meant going to Dinuba, our closest business district. The town boasted two major grocery stores, two branch banks, three pharmacies, a theater, two Five and Dime stores, a fire station, elementary and high school, a couple of Chinese restaurants, an ice cream shop, a blacksmith shop, an ice house, and a variety of other stores. The hamlet was located three miles north and one mile east of our home Forty.

Going to town was not an everyday kind of event in those days. Dad went perhaps once every two weeks, and Ray and I went maybe once every three months. With a grocery list in hand the three of us got into the 1929 Studebaker and were off to experience the greatest adventure two farm boys could imagine.

Dad's first stop was a visit to the Security First National Bank in the heart of town. In those days banks were hallowed institutions which adults only could enter. Once inside, it was noted that the tellers were ensconced in enclosures protected from the clients by a partition built of paneling and iron bars. The exchange of money was done through a small opening under the glass panel that separated the teller from the customer. The bank president and other officers had desks near the entry and were ready to assist customers with loans and other services.

While Dad was doing business, Ray and I had to stay outside the bank and wait for him to return. So what were two kids to do – just stand there and quietly wait? No. That would have been insane. We started to play tag with each other on the sidewalk outside the bank door. Suddenly, the bank president came charging out the door, grabbed us by the scruff of the neck, and sat us down on the sidewalk while threatening to call the police if we made such a disturbance again. Both Ray and I were so shocked our heartbeats raced to record levels and we were so scared we wet our pants. So much for our exciting adventure in town that day! We were both rather subdued as Dad came out of the bank and drove a block down the street to the Purity grocery store. There was also a Justesons grocery in town, but it was apparently the store where the more affluent citizens of Dinuba shopped. It was not for us poor farm folks.

We walked into the store where kids were welcomed and greeted by a grocer man who was glad to see us. We noted that most of the groceries were kept on shelves or behind glassed in counters, inaccessible to the public. Dad handed Mr. Grocer Man the list Mom had prepared. Mr Grocer Man took the list, and one by one gathered the items from the shelves. Self-service stores were unheard of in those days. One hundred pounds each of flour, potatoes, beans and sugar, two large cans of coffee, a 25-pound sack of ice cream salt, a carton with 24 boxes of Corn Flakes. The large amount of sugar was needed for canning fruit and making jam. After the items on the list had been placed on the counter where we waited, Dad asked the grocer man to add a sack of day-old bread. The bread had been removed from its original wrappers. The sack included bread rolls, pastries, and a variety of bakery breads collected over a period of a week or so. Most of it was dry and hard, and therefore resisted mold even though it was a week old. The sack of bread cost almost nothing. But when we got home, it was fun to go through its contents just to see what a bargain we got. We found a lot of good eating there. When soaked in a cup of coffee and spread with butter, it was better than the fresh stuff, or so we told ourselves.

After all items were collected, the grocer man added the total cost of the bill in his head and announced the amount. Dad had an arrangement with the grocer man that these items would be taken in trade for fresh eggs Dad had brought from our farm. When the value of the eggs was determined, it was an even trade. What a deal! If he had not had enough eggs to trade for the groceries he could have asked the grocer man to charge the difference. During those bleak days of the Depression many customers charged all their groceries and paid when they could. Some never did. But Dad preferred to keep accounts current.

Before going home that shopping day we made one more stop: the Five and Dime store back up the street. By this time Ray and I had recovered from our banking shake-up, so we excitedly entered the Dime store because Dad had given each of us five pennies and told us we could each pick five pieces of penny candy. Boy-oh-boy, was that ever the highlight of the day!

The penny candies were all out in the open on the counter. The five cent candy bars, however, were kept behind enclosed glass cases. There they were, the penny candies: Tootsie Rolls, Licorice Sticks, Sugar Daddy All Day Suckers, Saltwater Taffy, Jelly Beans, Boston Baked Beans, Rock Candy, Lemon Drops, Mint Rolls, and suckers that came in almost every flavor imaginable. The display included dozens of other varieties. So Ray and I stood there with our mouths drooling and our eyes wide open. How could we ever choose five pieces from such an assortment? Dad soon became impatient as he waited for us to make up our minds. Fifteen minutes later we walked out of the store as happy as ants at a picnic. Seldom had we experienced such a treat.

Occasionally our whole family went to town on Saturday nights. For many farm families this was their regular night out. We all parked our cars on an angle on Main Street. Most of the kids hurriedly got out of their cars and ran down the street, and for ten cents took in the double feature movie while Dad and Mom did some shopping. Teenagers met their friends, and if they included a member of the opposite sex, they walked the street hand in hand, talking and laughing, and then stopping at the drug store soda fountain for a banana split, sundae, or ten-cent milkshake. After dads and moms had done their shopping they simply sat in their cars and watched the people go by.

When our family came to town, none of us, of course, darkened the door of a movie theater. Nor did we go to the pool hall to shoot pool, as many others did. We mostly went to spend time with our friends, perhaps share a five-cent Coke, or enjoy a candy bar. After an hour or so, it was time to get home and make final preparations for Sunday.

Chapter 33
Saturdays On The Farm

It was another glorious Saturday morning. The sun was shining; the spring air clear and crisp. The Sierra Nevada mountain range stood in all its brilliance like a sentinel guarding our valley below. Directly to the east of our home, Mt. Whitney, its 14,505 foot peak the highest in the contiguous States, hid itself from view behind a closer snow capped peak. Paradoxically, Death Valley, at 282 feet below sea level, the lowest point on the North American Continent, lies just 70 miles, as a bird would fly, to the east.

The cows had been milked, the eggs gathered, the livestock and chickens fed, and the whole family was gathered around the dining room table. Mom and the girls had prepared a special breakfast of fried eggs, bacon, corn meal patties, and fresh strawberries picked from Mom's garden. But before we could start eating, Dad got out the worn Bible, read a Psalm and prayed. The prayer was not simply to bless the food. He prayed about many things: the church and pastor, missionaries, relatives that were sick, and members of the family who had special needs.

The moment Dad said 'Amen,' each of us made a mad dash for the plate of food nearest us. Our favorite dish on these mornings was a plate loaded with delectable golden brown corn meal patties.

Saturday morning breakfasts were often special at our house, not only because of the tasty food being served, but because they were designated as family time. After breakfast we stayed

> Recipe for Corn Meal Patties for 12
>
> The night before, make corn meal mush using about 10 cups of water and 3 cups of corn meal. Set 8 cups of the water to boiling. Stir the corn meal into the remaining water. Slowly pour the resulting paste into the boiling water and cook for 5 minutes, or until you have a mush of a rather heavy consistency. Pour the mush into a baking sheet or two and let stand in the ice box overnight.
>
> Just before serving the next morning, cut the mush into squares, fry on a lightly greased pancake griddle until lightly browned on both sides. Serve hot with butter and corn syrup or homemade molasses.

seated around the table and talked. Of course, Dad was head of the family and guided the conversation. Most of the time he just sat and listened while Mom and the kids shared concerns, ideas, gripes, or whatever was on our hearts. We were allowed to talk about anything and everything. Occasionally Dad interjected a comment or affirmed us in what we said. These were seldom, if ever, occasions for our parents to scold us or preach at us. Rather, they somehow had a way of pulling us together and making us feel good about being part of a family. After an hour or so we were ready to go to work at whatever needed to be done that day.

One of our favorite topics during these sessions was planning future projects for improving our home and farm. One morning we made plans for planting an orchard with a variety of fruit trees. At other sessions we made plans for such things as a cement sidewalk leading from our front door to the driveway, or a sprinkler system in the lawn, or an addition to the old house.

Between our front yard and the road was a 200 foot parcel of land which grew nothing better than weeds. A palm tree which had been planted next to the road stood as a landmark that identified our farm. Jack had graded a narrow strip of land next to the front lawn. We called it *lovers lane* because that's where the suitors parked to pick up my older sisters when they had dates.

Front yard area between the road and house that was always a problem.

We spent many Saturday sessions talking about this weedy piece of land. Mom insisted, "It must be good for something. I think it would be a good place for a vegetable garden." Some of us thought we ought to build a tennis court. Now that would have impressed our neighbors – a tennis court out here in the middle of nowhere! The idea never materialized. Mom finally won the argument. Water was piped to the plot so it could be irrigated and Mom started growing watermelons, cantaloupes, cucumbers, beets, and potatoes. As we had feared, what us kids wanted for a play area became a place for hard labor: hoeing weeds in the heat of summer, irrigating, and picking vegetables. That's why we dragged our feet when Mom suggested the garden.

After our planning and sharing sessions, the rest of each Saturday involved plenty of work for all of us. Seldom did we have to go out and do field work like making hay or picking cotton. The important job was to get ready for Sunday!

Alma was in charge of cleaning the house, with Eva and Rubena as her helpers. Caroline and Marie did the baking of breads and special pastries that would be served on Sunday – things like Zwieback, pies, cakes and coffee cakes. Lydia was in charge of cleaning the yard, especially raking the leaves that had fallen from the huge cottonwood trees. Ray and I were drafted as helpers. As I recall, Lydia was very precise about how the leaves should be raked. It was very important to her that the rake marks left on the ground would be in straight lines. The leaves didn't care about the rake marks left behind. But Ray and I soon learned that they mattered a lot to Lydia.

Ernie and Peter were responsible for mowing the front yard grass, trimming the hedge, making sure the garden was watered, and washing the car so it would be clean for going to church the next day. Jack helped Dad with things like gassing up the car, changing oil in the vehicles, and making repairs on the tractor and farm implements so they would be ready for the next week's field work.

Mom's main job was to butcher and clean several chickens for Sunday dinner. For this she conscripted the help of a couple of the boys to go into the hen house, catch a few roosters, taking them to the butcher block behind the garage, and, with an ax, chopping off their heads. A job we all detested. Mom then plucked the chickens' feathers, eviscerated their insides, and cut them up for frying the next day when the preacher and his wife often would join us for Sunday dinner.

When the evening chores had been done it was time for supper, after which we lined up for our baths in the single tub in the bathroom. Mom and Dad spent the evening preparing to teach Sunday school classes the next day. The older girls were occasionally permitted to go out on dates. The older boys were sometimes allowed to meet friends in town. The rest of us might get to listen to *Amos and Andy* on the radio.

By the end of the evening all was ready for church the next day.

A Reflection

Just days before Jesus was crucified, his disciples asked Him if there would be a sign to signal our Lord's return and the end of the world. Jesus pointed out several things that would indicate that the end was near. He then told them, *"You must be ready all the time. For the Son of Man will come when least expected,"* (Matthew 24:44 NLT). Being ready for church each week was really important to our family. How much more important it is for us to always be ready for the Lord's return.

Chapter 34
Sunday Church

At precisely ten minutes of nine on Sunday mornings, Ernie was out the door to back the family car out of the garage and drive it up to the back door of the house. He then sat behind the steering wheel and at exactly 5 minutes to 9:00 began intermittently to honk the horn, reminding the whole family that by 9 o'clock everyone needed to be in the car and ready to leave for church.

Since church was at the center and core of our family life we were all eager to attend the services of the day – Sunday school, morning service, 6:30 p.m. young people's meeting, and the 7:30 evening service. This was the day of the week to which we all looked forward. None of us stayed home unless we were deathly sick. Each of the services had its special emphasis and appeal. Besides the biblical training and spiritual nurture we received, this was our social life. This was where we met our friends and spent time together.

Sunday really was a special day for us. Each one had an ensemble of neat, clean, dress-up *Sunday clothes*. The outfits included a dress suit, white shirt and tie for Dad and the older boys, and dress pants, shirt (and coat during the winter months) and Sunday shoes for Ray and me. Mom and the girls each had a special Sunday dress, hat, dress shoes, purse and gloves. We wore these outfits only on Sundays. Even during the years of the Depression, Mom and Dad somehow managed to provide these clothes for us. Why? Because we were going to the meeting house where, in a mystical way, we entered into God's presence and worshiped Him. Mom often reminded us that sloppy dress was not acceptable in the House of God.

How we all crammed into the 1929 Studebaker sedan remains a puzzle to me. Fortunately, this model's trunk was a separate accessory attached to the back of the car, so it had a spacious back seat. I remember that I had to sit on someone's lap. So did Ray and Rubena. By staggering the seating arrangement in the back seat, one sitting forward and the next one to the back of the seat, we could get five across the seat. Four could easily sit in the front seat. The rest had to sit on the floor or stand.

The nine mile trip to our Mennonite Brethren Church in Reedley took about twenty minutes and our family was usually the first to get there, normally ten minutes early. I think we wanted to get there before anyone else so no one would see how the Gunther family had to cram into one car. Nine o'clock was the magical time to leave for church and it was Ernie's self-appointed calling in life to see that we departed at the scheduled moment. If we weren't in the car on time, he would get out of the car, come running into the house and yell, "Wes, aren't you finished dressing yet?"

"No, Ernie, the girls are using the bathroom."

Ernie would then run into the girls' room and say, "Rubena, you're late," or "Lydia, you can finish dressing in the car."

Ernie was forever micro-managing our family life. None of us ever moved quite fast enough and things never got done as soon as he thought they should. If only we would do things his way and as quickly as he did them we would all be a lot better off. He was sure he could milk a cow faster, plow the field with greater speed, pick more trays of grapes, and get more done in a day than the rest of us combined.

He had inherited Mom's temperament, looks, and way of talking. When he was not pleased with one of us, he spoke up without hesitation and with an angry voice told us what we had done wrong. His temper often flared up for almost no reason, but settled down almost as soon as it had erupted.

Ernie did work hard. So he set the pace for the rate of speed at which the rest of us worked and played. He had a generous streak in him that overshadowed his bossy nature, always looking for ways to help us out when we were falling behind, making a toy for some of us, sharing a piece of candy, and when he got his first car, giving us a ride in his 1939 maroon colored Pontiac. So when he started honking the horn on Sunday mornings we took it in stride.

"That's Ernie!" we said. And we all went about our regular routine of getting ready.

Sunday school started at 9:30 a.m. So the minute our family arrived on the church yard each of us scattered to get to the respective classes for our age groups. As young children, Ray and I met in classes in the basement. When we got to be teenagers, we went to classes held in the Sunday school building – a class taught by Peter Funk, an insurance agent, or Jack Enns, a car dealer. The rest of the family members scattered to classes held in the church balcony, the Bible School building, and every other nook and cranny of the various buildings on the church yard. Mom and Dad each taught classes, in the German language, for which they had prepared the night before. These were held in the main church building where classes were separated for the men and women.

Sunday School was a serious part of our education. As young children we learned Bible stories like Jonah and the fish and dozens of other stories from both the Old and New Testaments. Each class had a scroll with a beautiful picture portraying the

My Pastor, George B. Huebert
Photo Courtesy of Norman Huebert

lesson of the week. At the bottom of the picture was a Bible verse of the week. Before class was dismissed, the teacher handed each of us a card which included a small version of the picture and the Scripture verse. It was important that we take these home and memorize the verse for the following Sunday. Teaching Bible content was emphasized in all the classes, which meant we were not only expected to learn *about* the Bible, but to learn what the Bible actually said. As we grew older, we learned things like the names of the twelve disciples, the twelve tribes of Israel, and books of the Bible.

The morning service started at 10:30 a.m. and lasted until at least 12:00 noon. As we filed into church, the men sat in pews on the left and the women on the right. The center section was occupied by the more daring younger couples, with mothers and babies in the back center. During our childhood years, Ray and I were required to sit with our parents, either with Dad or Mom. It was utterly humiliating for us boys to have to sit with Mom in the women's section. In any case, I usually fell asleep when the preaching started. My Dad, having worked hard in the fields all week, often shared the nap time with me. When we got to be seven years old we were permitted to sit in the front rows of the center section – right under the preacher's glaring eyes. It was thought that having him stare down at us would keep us from whispering with our friends, but it didn't.

When Ray and I turned ten we got to move from under the preacher's nose to a small section of pews off to the right, facing the preacher from his left. The whispering and cutting up got worse as the church leadership failed to come up with a solution to the problem. By the time I reached age twelve I was allowed to sit with the other young people in the balcony. I soon discovered that all sorts of hanky panky went on up there.

The balcony was built in a U shape – the style found in many theater balconies of the day with the floor slightly tilted downward towards the front. Each row of pews was set on a riser that was about six inches higher than the one in front of it. The following is an example of some of the things that went on up there during the church service.

One Sunday morning, according to a preconceived plan, one of my friends brought a large marble to church. He was sitting in the back center of the balcony. It was agreed that he would drop the marble about the time the preacher was in the middle of his sermon. When he did, it started rolling toward the front of the balcony, making a loud plunk as it rolled from the edge of one riser to the next. By the time the marble got to the front of the balcony the preacher stopped preaching. There was suddenly a stone-cold silence throughout the church. When the marble hit the banister it started rolling along the curve of the balcony, and then to the very front corner where another friend, according to plan, was sitting to pick it up. He was rather stout, and happened to be wearing a pair of tight pants that morning. As he leaned over to pick up the marble, the back seam of his pants ripped open (not according to plan). Everyone knew immediately what had happened as the sound of the tear resonated throughout the church. During this time, the whole congregation and the preacher remained in stunned silence. Then, all at once, the choir broke into uncontrollable laughter. Before long, the whole congregation was in a state of pandemonium. Neither the preacher nor the ushers and *spotters* – the ones appointed to keep order among the young people – could do a thing about it. It wasn't long before the preacher pronounced the benediction and dismissed church for that Sunday.

There were other things that went on up there in the balcony. It was not uncommon for us to chew bubble gum to see who could make the biggest bubble, visit with our friends, make paper airplanes and sail them across the balcony, or even carve our initials in the back of a pew.

As I think about it now, there were probably two reasons why the children and young people created the problems they did. First of all, families were not encouraged to sit together as families. Apparently it was thought that segregating the women from the men was more important. Second, the church held on to the German language far too long. Whereas much of each church service was in English, a lot of the preaching was in High German. Low German and English were the common language of our homes and most of them could understand and speak them. But High German was the language of the church, and so different that it went over their heads. So as soon as the preacher started preaching in High German, they tuned him out. Just sitting there, they soon got bored and turned to doing other things.

There were many good and enjoyable things that happened in church. Each service was started with general singing. Henry Martens, a local car dealer, led the congregation in a time of lively singing of hymns and gospel songs from the Tabernacle Hymn Book. My sister Lydia was often at the piano accompanying the congregational singing. The church had a full choir that sang beautifully in four-part harmony under the direction of Frank Wiens, whose father was a missionary to China. The church also had a men's chorus directed by a local banker, Ernest Enns, that sang alternately with the choir. People formed quartets, trios, duets, or sang solos, and enriched the services with their musical talent.

All of my siblings sang in the choir at some point. Additionally, my sisters sang in quartets and trios. All of my brothers sang in the men's chorus. For some reason I was never invited to sing in any of the above. So now my readers know the quality of my singing voice as compared to that of my siblings.

One of the important parts of the morning service was the public prayer time. The congregation would stand or kneel and any member could lead out in public prayer. Most of the prayers were in German. Looking back, I realize that this prayer time gave vitality to the church because in prayer is where the real work of the church was done. They prayed for sister Kroeker who was sick, and for Mr. Bartsch who needed to be saved. They prayed for the church's missionaries in foreign lands, for its evangelists and pastors. They prayed for the Government and its leaders. These were the people communing directly with God. And God not only heard these prayers, but also answered them. It was believed that without prayer the work of the church would be in vain.

The 6:30 meeting, held in the church basement every Sunday night, was for young people, high school age and up. During my high school years, Henry Martens was in charge of this meeting. It started with singing gospel songs and choruses and included a *testimony time*, which gave anyone present an opportunity to stand up and tell about a life-changing experience he or she had had the week before. Many times these testimonies were as simple as quoting a familiar Bible verse or thanking God for a good week in school. Often the meeting concluded by having a special speaker give a short devotional. We usually liked these meetings because they were always in English and geared to the interests of young people.

The evening service started at 7:30 and lasted until 9 o'clock. A *preaching service* was alternated each week with a *Jugendverein* (Youth Endeavor) meeting. On the preaching night the congregation sang several lively gospel songs. The leader, often Brother Friesen, announced that members of the congregation could choose a song. So someone would call out, "Number 201." Brother Friesen would say, "*Trust and Obey*, that's a good one. Sing it out good and loud." A song we sang almost every night Brother Friesen was in charge was *Cleansing Wave*, page 149 in the No.2 Tabernacle Hymn book. We finally called him "Cleansing Wave Friesen."

The *Jugendverein* was organized with a committee that included a president and secretary. The committee planned each program of eight to ten items that usually included things like special music, testimony time, and the reading of a poem. The president of the *Jugendverein* led the meeting as the secretary sat at a table on the stage and took minutes which were read at the next meeting. Each meeting started with the singing of gospel songs. The one we liked best was *Wonderful Grace of Jesus*, page 348 in Tabernacle Hymn book No. 3. The whole congregation of 1,200 sang in full voice on this one. The verse was sung in full four-part harmony while the pianist played up and down the keyboard putting in every extra note and run she could manage:

> *"Wonderful grace of Jesus, Greater than all my sin.*
> *How shall my tongue describe it, Where shall its praise begin?*
> *Taking away my burden, Setting my spirit free;*
> *For the wonderful grace of Jesus reaches me."*

When we got to the chorus the men with their tenor and bass voices took the melody while the women sang an obligato:

> *"Wonderful the matchless grace of Jesus,*
> *Deeper than the might rolling sea;*
> *Higher than the mountain, sparkling like a fountain,*
> *All-sufficient grace for even me."*

At this point in the chorus, the women took the lead again:

> *"Broader than the scope of my transgressions,*
> *Greater far than all my sin and shame...*
> *O magnify the precious name of Jesus, Praise His name!"*
> Copyright, 1918, Charles M. Alexander

The last line climaxed in a crescendo with the sopranos reaching a high A-flat. We always sang all three verses. It was glorious!

Next to the singing of gospel songs like the one above, the highlight of each meeting was the reading of the program for the next meeting. For instance, we might hear the secretary announce, "Trio by Marie Gunther," or "Testimony by Ted Wiebe." That gave each of these persons their only notice that they were on the program for the next meeting. So we all waited with baited breath for that moment when we would be informed as to who was on the next meeting's program, thereby judging how good the next program would be.

So another Sunday, sadly, came to a close. On the way home I usually looked for my mother's lap – even until I was seven or eight years old. Her embrace was so warm and comfortable; I was sound asleep by the time we got home. It had been such a good day!

A Reflection

I was twenty-five years old when I stood behind the pulpit in a small church in East Los Angeles. In my audience were some of those men who had been my Sunday School teachers when I was a kid. Though my mouth went dry and my mind blank at that moment I stood up to deliver my very first sermon as a pastor, a warmth flooded my whole being. I knew I was surrounded by people who had helped mold my life and now stood with me as I entered into ministry as a servant of God. The Bible says, *"Think of ways to encourage one another to outbursts of love and good deeds. And let us not neglect our meeting together. ...But encourage and warn each other, especially now that the day of his coming back again is drawing near,"* (Hebrews 10: 24, 25 NLT).

Chapter 35
Boundaries

It was Sunday morning and Marie had gotten dressed for church wearing lipstick. She had painted her fingernails bright red the night before. As she emerged from her bedroom Dad took one look at her and said, "You look very pretty, Marie, but you don't expect to go to church that way, do you?"

Marie was, in fact, a very attractive young lady; meticulous in every way. She dressed neatly even if she was going to the barn to milk cows. Being well-groomed and well-dressed was as important to her as keeping a neat home and cooking the most delicious meals you ever tasted. I remember Marie as having a big heart, always ready for no special reason to give a small gift to one of us: a piece of candy, a special rock she had found, a handful of cookies she had baked.

Marie was a good student. While she attended the Bible Institute of Los Angeles she became acquainted with Pastor Sawtell who specialized in encouraging young people to memorize Scripture verses. Marie soon majored in committing Bible verses to memory. One day she brought Pastor Sawtell to our home for the purpose of getting all of us kids involved in memorizing Bible verses. As a result, I learned more than 1,000 verses in my youth as did most of my siblings. The Bible was Marie's favorite textbook. She knew it well and lived by its precepts.

One of the things that got to me while we were growing up was that Marie, even more than Alma, felt she had to have the last word in every matter that was on the table for discussion. When the family had one of its meetings, she usually gave the final verdict on what should or should not be done. I ultimately came to the conclusion that someone had to tell us what to do. Most of these matters were actually of little consequence, so why not let Marie do it?

However, on this particular Sunday morning when Marie had decided to wear makeup to church Dad had the final word. All of us knew he was the head of our household and *don't you forget it*! We did not leave for church that day until the makeup was gone.

It was the 1930s, and the traditional Mennonite Brethren church had certain standards for dress and behavior. Lipstick, painted fingernails, or makeup of any kind, were out of bounds. Wearing earrings was unheard of. It might be okay for them to wear pants while working on the farm, but certainly not elsewhere. But it was the Thirties, and times were changing. The younger women and girls were stretching the limits of the boundaries in spite of what the deacons said. Being a deacon, Dad tried his best to harness in the ways of the girls in his household. After all, what would the other deacons say if he permitted Marie to wear makeup to church?

The church had standards it felt were in keeping with consistent Christian living. Going to the movie theater, smoking, and drinking alcoholic beverages were discouraged. Dancing, playing cards, pool or bowling were frowned upon. Playing a game like baseball or basketball was probably acceptable on week days at school, but never on Sundays. One would certainly not go shopping or even buy a loaf of bread on Sundays. Of course it didn't matter, the stores were all closed on Sundays except for one of the three drug stores in

Dinuba which was open to take care of any medical emergencies. Working on Sundays was limited to doing necessary chores.

There were good reasons for the church's rules about Christian living. One of the distinguishing marks of the church was to follow the biblical injunction to be separate from the world. It based these teachings on such passages as the one in I John 2:15, 16: *"Love not the world, neither the things that are in the world. If anyone loves the world, the love of the Father is not in him. For all that is in the world, the lust of the flesh, and the lust of the eyes, and the pride of life, is not of the Father, but is of the world,"* (KJV). Our forefathers took such passages very seriously. They incorporated them into the very fabric of their daily lives. A simple lifestyle that was different from the world was a vital part of living out their faith. Those who where outside the faith could look at the way they lived and see that they were different: not in the sense of being peculiar, but in the sense of being good, moral, upright neighbors in the community. They were respected and trusted for their honesty and integrity.

Many of the things we should or should not do were established by our church. But there were also some boundaries which Dad and Mom expected their children to live within. We accepted these limits as part and parcel of life. Dad and Mom lived within them, so why shouldn't we?

Several years ago I was visiting my brother Peter and his wife Phyllis, who were living in Wheaton, Illinois. Peter was working for Moody Press which was sponsored by the Moody Bible Institute of Chicago.

After graduating from Dinuba High School, Peter went off to the Bible Institute of Los Angeles where he received a degree in Biblical Studies. From there he matriculated as a student at the prestigious Wheaton College in Illinois where he earned a Masters degree in Archeology.

My brother was the rebel in our family, bent on breaking the rules. For example, while at Biola he spoke out about the school's dress code and the poor food in the cafeteria. The matter became so serious he was about to be expelled. Had it not been for Dad's intervention, he would have been. One might say that throughout his student years he lived life on the edge. He was a good student, but also fun-loving, well-known among his fellow-students, and later his colleagues, for his fondness of teasing and telling jokes.

But Peter was a committed follower of Christ and steadfast in his faith. He had a strong work ethic, and was one whom God had endowed with gifts of leadership which Moody Press recognized by appointing him as Director of the Press, a position he held for many years. Moody was a very conservative institution and had all kinds of rules and regulations for its teachers and staff personnel like Peter.

So on the occasion of my visit, I said to my brother, "You are famous for having a hard time with boundaries, forever crossing the line during the years we were kids at home. How is it that you manage to work for an institution which imposes rules that are more strict than those of similar institutions?"

Peter responded, "Well, first of all, rules are made to be broken! But seriously, in working with large numbers of people, I finally came to the conclusion that rules are good as long as those who make them also live by them and enforce them fairly and in love. Moody's regulations are not unreasonable. I can live with them. And the reason I was able to keep the faith during my student years and not throw my church and religion overboard was because of what I just said. Mom and Dad lived within their own boundaries, and were fair in the way they expected us kids to live within them. When we stepped over the line, they corrected us in love."

I said, "After reflecting on those years, and the standards by which we were expected to live, I have come to the conclusion that the rules were not a legalistic discipline that would help get me to heaven. Rather, they were a means of helping me grow more Christ-like in my faith and in my daily walk with God. I was never hurt by living within the boundaries. On the other hand, they kept me from being hurt, even to the extent of adversely affecting my whole life."

Before Peter and I parted company that day we both agreed, however, that there were times when boundaries kind of hampered us in what we thought would have been fun things to do.

During our growing up years my siblings and I tried to live by the standards set by both my parents and the church, failing on occasion, and as a result getting a good lecture from Dad. As for me, the boundaries I grew up with somehow became so ingrained that when I broke them waves of guilt descended upon my conscience like hail on a wheat field. I finally decided that breaking across them wasn't worth it.

For instance, smoking was thought to be such a serious problem that I never so much as touched a cigarette in my life. As far as I know, none of my brothers or sisters ever took up smoking either. The pool hall in Dinuba was thought to be such a den of iniquity that I felt unclean just walking past it. I could only imagine what all went on inside that place: smoking, drinking, dancing, playing cards and pool.

Working on Sundays was something Dad hardly ever did. Nor did he ever expect any of us kids to do so. Mowing the lawn would have been unthinkable. One exception to no work on Sundays was occasionally changing the water while irrigating the crops in the heat of summer.

When we finally got a radio, a Sears Roebuck Silvertone console with an automatic dial, Mom kept it strictly under her control. We could listen to the news, but there were only a few comedies like *Jack Benny* and *Burns and Allen* to which we listened. *Bob Hope* was off the list.

As time passed some of the boundaries of both church and family were slowly relaxed but it amazes me how few I could shed. As of this writing, I have discarded some, but it took decades for me to make changes.

I recall taking Beverly and our children to our first movie in the 1970s. *The Sound of Music* was the number one box office attraction. When we got to our car after the movie, I discovered the car had a dead battery. Some months later we took our family to our second movie: *The Christmas Carol*. When we got back to our car we found that it had a flat tire. Should I have concluded that God was trying to tell me something?

A Reflection

As I reflect on my boyhood years, I am thankful that I was brought up in a home and church that had boundaries. I am especially grateful for parents who not only taught us to live clean, wholesome lives, but were a constant example of godly living. One of the proverbs in the Bible reads as follows. *"My child, never forget the things I have taught you. Store my commands in your heart, for they will give you a long and satisfying life. ...Then you will find favor with both God and people, and you will gain a good reputation,"* (Proverbs 3:1,2,4, NLT).

Chapter 36
I Thee Wed

It was December 5, 1936, and my oldest brother Jack was getting married to Helen Klassen. This wedding was going to be different from the run of the mill weddings held in our church, or any other Mennonite Brethren church, for that matter. Weddings were normally kept quite simple. No flowers, or candles, or bridal attendants. If there was a wedding march, the couple walked down the aisle together, up the steps to the platform, and faced the preacher while he exhorted them to remain true to each other for life, preached a serious sermon and finally, had them repeat vows. It was customary for both the bride and groom each to say a prayer while kneeling. The pastor then prayed a lengthy prayer after which he pronounced the couple husband and wife. Kissing the bride in public was considered obscene.

Jack and Helen did all the wrong things at their ceremony. They were a compatible couple in that they both liked to do things that would cause them to stand out in a crowd. Jack was the one in the family who got the finest suits at the upscale Harry Coffee's clothes for men in Fresno. He owned a new car before anyone else his age did. He bought an antique tractor even though it didn't run, just to have one. He planted flowers in circles rather than in rows, the old-fashioned way. He dried his raisins in a dehydrator, which made them turn yellow when dry instead of dark like regular raisins. He drove a flashy yellow convertible Studebaker coupe, the only one of its kind in the whole Valley. He liked doing things with pizzazz. Helen was like Jack in that she also liked to do things with style.

So that's how they did their wedding – with flair. They decorated the front of the church with huge bouquets of white flowers. Two brass candelabra, each holding twelve white tapers, were placed on either side of a kneeling bench that had been covered with satin. A lattice arch interwoven with ivy was placed over the kneeling bench. When the time came for the wedding to begin, a bridesmaid and maid of honor preceded the bride down the aisle. At the same time, two groomsmen accompanied the groom to the head of the aisle where they waited for the bride, escorted by her father, to make her appearance. And most conspicuous of all was the moment the couple would exchange rings right during the ceremony and kiss each other after being pronounced husband and wife. Such goings-on had never been done in our church before!

The wedding proceeded as planned and as far as our church was concerned most of its hallowed traditions were broken. The morning after, the church's deacons came calling at our house. They were there to admonish my father on the shameful way in which the wedding had been conducted.

"I mean, candles, bridesmaids, rings, and kissing," one Deacon said. "We can't allow it! Before we know it, other young couples will do the same things. We have to nip these kinds of worldly things in the bud."

Another deacon intoned, "You, after all, are one of the deacons and should have known better than to permit such a ceremony." The deacons next had a visit with Pastor Huebert and gave him a roasting for agreeing to such a wedding in his church.

Jack and Helen's wedding reception conformed more properly to the church's tradition for such events and did not incur the wrath of the deacons as the ceremony itself had. It was held in the church basement with 500 guests seated at tables. The bride's parents were responsible for supplying the traditional food that was served: ham sandwiches, Zwieback, potato salad, dill pickles, cake and coffee. I am not sure if special wedding cakes were a part of traditional Reedley church receptions in 1936. It didn't matter; Helen's reception table was adorned with a fancy five-layered cake. Anything stronger than coffee was strictly off the list of acceptable beverages. Thankfully, neither Helen nor Jack had a problem observing that regulation, although Jack had been known to imbibe a cold beer now and then.

After the guests had finished the meal they settled back for a program. The thing most anticipated about the program was to discover who had been selected as Toastmaster because he could make or break an otherwise successful wedding reception. The Toast-master had to be able to inject enough humor into the program to make people smile, but not enough to make them laugh out loud. He had to be able both to toast the couple and to deliver a sermonette – defined by Webster as "a scolding on a moral issue." The program included special music and a well-chosen poem. After the program, the couple stood in a reception line while the 500 guests came by to congratulate them and shake their hands. But there was no kissing of the bride.

All guests were expected to bring a gift for the couple. The bride had asked some of her friends to receive the gifts, open them the moment they arrived, and display them on tables set up for that purpose. One of the big things the guests looked forward to after the reception was to file past the gift table and see what kind of presents the couple had been given, and then to compare them to the gifts other couples had received at their weddings. You see, a family's popularity and wealth could be judged by the gifts received.

When the festivities had finally come to an end it was time for the couple to make a get away from the church. Friends of the groom tried to figure out which car the couple would use for their escape. If anyone knew for sure which one it would be, they decorated it and hung a wire strung with tin cans to the back of the car. After the couple got into the escape car, their friends lined up in their own cars and with horns honking, and driving reck-lessly, tried to follow the couple to the hotel in Fresno where they would spend their first night.

While the couple was on their honeymoon, some of their friends who knew where they would spend their first night upon their return would break in and shivaree their house. This included doing things like placing a bucket of water over the door so when they opened it the water would then pour down on the couple, putting rice in their bed or short-sheeting it. Friends became very resourceful when it came to doing a shivaree.

And so it was that, sure enough, before the deacons knew it, Jack and Helen's wedding had set a precedent to be followed for years to come.

A Reflection

I often wondered how Helen put up with Jack's rather eccentric characteristics during the many years of their marriage. After his home-going I asked Helen one day, "To what do you attribute the longevity of your marriage? She said, "Well you know, Wes, we promised to live together for better or for worse until 'death do us part.' I am sure I was often difficult to live with. I think every couple has its differences. But we made a commitment to each other and both of us were determined to keep it. Besides that, we loved each other deeply."

While Helen was sharing a bit of what married life was like, I was reminded of a verse in the Bible, "*So again I say, each man must love his wife as he loves himself, and the wife must respect her husband,*" (Ephesians 5:33, NLT). Jack and Helen had been married 58 years when the Lord took him home to Glory.

Chapter 37
Christmas

It was Christmas Eve, 1932, and we had just come home from church with our *Tuti*. Our church had a tradition in which the children gave the program on Christmas Eve, and each Sunday School class was expected to present a recitation of some kind. Usually these recitations involved having the members of the class file onto the stage and recite a line or two from a poem about Christmas or a verse from the Bible. Our class of five-year old boys stood meekly with hands in pockets and one by one walked up to the microphone and whispered his part of the poem:

Freddy: "I wish you a Merry Christmas,"
Donald: "I say it like a prayer. . ."
George: "When you wake Christmas morning"
Wesley: "May all you wish be there."

...And so on until all of us had said our part. We had memorized these lines at home so we knew them backwards and forwards. But when we faced an audience of 1,200 people, our minds went blank and we had to be helped by a prompter hidden in the back part of the stage. Invariably, one of the boys suddenly had a fascination for the microphone, put it up to his mouth and talked into it so loudly he woke up the old men in the audience who had already fallen asleep. Our teacher then came running to put him in his place. As we filed down to our seats we could see our proud mamas and papas smiling from ear to ear. "They were so cute," they whispered.

However good or bad our performances were, when the program came to a conclusion the Sunday School superintendent came to the stage and announced that the moment had come when each of us, young and old, would receive a *Tut*. One could sense an aura of excitement fill the whole meeting house. All the Sunday school teachers went down the aisles with grape picking pans filled with *Tuti*, passing them down each row. One for each man, woman, and child. Some took two, one for an invalid family member who couldn't come. Then, of course, there were those who took two, knowing they shouldn't. The superintendent, in the meantime, was warning the children to not open their *Tut* until they were out of the church building.

The *Tuti*, Low German for #8 brown paper bags and pronounced *Toota* for plural, and Toot (*tut*) for singular, were filled with a handful of hard candy, a few cream chocolates, and a stick or two of penny candy. They also included a handful of unshelled peanuts, a few almonds, a half dozen walnuts, plus an apple and an orange. I was not particularly thrilled with the walnuts because they were hard to crack and we had plenty of them at home. But all in all, the *Tuti* were the highlight of our Christmas Eve celebration. And what a relief to have that recitation over with!

Christmas Day at our house in 1932 was a pretty simple affair. Our whole family was up at the crack of dawn and ran to the dining room table. There we found plates, one with the name of each family member on it. The contents of these plates were our Christmas gifts from Mom and Dad. Mine had a few pieces of hard candy and a nail puzzle. My brother Ray had an identical gift, except that his nail puzzle was different from mine. Thus, each member of the family had a similar gift of about the same monetary value. It took Ray and me most of the day to figure out how our nails came apart.

Mom and Dad were not present in the dining room during this gift receiving time. Dad had already gone out to the barn to do the chores. Mom was busy in the kitchen preparing breakfast.

The skimpy gifts that year were made up for with delicious meals. Mom had prepared ham, eggs and biscuits for breakfast. For dinner, which was served at noon instead of the usual supper time, Mom had butchered and plucked pin feathers from two huge geese she had been fattening for this special occasion. These had been roasting in the wood stove oven all morning, creating a tempting aroma throughout the house. The girls helped her prepare a large amount of potatoes, mashed with real butter and cream. Jars of corn and green beans that had been canned the summer before were taken from the shelf and the vegetables heated. Cabbage from Mom's winter garden was steamed. Caroline had baked two chess pies and one green tomato pie. Baking the pies was something she did for our Christmas dinners for years, even after she was married.

Caroline had a special gift for baking the best pastries one could possibly imagine. They seemed to melt in our mouths. Her breads, cakes and pies were all delicious, but she eventually gained renown for her Zwieback. She lived in Reedley in her latter years and was featured with her Zwieback in a half-page article in the *Reedley Exponent*.

Chess Pie Recipe

3 tbs. sugar	½ c. cream or top milk
1/4 tsp. salt	1 tbs. butter
3 eggs	½ tsp. vanilla
1 c. dark corn syrup	½ c. chopped nuts
	½ c. raisins

Mix sugar and salt with well beaten eggs. Add syrup and melted butter and all other ingredients. Pour into unbaked pie shell and bake about 35 minutes at 350 degrees. May be served with whipped cream.

Mom's Green Tomato Pie

Slice 6 green tomatoes very thin. Let stand 5 minutes. Drain off some juice, then pour into pastry lined pie shell. Cover with 1 cup sugar, 2 tbs. flour, 1 ½ tsp. lemon extract (Watkins brand preferred). Cover with top crust. Bake in hot oven, 425 degrees, about 45 minutes. Tastes best with a huge scoop of ice cream. (I have personally made this pie, following Mom's recipe; quite good, I would say.)

Caroline's husband, Frank, was a meticulous farmer. Caroline was an immaculate housekeeper. We could have eaten off of her floors. Frank's tractors and equipment were kept in first class shape. Frank and Caroline had a well kept garden including many fragrant flowers. Their well manicured lawn was green the year 'round.

As I write this story today and think about my sister Caroline, one word comes to mind: *perfection*. Everything had to be just so. Nothing could be shabby, left half-done, or in a mess. If she started a project, she didn't quit until it was finished. And, of course, she expected the same of Frank and her children. Flawlessness was her passion. But at the same time, she was forgiving of those who didn't meet her standards. So when we kids who were younger didn't live up to her expectations we didn't worry about it. In fact, we sometimes deliberately made a mess of things just to see how she would react.

Ray and I were still small kids when Caroline and Frank were living on their farm on Road 56. As deacons, Dad and Mom spent one or two evenings a week visiting shut-ins and widows. On such evenings they often dropped the two of us off at Caroline's house so we could play with her kids who were almost as old as we. Even though their toys were well-used, they looked to us like they were new.

Sometimes Ray and I were allowed to stay at Caroline's house for night. This was really a special treat because we knew that the next morning we would have *Shredded Wheat* for breakfast instead of the usual *Cornflakes* we would have gotten at home. Often Caroline even sliced a banana into our cereal bowls! She was always doing special little things she knew we would like. So when she baked chess and green tomato pies for our Christmas dinners we knew we were in for another treat.

Dinner on that Christmas day in 1932 was served at one o'clock. All members of the family were present and accounted for. Mom's best white tablecloth had been spread and the table set with her finest china. Lydia had found a few late blooming flowers which she arranged in a vase and placed in the center of the table. Condiments included both sweet and dill pickles, home cured olives, and pickled beets. Alma had made the most delicious brown gravy from the drippings of the geese. Homemade butter and blackberry jam were served with Mom's homemade rye bread. A big pot of black coffee, rather than Postum, was made for the special occasion. It was a feast to be remembered!

A typical family dinner such as was enjoyed each Christmas.
L. side of table: Cecelia holding Candy on lap, Lindy , Kathy, Luella, Peter, Alan, Phyllis, Evan, Alma and Jack (Patz kowsky), Melvin (Patzkowsky), Jim, Caroline and Frank (Ens), Mom, Chris (Willadsen), L of table: Dad, Bud (Willadsen), Bill and Barbara (Martens), Next person unidentifiable, Eva (Willadsen), Helen, Bud (Willadsen), Jack Marilyn, Loretta, Carol (Ens), Ray, Sherry. (Persons without last name listed are Gunther).

The afternoon was spent singing carols in the parlor, with Alma at the piano, having us boys recite our parts in the program of the night before, reading the Christmas story from the Bible and a prayer offered by Dad. Before the gathering was brought to a close we all joined in singing a German carol:

"Du Kindlein in der Krippe, wir Kommen zu dir hin.
Wie hängt an deiner lippe, all unser Herz und Sinn.
Zu deinen Füssen legen, wir unsere Gaben dar.
O gibt uns deinen Segen, Du Kindlein wunderbar."
    –Composer unknown

"Dear Child, there in the cradle, to You we're drawing near –
With thoughts and words, with heart and soul, we're coming without fear.
We lay our gifts down at Your feet with thanks for God's great love.
Grant us Your blessing, wondrous Child, Your peace from God above."
    –Translated by Hans Kasdorf

This was Dad's favorite Christmas hymn, and no Christmas celebration was ever complete without it. Dad led out in his deep bass voice together with Mom in her rich alto, while the rest of us joined in singing the beautiful four-part harmony. Singing this carol became a family tradition throughout the years until about the year 2000 when there were only a few of us still living. I have looked for this hymn in a number of German songbooks without success, but have handwritten copies of it in my file.

By the time that 1932 celebration came to a conclusion, the fog was rolling in as the sun was setting in the west. It was past time, on that cold wintry day, for the menfolk to go out and do the chores and for Mom and the girls to straightened up the house. The much anticipated Christmas season had come to an end, and I was feeling low. I had hoped it would continue throughout the next year.

For the next several years, our Christmases followed the same pattern. The gifts were skimpy and were not a big part of our celebrations. But each year Mom spent enormous amounts of time preparing the plentiful food we always enjoyed. Besides the food described above, she and the girls baked a tub of Zwieback, a variety of Pfeffernüsse and cookies, coffee cakes and fruitcakes. The Zwieback were often toasted to keep them from spoiling. When dunked in coffee and spread with a pat of butter, they were a delightful treat.

No Christmas was complete without Mom's fruitcakes. As everyone knows, the main ingredients in fruitcakes are nuts and candied fruits. We had our own nut trees on the farm, but candied fruit was very expensive. So Mom made her own. Here is her recipe for candied orange and lemon peel:

Chop into cubes the peels from 12 oranges or lemons. Cover with water, bring to a boil and let stand for a while, then drain. Combine 3 cups sugar, and 1 cup water and bring to a boil, stirring constantly until sugar is dissolved. Add peel and let boil until thick, stirring to keep from browning the syrup. Pack in clean hot jars. When cold, seal with paraffin.

Mom's recipe book also included a method for making candied cherries, dozens of recipes for Pfeffernüsse, a variety of fruitcakes, candied nuts of all kinds, special Christmas pastries, and other goodies. Because Mom had the know-how for making these things from "scratch" and was willing to put the time and effort into doing so, she could afford them, even when times were financially hard. In this way she managed to provide a bountiful table even through the sparse 1930s.

As the Depression years passed, and our financial status began to improve, so did the way we celebrated Christmas, except that the Christmas Eve program at church continued unchanged even after I grew up and left home. Brother Jack and sisters Alma and Caroline had married in the mid-thirties and had begun to raise families of their own. The whole family, including in-laws and my nieces and nephews, came together for each year's celebration. New kinds of foods were brought to the festive table, adding to the enormous variety of the spread. By the early 1940s, there were usually about 25 of us at our gatherings and pure bedlam erupted. Everyone was talking at one time, and we kids were running around the house playing tag or hide and seek. Our method of giving and receiving gifts changed. We began choosing names, which meant that each of us became responsible for buying or making one gift for the person whose name we had drawn. That also meant that each of us received just one gift.

The time came when gift giving shifted from the early mornings to the afternoons. We gathered in a circle in the parlor. The Christmas tree had been sprayed white and decorated with blue lights. Gifts from under the tree were distributed. When Dad gave the signal, each of us tore into our gifts. On one or two occasions someone suggested that we quietly go around the circle and open our gifts one by one. It never worked.

By the 1940s, Dad and Mom were financially able to give each of us a gift in addition to the gift exchange. My most treasured gift from them was an Erector Set. Other than that, I was usually disappointed when all the gift giving was complete. I never got the model train set I had hoped for each year.

> Note: Christmas trees were a special part of celebrating the season. Ray and I excitedly counted the lit trees we could see in the windows of houses as we drove to church. We had a tree of some kind in our house from the time I can remember. The way it was decorated changed with the fashions of the times. At first it was a green tree with multicolored lights. Eventually, the white tree with blue lights became popular. Then the blue lights were left in the box and a blue spotlight lit the tree. The day came when aluminum trees replaced real trees.

A Reflection

The Christmas Eve program, the Tuti, the giving of gifts, the special baked goods and generous amounts of a great variety of food – all were traditions that held our family together. Perhaps the most important of those traditions was the singing of "*Du Kindlein in der Krippe*," reading the Christmas story, and Dad blessing us with his special prayer.

In the Old Testament, God instructed Israel through Moses to celebrate several festivals each year. At one place he said, "*Rejoice before the Lord your God for seven days. You must observe this festival to the Lord every year. This is a permanent law for you, and it must be kept by all future generations,*" (Leviticus 23:41 NLT). That's how important God considered traditions to be!

Chapter 38
School Days

My public school education began in 1932, the year our nation was in the depth of the Great Depression. Grandview was the rural elementary school I attended from the first through the eighth grades. The three room building, located on what is now Avenue 396 at Road 64 in Tulare County, was nearly three miles from home. Grades one and two were taught by Julia Ford; grades three, four, and five by Mary Shields. Zack Kleinsasser taught grades six, seven and eight in room 3, which doubled as an auditorium with a stage and a curtain, which opened and closed by pulling a rope just like in uptown theaters. Each classroom had an anteroom where we hung our coats and stored our lunch sacks. The school grounds included a softball field with a backstop of sorts and a basketball court, both of which were sanded so they could be used even after light rains had soaked the raw earth.

My older brothers, Ernie and Peter, had each gotten a bicycle when they were in the upper grades. Ernie rode a new *Schwinn* with 26 inch whitewall balloon tires, while Peter rode an old used, nameless bike with skinny tires on 28 inch wheels. When they finished eighth grade, the bikes were handed down to the next younger siblings. Since I was too small to ride a big bike like Ernie's when I started school, I had to walk with my older sister Rubena the three miles to and from school. Sometimes, if Dad happened to be driving in the direction of this institution of learning, he gave us kids a ride on the back of his truck. What outraged me with envy was that, while other school districts all around us had school buses, Grandview did not. Our neighbor kids who lived just a half mile to the south and were in the Wilson school district, had the leisurely delight of being bused to school every day. They kept reminding me of what a backwards school Grandview was as compared to Wilson. What could I say?

My brother Ray started school a year after I did. The two of us then began walking to school together. We did this until our older sisters finished elementary school and the bikes were handed down to us. By this time the bikes were well worn and needed constant repairs. For instance, the Schwinn's coaster brake needed to be disassembled every two weeks and cleaned. The nameless bike's tires went flat on a regular basis, so we needed to dismount them, repair the inner tubes with patches, reassemble them, and pump up the tires with a hand pump. I got to where I could take a bike apart and reassemble it with my eyes closed.

There were times when one or the other of the bikes needed major repairs and could not be used at all. So Ray and I rode the rideable bike in tandem. At such times, Ray sat on the seat while I sat on the book rack over the back tire and put my feet on the pedals while Ray put his feet on top of mine, thus both adding our muscle power to the pedals.

Note: As of this writing, Grandview is still a thriving elementary school at the same location as when I attended, but with new buildings. The original classic style building was, unfortunately, demolished rather than restored. Mrs. Ford died recently at age 98 I was elated to see Mr. Kleinsasser at my brother Peter's memorial service in Colorado Springs, Colorado in 1992. He has since passed away. I have lost track of Mrs. Shields.

My school days,
fourth grade.

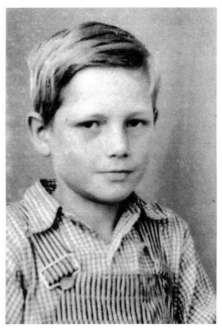

My brother, Raymond,
third grade.

About a half mile from home we had a neighbor who had a dog. It didn't seem to matter whether the sun was shining brightly or the fog was so thick it could not be stirred with a tornado, the dog came running to the road barking at us as if we were mailmen. We were always sure he was going to bite us, and one day he did. We felt it was a major daily victory to get past the dog unscathed.

One cold winter day, when I was in the sixth grade, I was riding the old nameless bike when for no apparent reason, it seemed, its front wheel skidded out from under me. Before I knew it, the bike and I both lay beside the road in a tangled mess and my arms and legs were bruised right through my shirt and pants, and bleeding. Fortunately, the accident happened not far from home, and I was able to hobble back so Mom could clean me up and bandage my wounds. She suggested that I not go back to school for several days after that – a conclusion with which I fully concurred. The old bike had to be scrapped.

Mom always packed a lunch which consisted of a bologna sandwich, a few potato chips, and an apple. A banana instead of the apple was a luxury. The same dry sandwiches every day! I guess I should have been thankful that we had any lunch at all during those difficult Depression years.

Grades one and two were not my best or easiest of school years. Reading was my biggest challenge. Mrs. Ford had three reading groups; the first included the best readers. I was always in group three, meaning that I was in the group with the most reading problems. I spent what were probably three of my happiest school years in second grade reading. But somehow I made it through the various subjects and was promoted to the next grade at the end of each year.

My reading problem followed me through all the years I was in school; elementary, high school, college, seminary, and throughout my life. When asked to read a chapter from the Bible for devotions at the breakfast table, my father often scolded me for my poor reading. Years later my seminary professor took me aside one day and scolded me for so poorly reading one of my research papers to the class. I attribute my inability to read well to the fact that all through life I have been unable to focus my eyes quickly. Perhaps I am dyslexic, but dyslexia was not even heard of during the years of my schooling, much less treated.

Mrs. Ford was a strict disciplinarian, which got me into trouble more than once. The day I was at the blackboard and not paying proper attention she left an unforgettable pain on the palm of my left hand with her trusty ruler. There were days when I apparently had disturbed the class once too often and I had to stay after school. I vividly recall the time I was sent to the principal's room. Boy-oh-boy, was that scary! I knew he had a whip hidden behind his desk and was known for using it from time to time.

When I was promoted to the sixth grade, Mr. Kleinsasser became my teacher. There were six rows of students in his classroom; two for each of the three grades he taught, with the sixth grade seated to his left. Goodness, what shenanigans we got by with because he had a left glass eye!

One day, when I was in the sixth grade, Mr. Brauer drove up to our school in his 1932 Essex coupe. Although he was probably about 45 years old, I immediately made up my mind that he was an old man and wondered why he had stopped by. He came into our classroom and announced that he would be visiting our school twice a week to teach us how to play band instruments. Well, that was some of the best news I had heard in a long time! I had recently inherited a swell, almost new trombone from my brother Peter who had graduated from high school the year before and had gone off to the Bible Institute of Los Angeles. Peter had played trombone all through his years at Dinuba high school. During this time there was a fire in the school's band room, and his original used instrument had been destroyed in the fire. Through the school's insurance, Peter received a brand new Conn, the best trombone maker in America. It was truly a fine trombone! Now it was mine.

For the next three years, Mr. Brauer came to our school as promised, and taught me and many of my fellow students how to play our instruments. By the time I was in the eighth grade, our little band was good enough to go to various towns where we were entered into band competitions. I continued to play my trombone during the two years I attended Dinuba High. For my last two high school years I transferred to Immanuel Bible Academy where I was part of a trombone quartet (the other members of the quartet were Pete Isaak, Paul Nickel and Louis Wiebe). We played in churches, migrant, and Conscientious Objector camps. What fun playing that trombone – all because the *old man*, Mr. Brauer, providentially came to Grandview that one day when I was in the sixth grade.

All through elementary school we had recesses, one in the morning and one in the afternoon. We also had an hour-long lunch period. During these times we could play ball; whatever sport was in season. If it was baseball or basketball season, we had team leaders who chose players for each of two teams. Although I wanted to play on one or the other of these teams, I always felt inconsequential. I was the last to be chosen by any team leader, if chosen at all. To make matters worse, I considered some of these leaders among my best friends.

The lunch hour was my favorite time of the day. A row of drinking fountains, with a bench on either side, was located on the back side of the school yard where a bunch of us boys (Terry Nishita, Joe Martzen, Robert Wineberg, August Gross, and others), ate our lunches. One of the group, Charlie Neufeld, was a great storyteller and often regaled us with his jokes and humor for the better part of the hour. Nothing helped digest my dry sandwich like a good story as told by Charlie!

One day while I was in the seventh grade, Mr. Just, a banker with the Bank of America in Dinuba, came to visit our school. The purpose of his visit was to introduce the students to the concept of saving money. He suggested that we take the nickels and dimes our parents gave us from time to time, and rather than buy candy, put them in the bank. A few weeks later he came back and helped each of us open a savings account. I recall that by being very careful I had been able to save 25 cents. I opened my first bank account with that huge amount of money. Mr. Just came to our school once a month during my seventh and eighth grades to collect our money and deposit it for us. By the end of my eighth grade I had $2.20 in my account earning interest and I thought I was the richest kid in the world!

All through our grade school years, Joe Martzen and I were the best of friends. We often walked home from school together. His house was about halfway between school and our house. So occasionally, on our way home from school, Ray and I stopped at Joe's house for a respite. Joe's mother usually had a glass of cold Root Beer waiting for us. Of course, we were late in getting home on such days, only to find Mom in her bedroom praying for our safe return. When we told her where we had been she gave us a mighty scolding and sent us off to do our chores.

When I finally reached the eighth grade, the most serious challenge of my education up to that point was at stake – to pass the *Constitution Test*. Before we could graduate from elementary school all students had to pass the test, which not only included questions about the Constitution of the United States, but also how and where our government was formed and how it functioned.

During that last year in grade school, Joe and I were in stiff competition as to who would get the best grades. As it turned out, we both got the same score on the Constitution Test. The question now was which of us would be chosen for valedictorian honors on the day we would graduate from elementary school. As it turned out, our friendship was put to the acid test, but persisted, even after it was announced that, out of a class of fourteen, Joe would receive the valedictorian honors.

After graduation from Grandview, I was enrolled as a student in Dinuba High School, which had a fleet of busses. In addition to the pleasure of riding the bus, a very beautiful neighbor girl was also a passenger. I had a secret crush on her, but was too bashful to ever speak to her.

Language was my most difficult subject in high school. I tried a year of Spanish and barely got a C. Mrs. Hawkins was my English teacher who tried to get me to use proper grammar by diagraming sentences according to nouns, verbs, adjectives, etcetera. I never caught on and have problems with grammar to this day. Physical Education was a required activity which I hated because I was never good at any sport. Band and wood shop were my favorite classes. In fact, I took two units of wood shop in my sophomore year. During that year, I created a bookcase from warped scraps of walnut wood that had been lying on the school's woodpile for years. The boards had to be lovingly sawed, planed, glued together and sanded. But the bookcase is proudly used in our home to this day.

During the two years at Dinuba High, I was always glad when Dad said he needed me to help on the farm, meaning I would not have to go to school that day. All that was about to change when, in the fall of that second year, I enrolled as a student in Immanuel Bible Academy.

Chapter 39
Immanuel

Immanuel Bible Academy was a high school level institution of learning sponsored by three Mennonite Brethren churches in the Reedley-Dinuba area. It had opened its doors in 1942 as a two-year school, but then added the third and fourth years of classes in '44 and '45 to make it an academy offering a diploma equivalent to one from a public high school. At that time, the school was located on the Reedley Mennonite Brethren meeting house grounds.

After two years as a student at Dinuba High, Dad and Mom finally agreed to allow me to transfer to Immanuel. The reason they were reluctant to let me make the change was because the school was known for allowing boys my age to goof off and have fun; no book-learnin' required. That was for me. These were the years when I hated school and, together with my best friends, was drifting off in the wrong direction.

So I started my Junior year of high school level classes at Immanuel. The first two weeks were a blast. My friends and I had a riot just being ornery and giving the teachers a bad time. But the party didn't last long. What we hadn't counted on was the new principal and teachers the school board had installed. Rev. J.N.C. Hiebert, principal, and Clarence Hofer, his assistant, soon clamped down on us and our frolicking ways. It was either shape up or get out. A couple of my friends got out. I stayed and decided to straighten up because I realized that if the teachers didn't do the job, my Dad would.

It wasn't long after starting school that year that I met a beautiful red-haired girl by the name of Beverly Friesen. She was a straight A student who had been the Valedictorian of her eighth grade class at Windsor school and had received the American Legion award as well. I soon learned that she was serious about getting a good education, and that she was a model student with no time for the likes of me. I was determined to get to know her. It was not easy because she had identified me as one of the rabble-rouser crowd and not her type.

It ultimately dawned on me that if I was going to win her friendship I would have to make some changes in the direction of my life, which I did. I began studying, even taking books home and doing homework, something I had never done in my career as a student. I found new friends who helped me get back on the straight and narrow. Mr. Hiebert became my favorite teacher and mentor. But all that did not guarantee that the ravishing red-head would ever notice me. What was a bashful kid like me to do, for land's sake?

The vintage Ford Model A bus dated back to about 1927, the year I was born, but it apparently was the best Immanuel could afford the year I began attending the school. The bus had plastic-like windows set in leather frames that could be moved up or down, depending on weather conditions. Instead of seats as in a normal bus, the seating arrangement included a long bench running length-wise on either side of the bus, plus a narrow bench down the middle.

Johnny Friesen and I lived at the far end of the fifteen mile bus route, so we became the designated drivers. It didn't matter that we were both barely sixteen years old and had only recently been qualified to get our first driver's license. No special training was asked for; none was given. We were simply handed the keys to the old bus and told to start driving. We picked up about twenty students at designated stops each morning. Some of the students had to walk up to a mile to get to the bus stop and wait in the freezing winter fog for the bus to get there. Parents gave no thought to any danger of having a young girl wait on an isolated country corner until the bus got there. We then dropped the students off in the afternoon and drove the bus home where it was parked and ready for the trip the next morning.

One of the concerns of the faculty and members of the school board was that Johnny and I would drive too fast. For goodness sake – the bus's top speed was 45 miles an hour! To ensure that we didn't drive at top speed, they took the bus in to the Jack Enns Auto agency where it was gassed and serviced regularly and equipped it with a *governor* on the carburetor, insuring that it could not be driven more than 35 miles an hour. If we tried to drive faster than that, the motor cut out until we got it below its designated speed.

The bus didn't always have very good brakes. There were times when we felt we needed to stick our feet through the floor board and drag them on the ground to help bring it to a stop. We usually had to down-shift it to a lower gear to slow it down. Even so, we often overshot a stop sign or a bus stop.

In spite of the many vicissitudes involved in driving the old bus, God's angel watched over Johnny and me, and we never had an accident and no one ever got hurt. I drove bus for the two years I attended Immanuel. My pay was free tuition which, as I recall, was $35.00 a semester.

Immanuel Academy Bus Fleet, the year after I graduated.
I drove the Ford shown on the left.

For me, the most memorable part of our whole bus driving career was the days Johnny was driving the bus and I was sitting at the front of the long bench, next to the door. It was a known fact that I had a crush on Beverly Friesen. She boarded the bus at a corner near Windsor school and sometimes sat a little further back on the same bench. I had arranged with Johnny that if Beverly ever sat on my bench with no one in between, I would give him a signal that at the next stop he was to put on the brakes as hard as he could. When he did,

Beverly came scooting down the bench and right into my waiting arms that reached out to save her from falling. I even waxed the benches from time to time to make sure this would happen. As crude as was my game, Beverly allowed me to court her for the next five years, after which she married me. The details of our courtship are told in another book entitled *Four Score and Ten*, which I wrote on the occasion of our fiftieth wedding anniversary.

After two years in Immanuel, I went to the Bible Institute of Los Angeles for one year, then on to Tabor College in Hillsboro, Kansas, mostly because that is where Beverly had decided to go. After three semesters of study in this great institution of learning, I spent a year farming with my father, during which time Beverly and I were married. In the fall, after our summer wedding, we were off to Los Angeles where I completed my under-graduate studies, and three years of seminary training. During my last year in seminary I was called into my first pastorate, City Terrace Mennonite Brethren Church, in the heart of East Los Angeles. The story of my life together with Beverly, from this point forward, is included in the anniversary book mentioned previously.

A Reflection

As I think back to those two critical years I spent at Immanuel, I have become aware of how important it is for young people to have role-models and mentors they can look up to. I thank God for godly teachers like Mr. Hiebert and Mr. Hofer. These were men we could emulate because they were genuine in living out their faith. In rehearsing those years, I am reminded of the Apostle Paul's words to Timothy, *"Be an example to all believers in what you teach, in the way you live, in your love, your faith, and your purity,"* (I Timothy 4:12, NLT). I completed my two years of high school at Immanuel and graduated with the first four-year graduating class. These teachers, together with the very beautiful young lady Beverly Friesen, who eventually became my wife, can be credited for the major changes I made in the direction of my life. I covet such role-models for every young person.

Chapter 40
The Garage

In 1934, Dad borrowed money, using the farm as collateral, to build a garage about 20 feet from the back door of the house. The family had agreed that it was a needed farm improvement. With the help of Uncle Pete, who seemed to know how to do most everything, the garage was built without plans. The structure was 60 feet long and 20 feet wide and included space for three cars. A 20 foot area closest to the house was partitioned off with the intention that it be used for storage space. As originally built, the garage had a dirt floor, but concrete flooring was added later. It had a pitched roof with asbestos shingles. We kids soon discovered that the structure was just right for playing Ante-Over, which we often did on summer evenings. One of the vehicle spaces was built with a mechanic's pit that could be covered with heavy planks when not in use. Otherwise the pit was used for changing oil in the farm vehicles and for overhauling a tractor from time to time.

A meagrope, used for rendering lard on hog butchering day and for making homemade soap, was installed in one corner of the storage space. A concrete enclosure surrounded it so a fire could be built under it. Mom's washing machine and laundry tubs were located just beyond the storage area. A door conveniently led from the back of the garage so Mom or the girls could carry the wet wash to the clotheslines. A water heater was added to the laundry area to provide hot water for the washing machine.

Two years after the garage was finished, the storage space referred to above found another purpose. Jack was engaged to be married to Helen

> Recipe for Homemade Soap
> From Mom's Looseleaf Recipe Book
> 4 ½ pints fat (drippings saved from cooking)
> Add 1 can lye and stir 5 minutes
> Add ½ cup ammonia and stir
> Add 3 pints water and stir until it boils
> Add a box of borax and stir until dissolved
> Stir off and on and add 1 more cup of water. "Always in between you can do something and don't stir constantly (it's not good). Let it settle and then stir again til its stiff enough to pour into containers and let stand till its ready to cut into bars." –Mom's instructions.
> (Recipe may be doubled or tripled if made in a meagrope, which Mom often did).

Klassen in December of 1936. He desperately needed a place where he could live with his new bride. Having a gift for smooth talk, proved by the fact that he later became an insurance salesman, and again attesting to his inventive mind, he soon had Mom and Dad convinced that he could convert the storage space into an apartment. With Uncle Pete's help, he did just that. The apartment included a kitchen just large enough for a sink, a small counter with hotplate, and a table for two. A double bed, chest of drawers, and chair barely fit into the bedroom. Between the kitchen and bedroom was a small sitting area that served as the apartment's livingroom. A tiny bathroom with shower off the west end of the kitchen was a great plus for the apartment, which was equipped with hot and cold running water. As the apartment neared completion, Jack's fiancee, Helen, who was a genius when it came to decorating a home, came to paint the walls and make curtains for the windows. By the time she had finished her job the apartment was invitingly livable.

I don't know how many years Jack and Helen lived in the apartment, but I do know that most of us siblings lived in the apartment for a period of time after we were married. Beverly and I got married in July of 1948. We lived in the apartment for four months. I don't know how we survived the heat of summer in that tiny place that had no insulation in the walls or ceiling. Our only ventilation was an open window and a small electric fan blowing warm air over us while we slept. But neither do I remember complaining about the heat. I guess we didn't know any better and we were too much in love.

A lean-to was eventually added to the back end of the garage for the intended purpose of serving as a tool shed. It actually became the nerve center of our farming operation because it housed all the tools and supplies needed to maintain and repair our farm equipment. A workbench with a place above it for hanging hammers and wrenches was built along one wall. Bins for holding an assortment of bolts, nuts and screws were built along another wall. This is where we kept our garden

The garage apartment.

tools and lawnmower. It was the ideal place for Ernie to build the toy farm implements Ray and I played with.

The lean-to that had been built onto the original house and had been the sleeping quarters for us boys was eventually torn down to make way for a substantial addition to the house. So the question arose as to where we would sleep while the addition was being built. Peter cleverly came up with the idea of converting the space above Jack and Helen's apartment into a loft. He was convinced that it would be just big enough for a couple of mattresses, and the four of us could comfortably make that our *bedroom*. It had just enough head room so that we could get to our beds by crawling on all fours. Mom agreed that it would be the perfect solution. One day Dad brought a stack of old boards from a junk store and before the sun had set that night they were nailed in place over the ceiling joists of the apartment. A ladder made of pieces of one-by-fours nailed to two studs of the partition gave us access from the garage floor to the loft.

Our new bedroom was functional in that the four of us boys had a place to sleep, but it also had some distinct disadvantages. Small as we were, climbing up that steep makeshift ladder was a bit of a challenge for Ray and me, and a bit dangerous if we had to use the outhouse in the dark of night. For another thing, it was stifling hot in summer and cold as an icebox in winter.

What we hadn't counted on was that the year we slept in the loft was the year a hor-rific scourge of rats invaded the garage. No one knew where they suddenly came from, but there they were, all summer long. The moment darkness filled the inside of the garage the rats began scurrying from one end to the other, running along one rafter and back across the other. They also found our bedroom and made themselves at home. It was not uncommon to have them run across our faces in the middle of the night. They could be heard chewing on the two-by-sixes and building nests in the dark corners of the garage with the intention of adding offspring to their pack. It wasn't long before the four of us opted to take our blankets and sleep out in the open on the front lawn. Soon after we moved out, the rats disappeared. It was assumed that they knew we were up there and their sole purpose for invading the ga-rage was to annoy us. Once we moved out they had no reason for being there. So they left.

As of this writing, the garage is still intact as built and the apartment is being used by renters. What vivid memories I have of that three-car garage and the loft that was our bed-room!

Chapter 41
The Hen House

Raising chickens for eggs, as well as for Sunday dinners, became an important part of our farming operation in the early 1930s. When the farm was purchased, it came with a small coop, but the chickens had the run of the farmyard. They were what are now referred to as free range chickens. Two roosters woke us up each morning and also made sure the flock sustained itself.

During one of our Saturday breakfast family meetings it was decided to go into the chicken business in a big way. First we needed to build a new hen house. Dad and Mom got together and agreed that the new building should be 100 feet long, 25 feet wide and would be built half way between the house and the cow barn. It should have a cement floor for easy cleaning and divider walls every 20 feet. The roof should slope with the high end facing the south. The south side should be screened with chicken wire. The yard in front of the building should be fenced in with chicken wire so the chickens could have limited free range.

Money for building such a large hen house was scarce in the depths of the Depression. Dad had already mortgaged the farm to buy other needed equipment. Always counting the family's pennies, Mom believed this project could be built with nickels and dimes from a piggy bank. One day she suggested to Dad that perhaps he and the boys could pour the cement for the floor of the building themselves. Neither Dad nor the boys had ever done such a thing. So, once again, we called on Uncle Pete for advice.

Since the major ingredient in cement is sand, it was decided that a lot of money could be saved by looking for a deposit of sand somewhere and hauling it to the building site. Sure enough, Dad found some in the bed of the canal that crossed Avenue 416 just west of the town of Dinuba. With the permission of the Alta Irrigation District, Jack, Ernie and Peter backed the '29 Chevrolet truck to the bank of the canal and pitched the sand, one shovelful at a time, onto the bed of the truck and hauled load after load, until they had enough for the cement that would make up the hen house floor. To break the monotony of the job, Peter occasionally dropped a handful of sand down the inside of Ernie's shirt. A sand-throwing fight usually ensued. While the boys were having *fun* hauling sand, Dad had the lumberyard in Dinuba deliver the gravel and bags of cement that would be needed for the project.

In preparation for the building project, Jack built a trough for mixing the cement. After the ground for the floor was graded and tamped smooth and the forms were in place, the men were in business. A wheelbarrow was filled with the cement which was mixed by using shovels and hoes, and hauled to the spot where the floor was taking shape. Uncle Pete had been hired to put the final finish on the cement. Just pouring the floor took two weeks of backbreaking work, but it turned out to be a beautiful piece of art.

When Dad had gone to the lumberyard for gravel and cement, he was told that he might consider buying rough-sawn, green lumber for such a project as a hen house directly from a sawmill up in the mountains. So one morning, with directions in hand, Dad loaded all of us boys into the Studebaker and we were off to the high country. We soon hit the Sierra Nevada foothills, and began to climb a very crooked, narrow road that eventually turned into a dirt trail. Ray soon began feeling carsick and vomited into a paper sack which smelled up the whole car, but Dad kept driving as if he knew where he was going. I doubt that he had ever driven on such a road. After three hours, we finally got to an area known as Whitaker Forest, just below the entrance to Sequoia and Kings Canyon National Parks. The huge redwoods, firs, and pines were so thick they blotted out the sun. Never had any of us seen such a forest, a marvel of God's handiwork.

I don't know how Dad ever found it, but suddenly a small sawmill powered by an old steam engine came into view. Two quaint mountain men, with cigarettes hanging from their lips, saw us coming, stopped their machines, and sauntered over to ask what we wanted. We were surprised they were not pointing guns at us. Dad pulled out the rough blueprint of the hen house he was planning to build, and asked whether they could provide the lumber. The men studied the plan for a while, told him what kind of lumber he would need, and how much. A deal was soon struck. The men agreed to deliver the lumber to the farm within four weeks.

The new building took shape rather slowly in between the spring farm work. Uncle Pete came over, when he could, to direct the construction. When it was finally finished, it included five separated pens with doors leading from one pen to the other. Roosts, nests, and watering troughs were added. Water was piped to the troughs with *floats* connected to the pipes. The floats would keep a constant supply of water in the troughs. The west end of the building included a storage area for feed and for cleaning and storing the eggs after the chickens started laying.

When the building was completed, Dad ordered 1,000 chicks from a hatchery. The day they arrived was filled with excitement – all those tiny, fuzzy, yellow chicks! I loved to pick them up and hold them. Dad had already bought brooders that would keep the chicks warm until they were old enough to grow feathers and run around on their own. It was not long before the first of the eggs were found in the nests.

What Ray and I had not anticipated in this whole project was that by the time the chickens were laying eggs, we would be just old enough to feed them and gather the eggs day after day. Not only that, but we soon learned that most of the eggs had been besmirched by chicken droppings while in the nests. The cleaning process involved sanding the droppings off with sandpaper attached to metal blocks. Each egg, then, had to be inspected, cleaned, weighed on a special scale and sorted – small, medium, or large – before being carefully placed in special egg crates for delivery to the stores.

Feeding chickens, plus gathering and cleaning the eggs, was a job Ray and I were entrusted with for years to come. In lieu of staying after school and playing basketball or baseball, it was something we could do as soon as we got home from school and before going out to milk the cows. We also learned that the hen house floor needed to be cleaned from time to time. Saturdays were often dedicated to scraping up the chicken droppings and spreading them in Mom's garden. She was always grateful: the manure made the flowers and vegetables grow so beautifully!

Occasionally, we caught Dad in the hen house in the middle of the day raiding a chicken nest. He picked up an egg, poked a hole in the small end with his pocket knife, put it to his mouth and sucked out it's contents, smacking his lips after he had swallowed it.

During the lean years of the Depression our chicken business proved to be a profitable venture in that it produced crates upon crates of eggs which Dad sold to the local grocery store in exchange for staple food items. Additionally, the roosters in the flock provided the family with the most delicious Sunday fried chicken dinners we could ever have imagined.

After a few of those special Sunday dinners, Ray and I agreed that all the work was worth it.

A Reflection

The wonder and beauty of Whitaker Forest, from the first time I saw it as a young lad, is forever etched upon my mind's drawing board. Beverly and I revisited the Forest a few years ago. It was just the way I remembered it – those massive, stately pines, redwoods and firs! Their density literally filtered out the sun, except that occasionally as we looked upward, the deep blue sky stood in vivid contrast to the shadowy silhouette of the majestic trees reaching to the heavens. The Psalmist must have had such a revelation when he wrote, *"Let the heavens be glad, and let the earth rejoice!. ...Let the fields and their crops burst forth with joy! Let the trees of the forest rustle with praise before the Lord!,"* (Psalm 96:11,12, NLT)

Chapter 42
House Addition

The early morning seven-alarm signal could be heard throughout the town of Dinuba as the volunteer firemen rushed to the station and on to a nearby house that was ablaze. It was a spectacle to behold! There had not been a major reason to pique the curiosity of the citizens of the town for years. Most of the townspeople got there before the firemen did.

After they were sure every family member was safely outside, the firemen began dousing the burning house with water from the nearby hydrant. It was too late. By the time the heroic firefighters had contained the flames, the house was beyond saving. The family would have to rebuild.

The news of the tragic fire spread throughout the county. My parents read about it in the *Dinuba Sentinel*. Months later they saw an advertisement. The lumber that had not been destroyed in the fire could be salvaged free of charge by anyone willing to tear down the house.

By coincidence, at about the time of the tragedy, our family decided it was time to build a major addition to our farm home. The lean-to that had served its purpose as the boys' bedroom for so many years would be torn down and replaced with the new addition. Dad and Jack went to Dinuba, surveyed the fire-damaged house, and decided to offer to salvage the building. "The lumber," Dad said, "will go a long way in building the addition we are planning." These were, after all, the Depression years, and a penny saved was a penny earned.

For the next month our whole family went out to the house every Saturday and dismantled it piece by piece. While the older men tore off the roof of the two-story building and hauled loads of shingles and charred lumber to the local dump, others pulled down the usable dimension lumber. Ray and I were given the job of pulling nails from salvaged two-by-fours.

Mom had warned us to be careful of boards with nails. One day, in spite of her concern, I stepped on a board with a rusty nail. It went right through the sole of my shoe and into the arch of my foot. Man-oh-man, did it ever hurt! While I was crying, Mom realized the danger of a rusty nail. I was immediately taken to Dr. Brigham's clinic in town to clean and dress the wound and get a tetanus shot. The shot hurt worse than stepping on the nail.

As we continued to work, the usable lumber piled up to a sizeable stack. We cleaned up the site of the burned-out house, hauled home the salvaged lumber, and stacked it near the building site for the new add-on. The next morning, Dad surveyed the stack of wood: the boards with burned edges and the warped two-by-fours scattered among the straight ones. In spite of the wood that might not be useable, Dad declared the salvage project a success.

It had been decided that the addition would be built in such a way as to create a "T" shaped house with a part of its roof line running at a 180 degree angle to the original house. The plan was to build a basement the length and width of the addition. It was also agreed that the inside configuration of the structure would include an entry with a sink and closet, a spacious kitchen, and a bedroom.

The lean-to was demolished. The two-by-four studs were saved to be reused. Dad then had a new water well dug smack dab in the middle of the area where the new basement would be. Before any building could proceed, we had to dig the hole for the basement. This would need to be 30 feet long, 25 feet wide and seven feet deep.

One day Dad asked Ernie and Peter to harness Kate and Beck and hitch them to the old Fresno scraper. With this implement and the team of mules, Dad started digging the basement cavity. One load after the other of hard packed dirt was slowly scraped out of the hole and piled up in our yard where it waited to be spread on the farm's low spots. Dad worked day after day. The hole got deeper; the work with the scraper got harder as the mules had to climb the incline out of the hole and up to the top of the dirt pile. In the meantime, the boys had to use hand shovels to clean up the sides and corners of the chasm – the places the mules and scraper could not get to. When the basement was finally deep enough and the sides long and wide enough, there was the huge incline Dad had

Note: As I sit here today and ponder the work involved in digging a hole the size of this basement with the crude implements, by today's standards, available to us, I cannot imagine Dad and our family committing to such a gigantic project. But I don't remember anyone, including Dad or Mom, having a moment of hesitation in moving forward with it.

used for getting the earth from the bottom of the basement to the ground level of the house. It had to be removed one shovelful at a time. The deeper the men dug into the hard packed dirt of the incline, the higher each shovelful had to be pitched. After a month of steady work, the hole was finally ready for the next step.

Dad again called on Uncle Pete to guide the men in the carpentry work. With hand saws, squares, hammers and nails, some of the salvaged lumber was put to good use as the men built forms to create the foundation and walls of the basement. Cement was mixed with a small electric mixer and poured into the forms, one wheelbarrow full at a time. After the concrete had hardened, the forms were removed and torn apart so the lumber could be reused in another part of the building process.

Since our regular farm work still needed to be done, framing and finishing the addition continued for the better part of a year. The kitchen cabinets were finally ready to be painted. The cabinet doors were made of panels of plywood edged with raised two-inch-wide frames. The panels were painted with a glossy white enamel. The frames of the doors were painted medium blue. Looking at the brightly painted cabinets I, with my youthful eyes, concluded that they were rather striking.

The kitchen counter was covered with the very latest in counter tops – linoleum with a rounded front edge, the color matching the blue of the cabinet borders. The floor was covered with blue linoleum. When the kitchen was finally finished, Mom stood at the door and surveyed her kitchen with its new electric stove and refrigerator, and smooth counter top! She was so pleased and proud. Even though cooking was not Mom's favorite job, she concluded that, compared to working in her old kitchen, cooking now would be a breeze. Her happiness, however, was rather short-lived.

During the time the remodeling job was in progress, Ray and I had begun a new hobby building model airplanes; kits could be purchased for a nickel or a dime. One evening,

House addition, perpendicular to the original house.

not long after our new kitchen was finished, we were working on our models. As we were cleaning up, I put the bottle of model airplane glue on Mom's new kitchen counter. In the process, the cap came off and the glue spilled on the back/center, burning a hole through the surface of the new linoleum. I became hysterical when I realized what had happened. So did my mother. I had seriously blemished her new counter. It was like driving a new car out of a showroom and wrecking a fender the first time it was driven. I cried myself to sleep that night. A few days later Mom found a solution for the blemish. It was just the right place to store our new electric toaster and hide the blemish completely. If my recollections are correct, that toaster was placed over the blemish from that day until a new counter replaced the linoleum many years later.

The entry to the new addition was quite large and spacious. It included a cabinet with sink and faucets with hot and cold running water. A mirror was hung above the sink. This is where the men washed up after working in the fields and where Dad shaved each morning after breakfast, using a straight-edged razor and a cup of shaving cream. As mentioned earlier, he was greatly amused when one of us kids walked by so he could take a dab of shaving cream and smear it on our cheeks or under our noses. A closet where the men kept their jackets and work shoes was located off to one side. A stairway led from the entry to the basement below.

The bedroom of the remodeled home was called the "boys' room." It was large enough for two double beds. My oldest brother Jack was married by this time, so the room was just the right size for the four of us: Ernie, Peter, Ray, and me. It was an exciting day when we moved from the attic of the garage to our new room. Never mind that I had to share a bed with Raymond until the day Ernie left for the army and Peter went off to Bible School. Nor did it matter that the room was as hot as an attic in the summer and cold as a refrigerator in the winter. A couple of years later Dad bought a little eight-inch electric fan which blew hot air over our heads while we tried to sleep during the heat of summer.

Our new basement added an immense amount of space to our family's living area. Several windows had been built into the uppermost part of the basement walls, with a small well on the outside of each window to provide a bit of daylight to the room. The basement is where Mom planned to store the hundreds of jars of precious fruits and vegetables she canned during the previous summer. This would have been the ideal place for an afternoon nap, or just to sit in a rocking chair and read. Please recall that a water well had been drilled in the middle of the basement. A pressure system (a pump with a one hundred gallon tank) had been installed and was intended to keep our house and garden supplied with water.

    Not long after our oasis from the heat of summer had been completed, it was discovered that it had one serious flaw. Because the ground water level in those days was so high, water began to seep through the cracks in the floor and wall almost as soon as the basement was finished. Within a short time a foot of water covered the whole floor! No matter how we tried to seal the cracks, the water found its way into the basement. The pressure system had to be raised immediately and installed on a two foot high platform. Mom's canned fruit had to be taken from the bottom shelves of the cabinets and stored up higher. It was useless for sleeping or sitting and relaxing. There were times when I had to wade through more than a foot of water to retrieve a jar of fruit for supper. What to do now?

One day Ernie, the resourceful brother that he was, came home with a hand pump. He and Dad bolted it to a cement slab outside one of the basement windows and led a steel pipe from the bottom of the pump through a window and into a hole that had been dug in a corner of the basement. By using the hand pump, it was now possible to pump the water out of the basement and into Mom's garden. For several years thereafter, the water had to be removed almost daily from the basement with the use of the hand pump. It was a job that took an hour or more, one that Ray and I inherited. Eventually, Dad had an electric sump pump installed in that hole in the corner. It kept the basement floor relatively free of an accumulation of water. But during the years I was growing up, that damp cavity under our new addition was never dry or free from seepage. As the years passed and the farmers irrigated their crops, the ground water level got lower and lower. As of this writing, the basement is dry as a desert pond and can be used for comfortably keeping cool and taking a nap on a hot summer day.

With a new electric stove in the kitchen, the old wood stove was junked, and we needed a different way to keep the house warm in winter. Our first heating stove was an upright, oil-burning unit placed in a corner of our dining room. The oil to feed the stove was piped from a 100-gallon tank located behind our garage. The stove kept our dining room toasty warm, but the rest of the house, especially the boys' room, was left cold as an igloo. It seemed that every winter morning in those days was below freezing. Ray and I often got out of bed, grabbed our clothes, ran to the dining room and stood next to the stove while getting dressed. It didn't matter that in the process other family members saw our exposed bodies. The comforts of a warm room overshadowed the need for privacy.

The upright stove was ultimately replaced with an oil burning floor furnace at the east end of our dining room. It was grand to come home from church on a wintry Sunday evening, stand over the furnace, and soak up its warmth.

Air conditioning was unheard of during the 1930s. In all those years our house became as hot as the business end of a branding iron during the summer time, especially while we still had a wood stove. Even the new addition did not change the temperature in the house, except that the kitchen was now less hot. One day in the early forties brother Jack, bless his unique inventive mind, came home with an electric motor and a fan blade attached to its arbor. He then proceeded to build a wire cage around it. Cooling pads were encased within the cage and a tube with running water fitted over the top of the pads. He then opened a front window in the parlor and hung the contraption from wires stretched to the ceiling of the front porch. His invention was, as it were, the forerunner of the present day evaporative cooler! And wonder of wonders, it worked, but cooled the parlor only a degree or two.

The house has been painted and repainted many times since its original yellow and green. I was sixteen years old when I was elected to give it another coat of paint. I had never handled a paintbrush in my life before I undertook the awesome task. By this time, Marie had married Lowell Wendt and they were pastoring a church in Los Angeles. The Vernons were members of the church and came to visit us the summer I was to paint the house. Mr. Vernon was a Los Angeles policeman in addition to being a professional painter. I had started to paint the house the day our guests were leaving to go back home. As Mr. Vernon came out the back door he stood for a few minutes and watched me paint. He then came over and gave me a few tips on painting that really improved the quality of the paint job. I have never forgotten his pointers. Mr. Vernon, gave me several basic pointers, but the one most amateur painters I have watched paint don't know, and I remember most vividly, is as follows:

"Wesley, when you are painting the wood siding of a house (which I was), after you have applied the paint, always make sure your last brush stroke is worked into the part that is already painted; never away from it. That way, you will not leave a brush mark on the finished product."

Through the years, I have found that this is important for anything I paint with a brush, no matter what I am painting or what kind of paint I am using.

Since Mom and Dad moved out of the house when they retired, it has undergone other structural changes but, as of this writing, the main part remains as it was remodeled so many years ago.

A Reflection

My first visual image of the house at age three is that it was not much more than a shack. However, through the years it was transformed into a beautiful home by the hands of loving parents. Even to this day, it holds many warm and sacred memories including the days before it was transformed and enlarged. As I think about it now, yes, the addition and improvements made life easier and more comfortable. But what amazes me is that we seemed to be just as happy and content in the original ramshackle house that was much too small for our large family as in the home it ultimately became. Perhaps it proves the wisdom of the old adage, *"Be it ever so humble, there's no place like home."*

Chapter 43
The Dairy

It was past 9 o'clock and the family was getting ready for bed after a long, hard day of work on the farm. Peter was already on his way to the garage where the four of us boys slept in the loft. He suddenly ran back into the house and yelled, "Dad, the cows are out!" We all ran outside and, sure enough, we could faintly see them in the alfalfa patch, grazing the fresh, sweet stems of the growing alfalfa. It was the spring of 1934 and our herd of cows, heifers and a bull, had grown to about thirty. They had broken through the pasture fence and were having a picnic.

Their favorite food was fresh alfalfa, but it was the worst and most dangerous kind of food a cow could eat. If they ate too much, it caused a gassy swelling of their abdomen which we called bloating. When a cow was severely bloated she would lie down and gasp for air. Unless the right medical attention was immediately given she would soon die.

One or two of our cows came dangerously close to bloating that spring night in '34. In fact, one of our most troublesome cows, Tillie, was already down. Dad knew there was only one thing to do – call for a long butcher knife. A veterinarian would have used a surgical instrument called a *trocar*, consisting of a sharp stylet (a slender probe) enclosed in a tube. There was neither time to call for a veterinarian, nor could Dad afford one. Ernie ran to the house as fast as he could, came back and handed Dad the knife. With the knife in his strong right hand, Dad plunged it into Tillie's stomach to release the gas that had accumulated. He immediately pulled the knife back out, stood back and waited for the gas to escape. After about an hour Tillie regained strength and struggled back to her feet.

In the meantime, the rest of us children rounded up the other cows and slowly herded them back into the corral. It was important to move them slowly lest the symptoms of bloating increase. Once we got them into the corral, we put hay into the stanchions and tried to get them to eat the dry hay – the anecdote for gas poisoning. Dad sat with Tillie the rest of the night to make sure she would not develop further problems.

As indicated earlier, when Dad bought the farm, several cows were thrown in with the deal. Dad had not owned a single cow since moving to California in 1920. Now, ten years later, the boys had to learn to milk on the very day we moved to the Forty. We started with just a few cows, but the herd increased as the cows had calves. The dairy was part of farm life during all of my growing-up years.

Our milk *parlor* was on the north side of the old barn which had been equipped with stanchions that could be locked around the cows' necks so they could not back out and leave the barn before they had been milked. In the early years, each of the seven stalls had to be locked in place one at a time. Dad later modernized the system so that by moving a long wooden arm, all the stalls could be closed or opened at one time. During those first years the milk parlor had a dirt floor. As could be expected, the cows often dirtied the barn. With a dirt floor, cleaning up after them was a messy and rather unsanitary job. After several years of this, Dad paved the floor with concrete which included a foot wide channel meant to act as sort of a cow toilet. The problem was, they often missed the mark. In order to avoid this, one of us boys ran for a shovel when we realized a cow was about to empty her bowel, held it next to her behind, and caught the fresh manure before it splattered all over the floor.

When a cow emptied her bladder there was not much to do but stand back and let the urine splatter far and wide on the concrete. This often happened right while we were milking the cow. Many times it was too late for the milker to stand back far enough. All we could do was let the urine dry on our pant-legs while we continued the milking chore.

The actual milking process was as follows. Each of us had a milk stool – a piece of four by four inch lumber about a foot in length with a board nailed to the top end of it. We sat on the stool with a three-gallon bucket between our legs. The act of milking was an art learned only with much practice. I started to milk when I was seven years old and kept milking day after day until I finished high school. Even so, some of us never became skilled in the art. It was with great humiliation that I finally had to admit one day that my sister, Marie, was the best milker in the family. Yes, dainty Marie, so petite and tidy in every way. She also knew what it meant to get sprayed by a cow.

Certain cows usually had to be hobbled (a chain clamped around the cow's back legs just above the knee) to keep them from kicking us while milking them. Tillie was one such cow. If she was not hobbled, she was likely to kick the milker's leg and send the bucket of milk we were holding between our legs flying, with the milk splashing on us and the floor. We lost many a gallon of milk by being too lazy to hobble certain cows that should have been hobbled. Dad was not very forgiving when this happened.

When we finished milking a cow, we emptied our buckets of milk into a strainer placed over a ten-gallon milk can. The purpose of the strainer was to catch specks of dirt or other foreign matter that fell into the bucket while milking. The strainer, however, was often the object of angry frustration for us boys. You see, we had several cats on the farm for the purpose of controlling the mouse population. These cats gathered around the barn at milking time. It was

My sister, Marie,
best milker in the family.

their habit to jump onto the rim of the strainer and help themselves to the milk as it slowly drained down into the can. It did not seem to matter how many times we tried to chase them off, they never learned their lesson. Every cat, as you know, has a mind of its own. The moment our backs were turned they were up on the strainer again. I lost my temper more than once over this situation. Perhaps this explains why, to this day, cats are not my favorite pet.

After the cows had all been milked and let back into the corral, it was time to clean the milk parlor. First the manure left behind had to be removed with a shovel. Then the floor was washed down with a forceful spray of water. While one of us was doing that, another was in the milk house washing the buckets and strainer. These were then sterilized in a contraption Jack had invented. The three or four ten-gallon cans of milk were put into a container in the milk house filled with cool water where they stayed until the milkman from the Danish Creamery came to pick them up – once every morning and once every evening. During the colder months of winter we had to put the cans onto a cart and take them out to the road so the milkman would not have to drive all the way to the barn.

The cart behind me was used for hauling milk cans to the road. Note the three-car garage in the background.

One of our favorite pastimes as boys was to scare the milkman. When he came driving to the barn at night we hid behind a tree or bush and would jump out, hollering at the top of our voices. Once we hot-wired the water tank in the milk house with a low voltage electric shock so the milkman got an electric charge when he picked up a milk can. We got by with this trick one time only because he tattled to Dad and threatened to stop picking up our milk.

While all the cleanup in the barn and milk house was going on, Dad, or one of my older brothers, went out to feed the cows. A long row of stanchions had been built along one side of the corral. Hay from the haystack was thrown down in front of the stanchions where the cows came to feed on the savory alfalfa hay. It seemed uncanny to me that each cow knew her place in the row of stanchions and if another cow greedily started feeding in the wrong spot, the two cows would tangle with each other until the matter was settled.

Dad always had a bull included in the herd of cows. The bull was usually mean and dangerous to tangle with and was therefore kept in a corral by himself. Only Dad knew how to manage the bull who learned to respect Dad's pitchfork.

There were times other than the one described earlier when the cows got out. One morning, while Dad and the older boys were working on another farm, the cows and the mean bull got out. I was the first to see them in our neighbor's alfalfa. I ran inside and yelled to Mom, "The cows are out!" She, Ray, and I, plus the girls that were home, came running out to try to herd them back into the corral. We panicked when we saw the bull among them. One of us ran to open the corral gate while the rest grabbed whatever sticks we could find. We carefully and gently, herded the cows toward the corral. The bull, however, had a mind of his own and stayed behind, mooing and kicking up dirt with his front paw. Boy-oh-boy, did he look mean! We finally had to call a neighbor to bring a pitchfork. Tensions were running high as the neighbor slowly approached the bull and after showing him who was boss, convinced him to make his way reluctantly into the corral.

It was only after Jack, Ernie and Peter were off to other pursuits that Dad broke down and bought a milking machine. With the machine, Ray and I could easily handle the milking by ourselves. It took about the same amount of time to do the milking, but with half the crew. There were, in fact, times when one of us did the milking without the help of anyone else.

Wes, holding the milking machines.

A Reflection

That small dairy sustained our family through the lean years of the Depression, providing the cash needed to buy other food and supplies. Although it bound us to the farm morning and evening, seven days a week, we were thankful for Tillie and Rose, and the rest of the cows (each with her own name) who so faithfully gave what they had to give – their life-sustaining milk – so necessary for giving us strong, healthy bodies.

The Apostle Peter uses milk as a symbol for keeping our inner lives strong. *"You must crave pure spiritual milk so that you can grow into the fullness of your salvation. Cry out for this nourishment as a baby cries for milk, now that you have had a taste of the Lord's kindness,"* (I Peter 2:2 NLT)

Chapter 44
Kate and Beck

Kate and Beck were a unique pair of mules, to say the least. I would hardly describe them as a team because they were so different one from the other and didn't always work together very well. Kate was high-spirited, Beck was laid back. When yoked together for work, Kate invariably took the lead while Beck had to be coaxed along. It appeared that while in the harness, Kate did more than her share of the work. Beck did what she had to.

My readers may remember that Kate and Beck were two of the animals that were thrown in with the deal when Dad bought the farm. Now in 1930, they were his only source of horse power. He had to depend on these two trusty mules to plow, harrow, plant and cultivate the land. Tractors were a common sight on most larger farms by the early 1930s. But there was simply no money for Dad to buy a tractor during these early Depression years. This dour pair of mules replaced the beautiful teams of horses Dad had in Kerman. As everyone knows, mules are a cross between a horse and a donkey. They are as smart and hard working as a horse, but they are by nature more like a donkey. Stubborn, contrary, obstinate and ornery are words that pretty well described Kate and Beck. But they also had some good qualities – strong, steadfast, tough, tenacious, and hard-working.

The mules, together with the cattle, were kept in the pasture on the back twenty of our farm. An irrigation ditch along Monson Road ran across the south end of the farm. It was a main ditch owned by the Alta Irrigation District (one of a system of such ditches that crisscrossed Tulare County) carrying irrigation water from the Sierra Nevada's snow-melt to the farmers in the valley below. Since it carried water much of the year, it provided the moisture needed for grass to grow on its banks even during most of the hot, dry summer months and was a favorite grazing area for Kate and Beck.

By the time we were ten years old, Dad considered Ray and me ready to harness the critters for work. The first thing we had to do on the mornings Dad planned to work the fields was to get the mules from the back end of the pasture and into the barn. The chore often provided a bit of a challenge. First, we had to walk what seemed like a mile to the ditch bank. We then had to try to sneak behind the mules and chase them toward the barn. The mules, however, were smarter than we. Rather than stay to-

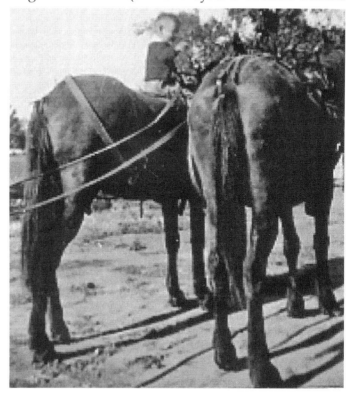

Mules Kate and Beck.
Little Jim Gunther is riding Kate.

gether as they did when grazing, they split up the moment they saw us coming. Kate made a beeline to one end of the ditch bank while Beck took off to the other. It often took a half hour of running back and forth before they finally got tired of teasing us and headed toward the barn and into their stalls. The barn had two stalls. Each mule knew which was hers. They never made the mistake of getting into the wrong stall. Kate would never have tolerated such nonsense.

The next challenge was harnessing the critters. Ray and I were usually a bit nervous when we had to do this. Mules, as everyone knows, can be very temperamental. The tricky part was placing the bridle over each one's head. We never knew whether one of them, especially Kate, would deliberately stomp on our feet while we were doing this. After finally getting their bridles in place, their collars were carefully placed around their necks and snugged up against their chests. The next step in the procedure was to throw the harnesses over their backs. This was the most dangerous part of the job because no mules liked to have something thrown onto their backs by small kids like my brother and me. While doing this we always had to be watchful of a kick in the pants by a mule's hind leg. Finally, we had to reach under their stomachs, grab the bellybands of the harnesses and secure them to their bodies. Kate and Beck were now ready for the day's work. Ray and I never felt safe until we had climbed out of the mules' stalls and were on our way back to the house for breakfast.

Kate and Beck were an incredible pair of mules. Many times Dad needed them to work on rented farmland that may have been seven or eight miles from home. To get there, he hitched the team to a vineyard wagon loaded with a plow or harrow. From the moment they headed down the road, they didn't walk – they trotted all the way. Dad then hitched them to the particular farm implement he was going to use, and worked the field with them all day. He then hitched them back to the vineyard wagon and they again trotted all the way back home, except that when they were within a mile from the barn, they broke into a full gallop. To think, they did all this after chasing Ray and me from one end of the ditch bank to the other in the early morning and working the field all day!

Who said Dad should get a tractor? He had Kate and Beck.

Chapter 45
Making Hay

It was the spring of 1933. The sun was coming up over the horizon of the Sierra Nevada mountains when Dad sent Ray and me to get the mules from the pasture so he could harness them. As usual, we found Kate and Beck grazing on the ditch bank at the far end of the Forty. For some reason, they cooperated that day and ran straight to the barn and into their stalls where Dad was waiting for them. Within twenty minutes he had them harnessed and hitched to the vineyard wagon. They were soon on their way to the Sultana farm, four miles northeast of Dinuba, eight miles from home.

The eighty-acre farm lay on the eastern slope of Smith Mountain, an isolated hill that rose 500 feet above sea level. It was the first of many foothills that gave entrance to the majestic Sierra Nevada mountain range beyond. The soil of the farm was perfect for alfalfa; light in texture, good drainage, not a spot of alkaline soil. And no sand burs.

It was time for the first alfalfa cutting of the season. Good alfalfa in the Valley had up to seven cuttings in one season. Dad had been to the farm a few days earlier to determine if it was ready for mowing. While there, he greased the mowing machine and installed a newly sharpened sickle blade. Today, after hitching the mules to the mowing machine, he picked up their reins and seated himself as comfortably as possible on its cast iron seat. When he

got to the corner of the alfalfa patch, he lowered the sickle and began cutting twenty acres of the eighty acres of sweet smelling alfalfa. Row after row, he went up one side of the Twenty and down the other. It was a two-day job.

By the time he had finished the mowing, the alfalfa was dry enough to be raked together. The type of rake he used at that time was known as a *dump* rake. With Dad on its seat, the rake gathered the alfalfa as it was pulled across the field by Kate and Beck. Each time he came to an irrigation levee (about twenty feet apart), Dad pushed a lever with his foot, causing the entire bank of 30 tines of the rake to lift just enough for the gathered hay to drop onto the levee, eventually forming a windrow where it continued to dry.

Depending on the weather, the alfalfa was dry enough to be called hay in a day or two. It was then ready to be formed into shocks. For this job, my brothers Jack, Ernie and Peter, each grabbed a pitchfork and went down each windrow, forming the shocks. At the same time, they collected hay the rake had missed and placed it on the shocks. More correctly, according to Webster, the little mounds of hay, about two feet in diameter and fifteen inches

Restored horse-drawn
alfalfa mowing machine.

Horse-drawn dump rake.
The *tongue* (a 12-foot piece of wood) is missing from this picture.

high, should have been called cocks. Wheat bundles were shocks. We always called our mounds of hay shocks, and never got in trouble with our English teachers for it. The hay was allowed to dry for another day or two before it was ready to be gathered and hauled to the haystack next to our dairy's feeding stanchions. Since moving to the Dinuba farm, Dad had acquired another flatbed truck, a dull green 1929 Chevrolet. So now we had two trucks for hauling hay: the Model-T and the Chevrolet. In earlier years the hay would have been loaded onto a mule-drawn wagon.

Loading the trucks with the hay required at least three strong men. The truck was driven between two rows of shocks, while a man with a pitchfork picked up the shocks on each side of the truck and placed them carefully on the edge of the truck's flatbed. One man was on top of the truck to make sure each shock was safely placed where it ought to be and

stomped the hay down so as to get as much hay as possible on the load. One person drove the truck slowly down the rows of shocks, stopping from time to time to allow the workers to catch up with the truck.

On the day the men started hauling hay that day in 1933, Jack and Dad, being the strongest, pitched the hay onto the truck. Ernie was on the truck, stomping the hay and keeping the load straight. Peter was in the cab, driving the truck.

Ernie had the most important but least desirable job in the hay hauling process. He was responsible for putting the shocks in place on the truck bed so they wouldn't fall off. He also had to make sure

Note: Driving a Model-T was quite different from driving later model trucks. A Model-T had three pedals on the floor, two levers on the steering column, and one hand lever to the left of the driver. The leftmost floor pedal, if depressed, moved the truck forward in first gear. If one wanted to shift into second gear, the hand lever to the driver's left was pushed forward. To put the truck in reverse, the driver pressed the middle floor pedal, while the rightmost pedal was the brake. The lever to the left was also the emergency brake when pulled all the way back. The right lever on the steering column was the gas, and the other lever was the spark. The engine, of course, had to be cranked by hand, and unless the gas and spark were set just right, one might crank the engine for an hour and not get the motor started – something that happened all too frequently.

the load was straight and balanced on each side of the truck bed as the hay was pitched onto the load. If not balanced the whole load might slide off the truck while driving home. Ernie was capable of building beautiful loads of hay. The downside of his job was that he was tromping on loose hay all morning long. Occasionally a shock of hay landed in his face, sometimes purposely, as it was being pitched. Another problem Ernie had was that Peter, driving the truck, would sometimes start moving the truck forward with a jerk, throwing Ernie off balance, landing him face down in the hay, with itchy alfalfa leaves inside his shirt. By age eight, I inherited the job of driving both the Model-T and the Chevrolet – my first lessons in driving. A couple of years later, I was promoted to Ernie's job.

It took most of the morning to load the two trucks with hay. Driving the eight miles back home was a challenge. A bump in the road or a sudden stop might shift the whole load, causing it to slide off the truck. If this happened, which it did from time to time, traffic on the narrow country roads was blocked while we reloaded the truck.

The best part of hauling hay was getting home with both trucks loaded and finding Mom with a big pitcher of homemade tomato juice waiting for us. Her juice was better at quenching our thirst than any Gatorade could have been.

After a very ample lunch prepared by Martha and Marie, the crew took a short nap before beginning to unload the hay. In the early days, the hay was pitched from the trucks onto the haystack, one shock at a time. Dad was now the one on the stack, making sure the sides of the stack were straight, and tromping the hay to keep it level.

A few years later, Dad bought a hay derrick. It was a post about twenty feet high and had arms in the form of a cross, extending ten to twelve feet to one side and six feet to the other. A steel cable was fed through pulleys at the end of each arm and across the top of the post. One end of the cable was attached to a grappling hook and the other end to our team of mules. The hook, capable of lifting six to eight shocks at a time, had curved tines three feet long.

Jack (left) and Dad in front of two truck-and-trailer loads of hay.
The front truck is a 1929 Chevrolet; the rear truck is the old Model T.

The kind of haystacks that Dad built for feeding cows.

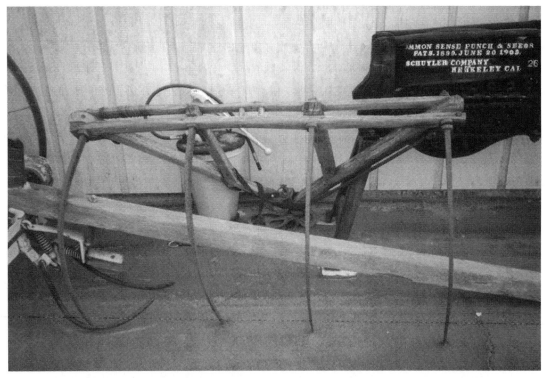

Grappling Fork for loading hay from trucks to stack. The piece of wood in the middle
of the picture is a tongue, to which horses were hitched for pulling machines.

When the men were ready to unload, the hook was pushed down into a stash of hay on the truck. Kate and Beck were hitched to one end of the cable. With their reins in his hand, Jack motioned for the mules to move forward, raising the hook with its hay. When the hook was at the right height, Jack would hold the mules reins tight and yell "whoa." Hopefully, the mules would stop. If they didn't, the whole derrick would come crashing down. It was a danger the men lived with each time the derrick was used. And, sure enough, it happened one day. But Mom's prayers were answered. It fell where no one was standing. Everyone was safe. A few years later a tractor replaced the mules.

If everything went as it should, the hook with its load of hay was swung across the haystack to where Dad wanted it. He then yelled "hack" and Ernie, on the ground, holding a rope attached to the hook pulled the rope, releasing the hay from the hook. Dad's job on top of the stack was a dangerous one because the tines of the hook swung back and forth after the hay was released and could easily have hit Dad and caused serious injury. Backing away from it, he could also have mis-stepped and fallen off the stack. For these reasons, he never allowed any of us boys to take this job. Through the years Dad built some beautiful haystacks, many of them forty feet long, twenty feet wide, and fifteen feet high.

There were years when we grew more alfalfa hay than we needed, so Dad sold the surplus. It was often sold to our Armenian neighbors who were very finicky about the quality of the hay and always wanted it stored in their barns. That was a job of a different color! When unloading the trucks, the hay had to be carried, one fork full at a time, into the barn where the temperature was 110 degrees or more, and pitched up into its loft. When selling to these neighbors, we felt we earned every dime they paid us for it.

During the early 1940s, Dad was able to afford more up-to-date machinery for making hay. We had a mower that was hooked directly to our tractor and could now mow a field in one-third the time a horse drawn mower could do the job. Mowing the alfalfa became one of Ernie's favorite jobs. He usually had the tractor in fifth gear when he mowed. Years later, when I was old enough to run the tractor and mower, third gear was fast enough for me.

Side-delivery rakes came into general use by the '40s. These rakes gathered the hay into windrows as tractors pulled them across the field. Balers also came into popular use. They compacted the hay, made it easier to handle, and used less storage space.

Being the entrepreneur that he was, Jack bought a hay baler soon after he was married in 1936. His intention was to contract with alfalfa farmers to bale their hay for them. The baler was one of the original models which could be pulled by horses or a tractor. It was a six-man operation. The shocks of hay had to be pitched onto a deck by two men and fed by hand into the baler by one man who was standing on the deck. When the bales came out at the back of the machine, they needed to be tied with three strands of baling wire. This part of the operation required one man sitting on each side of the baler, one feeding the wire around the ends of the bale, and the other tying the wires. The sixth man drove the tractor. Each of these bales weighed up to 150 pounds and took two strong men to lift onto the bed of a truck for hauling to the stack. Jack's baling business lasted but a year or two as more up-to-date equipment became available.

In spite of the popularity of the baling machines in the 1940s, Dad continued to favor the only way he had ever made hay – in shocks and pitched loose onto a haystack. He did this until he sold his dairy the year after I got married in 1948.

Making hay in the 1930s was to the farmer what working on the railroad was to other men – a lot of hard work! The former had one distinct advantage – ah the sweet smell of freshly mowed alfalfa!

A Reflection

Making hay was a team effort. It required several men to precisely coordinate their energies in loading a truck with hay and then getting it onto a stack. It has occurred to me that for us, family life functioned the same way. Each of us, whether young or old, had a job to do in order to create a successful and healthy family. The Bible compares our bodies to this kind of teamwork. *"Now the body is not made up of one part but of many. If the foot should say, 'because I am not a hand, I do not belong to the body, it would not for that reason cease to be part of the body.' ...If they were all one part, where would the body be? As it is, there are many parts, but one body."*

In the above passage the Apostle Paul illustrates how God intends the church to function – each member having been given a gift to be used in serving Christ and His church. When we do so, *"This makes for harmony among the members, so that all the members care for each other equally,"* (I Corinthians 12:14 - 25, NLT).

Chapter 46
Cotton Farmer

It was April 1, and Kate and Beck were harnessed and hitched to the two-row cotton planter. Dad and the team were soon on their way to the Anderson farm, just a mile to the north, where he would begin the process of planting forty acres of cotton. When he got to the farm, he filled the two canisters of the planter with seed from sacks he had dropped along the road the day before. He had no fear in those days of someone stealing the seed. After making final adjustments as to how deep to plant the seed, and dropping a marker that would tell him exactly how far from the first two rows he should plant the next ones, he set out to plant his cotton. The job would take several long days of sitting on the hard seat of the planter, keeping the team in line, and making sure the right amount of seed was being planted at the right depth.

His concern in planting those first rows was to make them as straight as possible because every row after that would be no straighter than the first. It was a matter of pride with farmers to have straight columns of anything they planted: cotton, corn, beans, or whatever. Dad set his sights on a post at the far end of the field he would be planting. He knew that if he kept his eyes on that post, and Kate and Beck cooperated, he would have fairly straight rows.

The first weeks of April were the ideal time for planting cotton in the San Joaquin valley. If planted too early, a late frost might destroy the seedlings. If planted too late, the crop would not mature properly in the fall. It was also important that the soil have the proper amount of moisture to cause the seeds to sprout. The normal rains of winter usually kept the mois-

A horse-drawn cotton planter with a *tongue*.

ture content of the soil just right for April planting.

It took two anxiety-filled weeks for the seeds to sprout. Even a light rain during this time would form a crust on the soil – a crust the seedlings could not penetrate. In that case, Dad would have to replant. A very expensive operation. After about ten days of nervous waiting, he went to the farm each day to check on the seedlings. It was always a great relief when he could look down each row and see the tiny green cotton plants coming to life – almost as thrilling as seeing a baby being born. The Sunday after he could see the green rows of cotton and we were on our way to church, he stopped the car to show Mom and the rest of us the beautiful, straight rows he had planted. We all chimed in, "You did a good job, Dad!" He was so proud. Seeing the tiny plants in every row made us all feel good.

When the young plants were from two to three inches tall, it was cotton chopping time. The seeds had been planted in such a way that there was a continuous row of plants. But to allow that many plants to mature, they would have crowded each other out, and in the end lessened the yield of cotton. Each row of cotton had to be thinned so just one plant was left to grow within the space of ten to twelve inches. It was at this point that all of us kids in the family became involved. Every Saturday and every weekday after school, we went out to chop cotton. We not only thinned each row, but hoed the weeds that had sprouted along with the cotton. In those days, before weed killing treatments were even heard of, the job of controlling the weeds was more work than thinning the cotton. Through the years, other varieties of cotton have been developed, and the methods of growing it have changed immensely.

None of us, of course, got paid for chopping cotton. It was assumed the job was part of being a farm kid. So to motivate us, we made a game of it. The one who got to the end of the row first was the winner. We worked with a hoe that was nine inches wide. Chop, chop, chop. One swing of the hoe usually left just one plant standing. But oh-oh, we sometimes missed and chopped a plant that should have been left to grow. By the middle of the day, sweat was running down our faces and into our eyes. Our arms and shoulders ached from the repeated swing of the hoe. As it turned out, Lydia was the best and fastest cotton chopper on the team, even faster than Peter or Ernie.

The cotton then needed to be cultivated to help with the weed control, a job Dad also did with Kate and Beck before we had a tractor. Six weeks after the first chopping we had to repeat the job; this time, not to thin the cotton, but to hoe all the weeds the cultivator had missed. Our fields were usually invaded by several types of weeds that, in spite of regular hoeing, sprang up again and again. Several varieties of these weeds were vines or grasses

Ernie (left) and Peter on the cotton planter, as seen from its back.

that spread their root systems just beneath the surface of the ground. The worst of them was *Johnson Grass*. If left unattended, it could overtake a whole field. Our Anderson farm had several of these infected spots. The roots were so thick, tough and intertwined that our hoes could only penetrate the matted mess by putting every muscle into the swing of the hoe. Sometimes it seemed useless to try to chop the invasive weed. If we went back the next day, we could see that it had started to grow again. If left unhoed, it grew five or six feet tall and the area it covered was soon twice as big. So the grass had to be hoed several times each summer. The job was almost as bad as picking grapes.

After the second hoeing, it was time to prepare the soil for irrigating. The cultivator was equipped with an attachment that drew a furrow between each row. The crop needed to be irrigated several times each summer.

By mid-July the cotton plants had blossoms that were white and slowly turned to purple. It was a marvel that went unnoticed by the rest of the world. But for every cotton farmer it was a beautiful sight to behold. By this time the cotton was almost as tall as my Dad with his six-foot frame. He often walked down row after row just to examine the miracle of nature. Each of those blossoms would turn into a cotton boll. By early October the bolls would open and the crop would be ready for harvest.

Since his usual workforce, us kids, was back in school, Dad had to hire a crew to pick the cotton. During the 1930s, the pickers were what John Steinbeck called "Okies" in his classic book, *The Grapes of Wrath*. They were families who had fled Oklahoma, Arkansas and parts of Texas. The years of the Dust Bowl and the Depression had simultaneously created an economic disaster for these people. They had heard there was work for them in the central valley of California. When they got to California they moved up and down the Valley during the summer months, picking fruit and grapes. By cotton harvest time, mid-October and November, there was no more fruit to be picked. So they were glad there was cotton to be harvested.

Fluffy bolls of cotton, ready for harvest.

On the day cotton harvest began, 50 to 75 pickers (including children who should have been in school but weren't because the family needed the money they would earn by helping to pick) descended on Dad's fields. Each of them carried a heavy canvas sack under his or her arm. The sack was about fifteen inches in diameter. Its length depended on the picker. Some men had twelve foot sacks. Women's sacks were usually nine feet in length. Each sack had a band at the top, which was slung over the picker's head and hung from the shoulder.

Picking cotton by hand.

Many of these pickers came to Dad's cotton fields year after year so we knew them quite well. As the years passed and I got older, I was from time to time put in charge of weighing the cotton as it was being picked. Two of the pickers, Ned and Claire Williams, had been coming to pick cotton for Dad for several years. I admired Ned and Claire. They were friendly, fast, and dependable pickers. During lunch time one day, I asked them to tell their story of where they came from and how they got to California.

They started their story by saying, "We was born and raised in Arkansas. When we got hitched, we was sharecroppers, raisin' cotton and wheat in western Arkansas. In 1930, it stopped rainin' and the win' started a-blowin' – sometimes 50, 60 mile a hour. Without rain, the fields was bare. The win' kept a-comin' an' carried the fine dirt with it. It wen' on like this ever' day fer months. Blowed the soil all the way ta the nex' county. Dust were so heavy we coudn' see more-n ten foot in front of us. Ev'n when we stayed indoors and kep' windows an' doors shut, the dust come thru' ev'r crack so we coudn' breathe."

"So what happened to your farm," I asked.

"We don' have no crop fer three years. The Depression set in and there was no jobs to be had in all of Arkansas. We heared there was a need fer fruit pickers in Californy, so we loaded our old Model-T truck with ev'rthin' we had, and headed on down Route 66 to Californy in 1933. When we finally git here, we see thousands of others who 'ad run from the Dust Bowl was a'ready here. An' the farmers don' need no more workers. But what was a man ta do? We was a'ready here. Fer the las' three years we barely make it. As we truck'd up the Valley from Bakersfield, we foun' a job pickin' cotton. We are so thankful we fin' yore father's farm."

"Why do you say that?" I asked.

"Furst of all," Claire said, "yer father has been good to us. He lent us money when we was short. Fer 3, 4 winters, after the cotton was all picked, he let us stay in a barn on one of his farms – di'nt charge us a dime. We dn't know what we'd a done otherwise. That barn was fixed up like a house. Without it, we'd froze ta death during the cold of winter – e'n here in Californy."

Ned added, "Besides that, we like pickin' cotton."

I responded, "You are some of the best pickers I have seen. We appreciate that we can depend on you coming back each year. You don't grumble, like others do, when the picking isn't as good as it could be. As you know, now that World War II has started, it's hard to get pickers. We have come to depend on you more than ever. But tell me, what was it like the first time you put a cotton sack across your shoulders and started picking?"

Ned spoke up, "Wes, as you know, pickin' cotton is hard work, harder than it looks."

"I know. Through the years, I have picked a few sacks of cotton myself – not many, but a few."

"The furst few days of the season is the hardes'," Ned continued. "Them fluffy bolls a' cotton fool ya. When ya reach out ta pull out the cotton, ya fin' that hiden' under them soft tufts are them sharp prongs o' the boll. Until we git the swing of just where ta put our han's, them prongs seem ta reach out and bite our han's until they is sore and bleedin'. The other thing is, ta do the job fas', we got ta git down on our knees. Before we know it, them knees is a-bleedin' from crawlin' on the rough clods on this here heavy dirt of yur'ns – an' our backs start ta ache from pullin' them heavy cotton sacks. After a few days, though, we git used to it, so now we like pickin' cotton."

When Ned and Claire had finished their lunches, they picked up their sacks and were off to the field again. I watched as they stuffed one handful of cotton after the other into the opening of their sacks which were dragging on the ground behind them. Within less than two hours, their sacks were full. By this time they had reached the far end of the field. It was incredible, the way they picked up those heavy sacks of cotton, threw them over their shoulders, and carried them almost a quarter of a mile to where the cotton trailer was parked.

Mom and Dad weighing cotton. Picture shows Dad's trailers
into which sacks of cotton were dumped.

I was there to man the scale and weigh their sacks. Each picker was paid by the pound, so it was important that each sack be weighed and the weight carefully recorded in a book we kept for that purpose. Every picker had his own book in which he kept his record of each weigh-in.

"You really filled those sacks in a hurry," I said. "Let's see how many pounds we have here." Ned's sack weighed 106 pounds; Claire's was 92 pounds. "I don't see how you manage to get these sacks so full, and then carry them all that distance. You must have very tough muscles by now."

"Yeah," Claire said, "an' now we got ta crawl up that shaky ladder ta the top of yur'ns trailer, and stan' on that wobbly plank while we empty them sacks. Maybe you all would like ta do it fer us, Wes, while we take a little res'!"

"I wouldn't mind, if I could, but I don't think I could even get that sack on my shoulder, much less crawl up that ladder."

Claire jokingly said, "Maybe tha's somethin' you should work on."

Paydays were on Saturdays. The pickers felt they had done a week's work by noon of that day. Dad was there in the shade of the trailer with the weight book. He had tallied the number of pounds each one had picked. "Ned," he said, "according to my records, the two of you picked 492 pounds on Monday, 467 on Tuesday, 489 on Wednesday, 493 on Thursday, 429 on Friday, and 192 this morning. Does that agree with your records?"

"Ya got it right," Ned said. "That adds up to 2,562 pounds fer the week."

Dad carefully weighing a full sack of cotton. Pickers in the background.

"And at 2 cents a pound, you earned $51.24. That's a week of good, hard work, Ned."

In that way, Dad payed each picker in cold cash. The price Dad paid per pound for picking in the early 1940s was considerably higher than it had been in the 1930s, when some farmers paid less than one cent a pound for picking their cotton. As the war continued and the shortage of pickers became more acute, the price farmers had to pay workers increased steadily.

After being paid, each family hurried home, changed clothes, and went to town to spend their hard earned money. The more sensible ones went first to the grocery store to buy food for the next week. Others went straight to the taverns to drink and smoke while their children enjoyed a picture show. If, at the end of the evening they had any money left, they bought a few groceries. For the careless ones, little thought was given to the need to pay rent on whatever tenement house they might be living in, or to buy gas for their car.

Most of them came back the next Monday completely broke, but ready to start the week over again. They had, however, bought enough cigarettes to carry them through the week. As Frank in the comic strip once said to Ernest, "Between my income and outgo, I don't have any standstill."

By the end of each day, the pickers had filled at least a truck and trailer load of cotton which then needed to be taken to the cotton gin five to six miles from the fields. At the height of the season, the huge trailers filled with freshly picked cotton were lined up by the dozens, waiting to be unloaded. Dad would often have to wait halfway through the night to get his truck and trailer unloaded.

As anyone who has studied history knows, the cotton gin was invented in 1793, by Eli Whitney. Each tuft of cotton, when it comes out of the fields, is saturated with seeds the size of small beans. Before the cotton can be of any practical use, the seeds need to be removed. Before the invention of the gin, removing the seeds was a tedious job done by hand. A skilled worker could, at best, remove the seeds from one pound of cotton a day. With Whitney's machine, the seeds of 50 pounds of cotton could be removed in a day. Depending on the size of the gin, as it was improved, it could remove seeds from hundreds of pounds within an hour. It is generally agreed that the invention of the cotton gin ushered in America's Industrial Revolution, and the production of cotton multiplied in fields around the world.

So when Dad took his cotton to the gin for the removal of its seeds in the 1930s, Eli Whitney's invention was an established industry taken for granted by every cotton farmer. Not only did the gin remove the seeds, but also cleaned the cotton and compressed it into 500-pound bales for easy handling. I use the term with hesitation, because who could handle a 500-pound bale easily? It was a two-man job just to roll it over and onto a trailer to be hauled to the gin yard and picked up later with a mechanical hoist. The gin owners kept the seeds as payment for their work.

Occasionally Dad would allow me to go to the gin with him. I was utterly fascinated as I watched the fluffy bolls of cotton being unloaded from Dad's truck by a huge vacuum pipe that sucked up the cotton and sent it through the ginning process at the speed of lightning and into the press that formed the bales. In those days, my brother-in-law Frank Ens, worked at the gin's press. Had it not been for him working there, I would not have been allowed to visit the gin because it was thought too dangerous for a small kid like me to be near the huge machines.

On some of the nights I went to the gin with Dad it was almost midnight before we could go home. I fell asleep by the time Dad turned onto the road from the gin yard. When we got home Mom had a bowl of soup waiting for us. The next day Dad started the process all over again. The harvest season often lasted two months.

Although Dad grew a lot of alfalfa during the years he farmed in California, cotton slowly became the crop in which he majored. He had first learned cotton farming back in the days he and Mom lived in Oklahoma. He planted some cotton in Rosedale and Kerman, but when we moved to the Forty south of Dinuba he got into the business of cultivating cotton in a big way. He was, in fact, the first one to introduce cotton to the Dinuba-Reedley areas of Tulare and Fresno Counties.

Our neighbors were all into growing grapes during the 1930s. The unspoken gospel truth was that if you didn't grow grapes, you were kind of odd and didn't belong. His Mennonite brothers, especially, attached a certain stigma to cotton farmers. So during the 1930s, Dad was the butt of many of their jokes. Didn't he know that there was more money in grapes? Why did he insist on growing a *poor man's* crop? Dad could have gotten into grapes, but they never interested him. During the 1940s, he bought a farm that had 20 acres of vineyard. Before the year was out, he pulled half of them and planted cotton, keeping just ten acres of grapes.

As I recall, during the 1930s the price of cotton was about eight cents a pound and hard to sell because the world market was flooded with an abundance of the crop. There were years when the crop could not be sold until the following year, which meant that Dad did not get paid until the cotton was finally sold. But he soon learned that by waiting for his money, he always came out on the surplus side of farming. His grape-growing brothers often lost money on their crops during those years. They had not become savvy to Dad's little secret that there was money to be made with cotton even during the Depression years.

In the 1940s when America became involved in World War II, there was a sudden demand for cotton to make uniforms for the thousands of soldiers who had been drafted into the Armed Forces. The price of cotton immediately shot up to 40 cents a pound. Now his grape-growing brothers began to look at Dad with envy. He was making huge profits on his crops, while the demand for grapes and raisins stagnated. All at once we noticed that the grape-growers were pulling out their vines and coming to Dad, asking questions about how to raise cotton!

During the decade of the Thirties there was an overabundance of manpower available to harvest the cotton crop. As men were drafted into the Armed Services, and others, including women, joined the military workforce, the supply of workers needed to pick cotton dwindled to almost zero. It was then that immigrants from Mexico began filtering across the border and came to the aid of the agricultural workforce. The Okie cotton pickers of the Thirties were replaced by Mexicans. During those critical years, Dad's crew of workers was almost exclusively people of Mexican descent. By this time I was old enough to notice the difference between the two types of workers. The Mexicans, much like Ned and Claire who were topnotch

An early model of a one-row cotton picking machine.

workers, really put themselves into their work. I loved to man the scales when we had a Mexican crew. These people sang or told stories and jokes all day long. Each day seemed like a party – they were having a good time.

The day came in the 1940s, when the mechanical cotton picker was invented. This invention changed the complexion of cotton farming in much the same way as did the invention of the cotton gin. Suddenly, the need for a crew of pickers was replaced by a single machine which could do the work of fifty pickers. It was not long before Dad purchased his first mechanical picker. It was made by John Deere and could be attached to our three-wheel tractor by running the tractor in reverse. It took us two days to convert the tractor into a picker, but well worth the effort.

I was privileged to drive the picker two or three seasons before I got married and left home. The farm-boy in me came into full-bloom on the fall mornings when I climbed into the driver's seat, started the motor of the machine, and moved down a row of cotton. I was continually fascinated as I watched the dozens of spindles whirl into action, catching the hundreds of fluffy-white bolls of cotton and sending them into the huge hopper behind me.

The farm home where I grew up.
This picture is from the late 1940s. Mature cotton is seen in the foreground.
The buildings behind the house are the garage and the hen house.

A Reflection

It was a sad day when I left Dad to continue farming without me. We had developed an intimate relationship – a bond that was so very difficult to break. I would gladly have remained on the farm and grown cotton the rest of my life (hence the picture on the back cover of this book) just to keep from breaking that tie between us. But God apparently had different plans for my life's work. While reading my Bible one day, the words of 2 Timothy 4:2 seemed to speak directly to me, *"Preach the word, be instant in season, out of season; reprove, rebuke, exhort with all long suffering and doctrine."* (King James Version). By the time I was twenty-one years old, I was destined to prepare myself for church ministries.

Chapter 47
Picking Grapes

It was grape picking season in the Valley. As usual, our family was transformed into a crew that included every member of the family, from Marie on down. My older siblings were already married and on their own. For the two weeks just before school started in the fall, we picked raisin grapes. Picking grapes that would be sold to a winery was frowned upon by the church.

I became a member of the crew at age seven and was given the job of water boy. It was my responsibility to carry a canteen of fresh water and make a circuit of the crew about every half hour to offer each one a drink. It was, indeed, a monotonous job which I was not fond of. I sometimes lay down in the shade of a grape vine and fell asleep between rounds before being rudely awakened by a crew member yelling, "Water, water! Wes, where are you? I need water." If I didn't show up within a few minutes I was soundly scolded for not doing my job. We all drank from the same canteen, putting our lips to the same spigot. Sometimes I filled the canteen with the water from a nearby irrigation ditch. No, we didn't have sparkling spring water with a bottle for each crew member. And none of us ever got sick or caught a dreaded disease from the water.

My job also included keeping the crew members supplied with paper trays. This was even worse than carrying water. I had to trudge through the hot, loose dirt a quarter of a mile with the heavy trays. This thankless job lasted for one season. After this Ray took over and I became a regular grape picker. After Ray was promoted to a picker, Dad often came back to the field and carried the water after doing the morning chores.

> Note: When Alma got married she thought she had graduated from a grape picker to a housewife. She married Jack Patzkowski, and they promptly bought a farm adjoining our Forty to the north. Through most of my growing up years, they were our neighbors. Their farm included twenty acres of grapes. Ironically, Alma was soon back to picking grapes with Jack. When their children were old enough they were also conscripted as grape pickers. Sometimes Ray and I helped.

A typical grape picking day proceeded as follows. Mom and Dad were up by 4: 00 a.m. to begin preparations for each big day, packing lunches and making breakfast. By 5:00 a.m. Ernie was yelling, "Wes, Ray, it's time to get up!" I slowly pulled myself out of bed, realizing that every muscle and bone in my body was stiff and sore. It was an effort to get dressed into my oldest and most worn clothes. Grape picking was a dirty job and hard on clothes. My overalls had not been washed from the day before, so they were stiff from the juice of grapes and smelled of sweat. Breakfast was ready by the time I had washed the sleep out of my face.

Occasionally during these two weeks, the breakfast consisted of eggs, bacon and fried potatoes. More often it was no more than a bowl of cold cereal and several slices of homemade rye bread with butter and peach jam. The cereal, however, was *Pep*, a more expensive variety than the usual corn flakes. The *Pep* was a huge treat compared to the regular fare.

It was served only during grape picking season. The very name of the cereal was reason enough to eat it, because I knew I would need every ounce of pep it was purported to give to get me through the day.

By 5:30 I had finished breakfast, sharpened my grape picking knife and collected my grape pan. With a shiver, I stepped out the door into the cold morning air. I climbed onto the bed of the old 1929 Chevy truck, which was waiting with its motor running, and dangled my legs over its edge.

Once all were on board, Dad shifted the transmission into low gear and took off with such a jerk I had to hang on for dear life. I thought I would freeze to death as the wind blew right though my light clothing. But I endured the cold, knowing that within two hours sweat would be running down my back. Dad drove us to the Isaak farm, two miles north of Dinuba and six miles from home, where we were to pick grapes that day. The sun was just beginning to peek over the horizon when we got to the vineyard. By this time I was fully awake. I jumped off the back of the truck with the rest of the crew, and grabbed my knife, pan and sack lunch as Dad drove off to milk the cows and do the chores back home.

My goal, as a regular crew member that first year, was to pick 150 trays a day. By that time Marie, Lydia, Eva and Rubena were picking 350, Peter 400, and Ernie 450 to 500 trays a day. As I got older, I eventually worked my way up to 400. It was hard to accept the fact that Ernie could pick more trays than any of the rest of us. We accused him of not filling his grape pan as full as we did and doing a sloppy job of spreading his trays. Actually, we knew he was the hardest and fastest worker among us.

When we arrived at the Isaak vineyard, Marie immediately claimed row one, which she knew always had the best grapes. Ernie had to settle for row two. I, being the youngest member of the crew, was assigned to row seven. I picked up four packs of paper trays (a heavy load for an eight year old) from the bundle that had been dropped at the head of the first row and headed for my assigned row. By this time my adrenalin had kicked in. The rest of the day was a race to see if each of us would reach our self-imposed quota. Even though all the money we earned flowed into the family treasury, we considered it a matter of honor to reach our goals.

We were paid by the tray, so it was important that we pick as many trays a day as possible. During the early 1930s, in the depths of the Depression, we were paid 1 ½ cents a tray. That meant that Peter who picked 400 trays a day, was making $6.00 a day compared to the average day laborer who was glad to make $1.00 a day. Toward the end of the 1930s we were being paid 2 ½ to 3 cents a tray. In the 1940s, we got up to 4 and even 5 cents a tray.

Days before the crew got to the field, Mr. Isaak had used a *sled* or *drag* to smooth the ground between every other row of grapes. When picked, the grapes were dumped on paper trays on the smooth dirt where they would dry in the hot sun and turn into raisins. Each tray was a bit larger than a page of open newspaper. Our round, tin metal grape pans were about eighteen inches in diameter and eight inches deep, just big enough that when filled with grapes and dumped, could fill one tray. After the grapes were dumped on the tray they had to be spread neatly over the entire tray so they would dry evenly.

The first morning of the picking season I attacked that first grape vine with a vengeance. Every good grape picker knew that we couldn't just bend over and work while standing; we had to get down on our knees. So there I was, down on my knees in the dirt that had clods as big as baseballs. By noon of the first day both knees were raw with blisters. I soon had pains in my back and legs from getting up and down as I filled the pan repeatedly, carried it to the center of the row, opened a tray, dumped the grapes, and then got on my knees to spread them. Since Mr. Isaak had only smoothed every other row, I had to pick the grapes on both sides of the row. The sun beat mercilessly on the north side of the row while the south side was more shady and cool. How I dreaded to pick that north side!

As the day progressed the sun got hotter and hotter, causing sweat to run from the brim of my hat into my eyes and made them burn. By noon my muscles ached and I had already nicked my hands at several places and made them bleed. When I looked up at the sun and saw it was high in the sky, I automatically knew it was lunch time. I made my way to the shade of a huge poplar tree in the Isaak's front yard and stretched out on the grass. It felt like a bit of heaven. I gobbled down the sandwich, potato chips, apple and cookie Mom had packed. Sometimes, instead of the sandwich, Mom stuck a can of pork and beans into the sack. Cold pork and beans – they were sooo good! Dad had bought the beans by the case at 6 cents a can. After lunch, I had just enough time to stretch out on the grass for a short nap. Within half an hour Peter called out, "Time to get back to work."

It took nearly the whole day to pick my row of grapes. When I got to the end I walked back to the starting point, counting the number of trays in the row. I then cleared a small corner of the first tray and, taking a grape berry, squeezed the juice gently as I wrote the number of trays I had counted. I sprinkled a bit of dirt over the juice, making the number quite legible. After finishing their row, each member of the crew did the same. When we finished picking Mr. Isaak's field he added up the number of trays in each row and paid Dad accordingly.

I continued picking until almost sunset and met my goal of 150 trays. What really kept me going during the hot afternoon was the special treat awaiting me at day's end. Across the road from the Isaak's farm was a small gas station that sold cold soda pop. The moment I finished picking, I made a beeline for the store and pulled a nickel out of my pocket, just enough

Picked grapes on paper trays spread out for drying into raisins.

for a bottle of pop. The sweet Nehi strawberry soda trickling down my parched throat was even closer to heaven than the lunch time under the tree. By that time Dad was back with the truck to take us home for a shower, a huge supper, and a soft bed. The next morning just came too early.

There were several insects grape pickers had to constantly contend with: ants, black widow spiders, and hornets. I was told that the spiders could kill me if they got their poisonous venom beneath my skin. I was deathly afraid of the spiders and found one here and there but thankfully was never bitten by one. The hornets were more frequent visitors. They built their nests right in the middle between two grape vines where the best grapes hung. I tried to remember to shake each vine before diving in under it to pick the grapes. The hornets usually started buzzing if disturbed. If I found a hornet's nest, I took a piece of paper tray, rolled it up, lit it with a match and held it under the nest. Each of us carried a pack of matches for that purpose. The hornets could not tolerate the smoke, so they quickly left their nest, but only long enough for me to pick the grapes around it.

One day I forgot to shake a vine. I was down on my knees cutting the first bunches of beautiful grapes, when I felt a terrible hornet sting on my forearm. I was on my feet in a split second. Man-oh-man did it hurt! I jumped up and down and tried to suck the venom out of the sting. Nothing helped. Before long the sting had created a swelling on my arm the size of a banana. Eva, picking just a couple of rows from me, heard the commotion and came running.

Eva was the member of the family who was the first to come to the rescue of any of us when we got hurt or needed help. She apparently was born with a caring heart. Perhaps that is why she later became a nurse. Her temperament was much like Dad's; seldom showing anger or letting her temper get out of control. When she came to bandage our wounds or listen to our problems, her presence was calm and reassuring.

Unlike Marie, Eva did not concern herself with wearing the latest fashions. Wearing just the right color or amount of make-up was not important. That is not to say she did not take care of herself or did not look presentable when she went out.

God had gifted Eva with a special musical talent. She had a rich, mellow voice that simply melted the hearts of her listeners. Just today I was given a copy of the 1942 Yearbook of Reedley Junior College. There I found her pictured as a member of the A Cappella Choir, an honor few others enjoyed. Besides singing in choirs, duets, and trios, she was the soloist in the family. Peter and Raymond were also soloists, but her voice had a special quality. Most importantly, when she sang, it was apparent that she did so from her heart, the result of a close walk with the God whom she loved and served.

But to continue my hornet story. I thought I was going to die from that sting. But Eva kept telling me, "Wes, you're going to be okay. It's going to hurt for a while but you will live." She then calmly got some water, made a compress of mud and applied it to the bump on my arm. The cool mud helped a little, but it took several hours before I was ready to start picking again. I had trouble sleeping that night. The next morning the bite itched so badly I wanted to continuously scratch it, but Mom warned me that scratching would only make it worse. I had to endure the suffering of that sting for the next three days.

After the grapes had been picked, it took about two weeks of ideal hot summer sun to dry them enough to be turned. At that point, the grapes on each tray had to be turned upside down onto another tray, so the underside of the grapes would dry. Turning trays was a tedious process; few had the stamina and back strong enough for this job. It took two men working side by side to do it efficiently. Ernie and Peter teamed up and turned trays with speed. Dad promised them that they could keep the money they earned. They were well paid. Ray and I could have made a team but I guess we were worn out from the rigors of the picking season.

Packages of raisins - grapes that have been dried and are ready for boxing.

After the grapes had dried to just the right consistency, the trays had to be rolled into bundles and left to *cure* in the field for a week or two. The final step in the raisin making process was to *box* them. Wooden sweat boxes, about two feet wide, three and a half feet long and eight inches deep, were loaded onto a *vineyard wagon*. A vineyard wagon was just wide enough to fit between two rows of grapes and was drawn by horses in the early days. As the wagon moved slowly down the vineyard row the bundles of raisins were pitched into the boxes where one man would remove the raisins from the trays, discard the trays and keep the raisins neatly spread in each box until it was full. The discarded trays were later gathered and burned. The heavy sweat boxes filled with raisins had to be offloaded from the vineyard wagon and stacked one on top of the other before being sold and hauled to the processors.

Besides picking for Mr. Isaak, our crew picked grapes for several neighbors closer to home. One of these farmers was the father of Ernie's fiancée at the time. Half of his forty-acre vineyard had good Thompson seedless grapes that were easy to pick and the most common variety in the area. Half of his vineyard was planted with *Sultanas*, a variety which was very juicy

An old vineyard wagon. This one is loaded with *wooden* trays used before paper trays were used.

and squishy. When we picked them our hands were soon sticky and covered with mud because of the juiciness of the grapes and the dust on the vines. Yuk! Additionally, half of the vines in some rows of grapes were missing, so when picking, we had to run from one vine to the next just to fill one pan of grapes. On top of that, this farmer was very fussy about how his grapes were picked. He came out twice a day to see if we had left bunches that should have been picked, or to see if our trays were well-filled and spread evenly. How we dreaded picking those grapes! But because he was the father of Ernie's fianée, we had no choice.

We also picked the grapes of Paul Hofer, John Hofer and Mr. Kleinssaser. They all lived on *Hofer* road, just a mile to the west of our farm. We didn't mind picking for them because they had good vineyards and we could easily meet our goals for the number of trays we hoped to pick each day.

After two weeks of picking, Dad gave us a choice. We could quit picking grapes at the end of two weeks or we could continue to pick for another day or two and keep the money we earned. Most of us picked for another two days.

Chapter 48
A Day in Fresno

The 1936 grape picking season had just come to an end and it was time for our family's annual trek to Fresno for a day of shopping. It was a tradition we had established when moving to the farm south of Dinuba and continued to keep into the mid 1940s when the last of us went off to college.

As everyone knows, the Depression continued through the decade of the Thirties. Although he could hardly afford it, Dad struck a bargain with the Studebaker dealer in Fresno, and ordered a new car. Because of the size of our family, Dad ordered the biggest Studebaker made, a black sedan. In those days cars lasted only about two years, and it was cheaper to trade the old one for a new model than to have the old one repaired, or so Dad insisted while talking it over with Mom. Brother Jack was planning to get married later that year, so he ordered a shiny blue sport coupe at the same time Dad ordered his. According to plan, Dad and Jack traveled by train to the Studebaker factory in South Bend, Indiana in the spring of 1936 and took delivery on their new cars, a scheme which was cheaper than having them shipped to the dealer.

Our shopping trip to Fresno that year would be the first *long* trip in our new car. Before we left home, Dad ordered *roll call* to make sure no one was left behind. Let's see, Dad and Mom, Marie, Ernie, Peter, Lydia, Eva, Rubena, Ray and me, ten of us. Jack didn't go because he was too busy getting the apartment in the garage ready for his bride-to-be. Alma and Caroline were already married.

Getting the whole family into the spanking new car was like putting a jigsaw puzzle together. After a few tries, we all found our places. We didn't mind being crammed together. We were, after all, going to Fresno after a tough grape picking season. The outing was more exciting than opening presents on Christmas day.

It was a forty-mile trip, and Peter had just gotten his driver's license, so Dad let him do the driving. We were a little leery of having a greenhorn at the wheel of our fancy new car, but if Dad trusted him, why shouldn't we? When we got to the Fresno city limits, we stopped and Dad took over the driving because he knew the streets of the city like the back of his hand from the many years of taking his cotton crops from Kerman to the Fresno cotton gin.

The one-hour trip got us downtown by 10:30 a.m. The streets were already bustling with crowds of people going in every direction. We finally found a place to park way out on the north end of Broadway, but it was just a block east to Fulton Street where streetcars ran in both directions every few minutes. It would have been fun to ride the streetcar, but the fare for ten of us could more wisely be spent on other things. The closer we got to the corner of Fulton and Fresno Streets the busier the sidewalks became. They were, in fact, so jammed with people it was hard to keep our family together. Mom made sure Marie was holding my hand and Ernie was holding Ray's hand as we crossed each street, while Dad kept a constant eye out for each of us.

We all needed new shoes for the winter season. So the first store we went into was Leed's shoe store. I remember seeing the manager's eyes light up when he saw us coming in. He anticipated that this might be his biggest sale of the day, or even the week. There weren't enough chairs in the store for all of us to sit at the same time, so some had to stand and wait while others were fitted for their shoes. The girls had already studied the display of shoes in the window and knew which ones they wanted. We boys were less particular. After all, shoes were shoes. An older female clerk started measuring the girls' foot sizes and getting out the shoes they had seen in the window.

"We are sorry," she said to Marie, "We are out of your size in that shoe."

Marie was visibly upset. She was so fussy about what she wore, and she had set her heart on those shoes. It took a while before each of the girls got the shoes they wanted in the size they needed. After the girls had gotten their shoes, it was Mom's turn. She almost blushed while we all watched her being fitted with the nicest pair of shoes in the store.

In the meantime, a male clerk was measuring foot sizes for us boys. Ernie had seen a pair of shiny black dress shoes in the window. Dad nixed that choice, saying he needed more sturdy school shoes. I was overjoyed with my new pair of rubber soled brown shoes. Dad got a plain pair of new work shoes.

We had all been fitted with a pair of shoes within the hour. Dad got up to pay the bill from the money we had earned picking grapes: $46.50 including tax; it would have been $604.50 in 2006 currency.

It was almost lunchtime as we filed out of the shoe store. Normally, we would have gone just a block east to Courthouse park to have a picnic lunch. But Mom was tired of packing lunches during the grape picking season, and would soon be packing school lunches, so we headed to Hart's Cafeteria on Tulare Street where we could get a good lunch for 40 cents.

After lunch, we covered the town. We were so excited we almost ran to National Shirt Shop where I got two new school shirts, and the rest of the family got similar pieces of clothing. Walter Smith's on Broadway was the store for work shirts, overalls and jeans. Mom and the girls toured through the huge J.C. Pennys and Gottschalks department stores for their clothing. Our last stop was at Harry Coffee's store for men. Coffee's was the finest men's clothing store in Fresno and Dad needed a new Sunday suit.

The whole family followed Dad into the store. As usual, Mr. Coffee was at the door to greet us and guide us to the right department. He knew Dad by name, as he did all his regular customers. It was a delight to walk into his store because of his friendly manner and the good service his store provided. A knowledgeable salesman was waiting for Dad in the suit department. He measured Dad for size, then started pulling out several suits he thought might look good on him. It wasn't long before Dad's eye fell on a black wool with a fine stripe.

"This is it," Dad said. We all agreed.

"How much," Dad asked.

"This one is $65.00," the salesman replied. "Suits are kind of expensive, you know." Dad shook his head and said, "I can't spend that much of my children's hard-earned money." (Sixty-five dollars would be $845.00 in 2006 currency. That was more than our whole crew earned in a day of picking grapes.)

Marie spoke up, "That's alright, Dad. You haven't had a new suit for so long and you have worked so hard for all of us for so many years. We want you to have it." We all chimed in, agreeing with Marie. After trying it on, Dad looked at himself in the mirror once more as he admired the suit. Mom shook her head in agreement, thinking to herself, *he really is a fine looking man in that suit.* Dad reluctantly gave a nod to the salesman, "I'll take it." The store's tailor came out to make adjustments on the fit of the suit and told him it would be waiting for him the next time he was in Fresno.

By 3:30 that afternoon our clothes had been bought and we had made quite a dent in the $5,000 we had earned picking grapes that season. It was time to head for home. Our car was hot as an oven as we all climbed in for the trip back home. We opened all the windows, but the September afternoon air was still stifling. When we got to the edge of the city, Dad told Ernie who was driving the car,

"Stop at Hall's Restaurant and we will each have an ice cream cone."

We all cried out, "Yea!" The double-decker cones were 5 cents each.

Tired, but happy, I dozed off, leaning on Mom's shoulder for the hot trip back home.

A Reflection

As of this writing, Hall's is still the same restaurant at the same location, (2395 South "G" Street, Fresno) but is now know as Café 309. About fifty years ago a group of men from First Presbyterian Church in downtown Fresno began meeting at this restaurant every Friday morning for breakfast and Bible study. Nine years ago I began attending this meeting, and have been a regular member ever since. What a great way to follow the instructions of Paul as he wrote a letter to young pastor Timothy and said, *"Study to show yourself approved unto God, a workman that needs not to be ashamed, rightly dividing the word of truth,"* (2 Timothy 2:15, KJV).

Chapter 49
Irrigating the Land

Soon after we moved to the Dinuba area in 1930, Dad began renting the eighty acre Zeipke farm, located halfway between Dinuba and Reedley. It was an excellent piece of land for growing alfalfa. The farm had but one problem – the irrigation pump, driven by a belt between it and an ancient flywheel gas engine. The engine was a one-cylinder job that could only be started by turning one of two huge flywheels located on either side. The engine used gasoline for fuel. Instead of a sparkplug (like more up-to-date gasoline engines have), it was equipped with a magneto to create the spark needed to keep the engine running. The first time Dad tried to start it, he set the spark and made other intricate adjustments. He then grabbed hold of one of the wheels, and with his strong arms, began turning it. He turned and turned and made other adjustments on the spark and throttle, nothing happened. It seemed dead as a door nail. He was about to give up, when a half hour later, he suddenly realized the wheels were turning on their own. Putt–putt–putt –sputter – putt–putt –sputter –putt. The engine was known for its unsteady sound that could be heard a half mile away. As long as it ran, the pump produced an acceptable stream of water, enough to keep the Eighty irrigated.

Dad usually started the alfalfa irrigation season in early spring. It was a job that continued through the entire summer. After getting the pump going, the water ran down the ditch he had made and to the checks, the space between two levees, he planned to irrigate that day. Once he started the irrigating process, the pump had to run day and night, which meant he often had to get up in the middle of the night and drive to the farm to change the water.

A restored gas engine much like the one Dad used for irrigating the Zeipke farm.

Since changing the water at night was a two-man job, he usually took Jack or Ernie with him. I asked Jack some years later what it was like to have to get up in the middle of the night to go with Dad to change the water.

"Dad was a remarkable man," Jack began. "He never, in all his life, owned an alarm clock. But if he had to get up at 2 a.m. to change the water, he fixed that time in his mind before he went to bed. Sure enough, he woke up on schedule at 2 a.m. If he needed to get up at 3 a.m., he did the same. He then woke me up, and while I was still half asleep, drove the old Model-T the six miles to the Zeipke farm. The minute we stepped out of the truck the mosquitoes swarmed around us like bees surround a hive. Dad lit two kerosene lanterns, gave me one and kept the other. We first inspected the check of alfalfa that was supposed to be getting the water. If it hadn't filled the check, we might have to wait an hour or two. If the check was full, we walked to the end where the ditch was, and he changed the water while I held the lanterns."

"Is that the only reason he needed to have you go with him?" I asked. "It seems that Dad could have easily done the job himself."

"No, he didn't really need me for that, but quite often we got to the farm only to find that for no reason at all the old flywheel engine had stopped running during the night, which meant we faced some major problems. First of all, the alfalfa that didn't get watered threw off our whole irrigation schedule. The other problem was getting the engine started again in the middle of the night! I stood next to the spark and gas throttles and made adjustments. Dad worked the heavy flywheel. We eventually got it going again, but not without exhausting effort."

"Knowing Dad the way I do," I said, "how did Dad react when he had trouble restarting the engine. Was he able to keep calm or did he get angry and lose his temper?"

I wasn't surprised when Jack said, "Yes, Dad sometimes got angry, but I never saw him lose his temper, take out his anger on me, say a single curse word or throw a wrench at the engine. I would rather believe he was silently praying it would start. He may have gone home with a dour disposition, but by the next morning he was his normal self."

Irrigating through the summer months was a job every farmer in the San Joaquin Valley had to put up with. It was the only way of getting most crops through the hot, dry season to harvest time in the fall. Through all the years Dad farmed, he rented land in addition to the home place. Each farm had a different type pump and a different type of motor to run it. Some worked well, some were nothing but trouble. But the pump was the most crucial piece of equipment on each farm.

Dad finally gave up on renting the Zeipke farm because of the antiquated pump; instead he rented various other farms in the area. The most common pumps used in our area were what we called a deep well variety, with an electric motor mounted vertically on top of the pump. Several years later Dad rented land from my brother Jack. It had what we called a *centrifugal* type pump, which was mounted horizontally over the well. The performance of the two types of pumps might be compared to a man who stands on his feet while he works, and one who tries to work while lying down.

A major problem Dad had with the centrifugal pump was that it had to be primed by pouring buckets of water into the well each time it had to be started. Sometimes it lost its prime in the middle of the night and ran for hours without pumping a drop of water. When it did work, it produced half the volume of water compared to a deep well pump. Because the watertable in those days was so high, the pump was set on top of an eight-foot deep pit in the spring of the year. (The watertable is defined as the depth at which one could find an ample supply of water below the earth's surface.) As the irrigating season progressed through the summer, the watertable fell significantly. So in order to keep the pump working, it had to be lowered to the bottom of the pit with block and tackle. It took Dad and three other strong men a whole day to do the chore. Don't think for a minute that Dad looked forward to that.

So much for pump problems. Now, a word about the irrigation process itself.

During the first year or two after moving to our Forty, Dad raised mostly alfalfa and milo to keep our livestock fed. In 1932, he planted his first crop of cotton. Irrigating cotton rather than alfalfa was like the difference between pouring water on the chicken barn floor to quench the thirst of the birds and running it into a water trough. Alfalfa was irrigated by making levees and checks. For irrigating cotton, furrows had to be drawn between the rows of cotton.

After the furrows in the cotton patch had been drawn, a ditch had to be made that would carry the water from the pump to the field. In the early years, Dad used Kate and Beck hitched to a plow and plowed in such a way that the moldboard threw the earth in one direction; then he turned around and followed the same furrow to throw it in the other direction. He did this several times, creating a wide furrow. He then hitched the mules to what we called a "vee" which consisted of two pieces of iron about eight feet long, twelve inches wide and an inch thick (a heavy and unwieldy contraption) put together in the shape of the letter "V". This crude implement, made by a local blacksmith, was used to finish the ditch making process. In order to make it work properly, Dad had to stand on the vee with his left foot on one side, and his right foot on the other side and for dear life hold with both hands onto a handle affixed to the vee. When dragged through the plowed furrow correctly, it pushed the earth out of the furrow to form a bank on either side The result was a smooth ditch about four feet wide and three feet deep. The day came when our tractor replaced the mules, but it was still a labor intensive and dangerous job, so dangerous that Dad never allowed any of his boys to handle the vee. Many years later a vee was invented to be attached directly to a tractor from a three-point hookup and the job could be done by the tractor and driver alone.

After the ditch was made, each row of cotton had to be prepared in such a way as to be watered individually. Wooden pipes were used to make sure each row got the same amount of water. These pipes, about two inches square and twenty inches long, were made of redwood and nailed together by hand. We carried them by the arm-full from the truck and dropped one in each furrow and later came back and threw a bank of dirt over each pipe. By the time I was eight years old, it became my job to set the pipes and then wait until Peter or Ernie started the water down the ditch and into the pipes. Many times, water seeped through the dirt that was covering the pipe, allowing the water to rush down the one furrow and leaving the others dry. How frustrated, no angry, I got when pipe after pipe had to be reset! This usually happened when the dirt was either too heavy with clods, or too light and sandy. After resetting the pipes I had to watch to make sure they didn't wash out again.

These pipes were later replaced by syphons, a curved piece of plastic pipe which could be submerged in water from the ditch. Then, by holding one's hand over the end of the pipe, he would throw it over the bank. Miracle of miracles, the water was drawn from the end of the pipe in the ditch, over the bank, out the other end and into the furrow! I often wondered why it took some genius so long to invent the simple syphon. I have noticed that, as of this writing, these syphons are still used by farmers to irrigate their row crops.

After the ditches were made and the pipes (or syphons) were set, the irrigation season was, for the most part, an enjoyable part of farming. On those days when I was doing the irrigating, I could get the water started in the morning, let it run all day, and not have to change it until the evening. That left much of the day free to do some of the fun things I never had time to do otherwise.

The evening setting of the water had just one drawback – mosquitos! Swarms of them surrounded me the moment I stepped out of the truck. They apparently had taken a liking to me. I once had a talk with them and asked them, "Why me? There must be other people around here that would appreciate a visit from you."

"No," they said, "we like you best."

It made me feel so special to know that I was loved by pesky little mosquitos even though I suffered severe discomfort from their innocent bites.

Irrigating our home place was quite an improvement over irrigating our rented land. Earlier when describing the pump on the Forty, I referred to a cement *stand* into which the water from our pump flowed. It was then led in one of two directions into twelve inch cement pipes buried deep in the soil. In the early days these pipes extended only about 300 feet in each direction. From there ditches had to be drawn to carry the water to the field. As Dad could afford to make improvements on the farm, he extended the pipelines all the way across the north end of the Forty. We boys had the pleasure of digging trenches, eighteen inches wide and three feet deep, with regular hand shovels. We worked for days, sometimes wondering if we had been drafted into the Army. Each twelve-inch pipe was four feet long and had to be carefully set with cement where one was connected to the other. A valve was installed every twenty feet so all we had to do was to open a valve when irrigating the pasture or alfalfa. Once the pipeline was installed, the dirt had to be shoveled back into the trench, and we decided that, sure enough, we were in the Army! But when it came time to irrigate, we decided the pipeline was worth the backbreaking effort.

An irrigation stand with a full discharge pipe of water from a pump.

A Reflection

I was in the fourth grade at Grandview school when I was handed my first California history book, a copy of which I was able to find in a used book store recently. I opened the first page and read the story of Billy who woke up in the middle of the night and called out to his mother, "I want water! I want a drink of water!"

Just as our land needed water in order to allow the crops to grow, so do our bodies. When we get real thirsty, our bodies literally cry out for water. We want it, and we want it now!

But each of us have an even deeper need – spiritual water to satisfy our souls. The Bible often makes reference to this need. One day Jesus met a woman at a well in Samaria and said to her, "*If you only knew the gift God has for you and who I am, you would ask me, and I would give you living water. ...The water I give takes away thirst altogether. It becomes a perpetual spring within, giving eternal life,*" (John 4:10 and 14 Paraphrased).

The Prophet Isaiah wrote, "*Is anyone thirsty? Come and drink – even if you have no money!*" (Isaiah 55:1, NLT). This living water is still available to all who open their hearts and allow Jesus to satisfy that deep thirst in their souls.

Chapter 50
Farm Boy

As a boy working on the farm, things happened that made an indelible impression on me. Some involved doing ordinary work that any farm boy might be expected to do. Some jobs were a bit more dangerous, jobs that, at the time, I was probably too young to handle. Some I took in stride. Others I faced with fear and trepidation. Let me recall some of these incidents that vividly stand out in my memory.

Changing Water

I was just a thirteen-year-old kid when, one summer day, Dad sent me on our 1934 Ford pickup (never mind that I should not have been driving a truck at that age) to the Anderson farm to change water in the alfalfa. Changing water in those days meant causing the water from an irrigation ditch to flow from one *check* to another. (A check was a 20 foot strip of land between two levees.)

The soil on the Anderson farm was rather sandy and not well graded for irrigation purposes. So the ditch Dad had made at the far end of the Eighty ran near peak levels at some places and low at others. To change the water I needed to move the tin (a piece of sheet metal in the shape of a half moon) that created a dam in the ditch so the water would not continue to run the full length of the ditch. For a kid my age, this was always a nerve-wracking job especially in sandy soil and where the water was running high in the ditch. The first thing I had to do was grab the wooden handle that ran across the top of the tin, lift the heavy thing from where it had been set and drag it twenty feet further down the ditch where I had to reset it. I knew the water backed up behind the tin in the ditch would come rushing down to the new dam I was creating. So this had to be done in mere seconds. If I didn't get it set just right and on time, water would begin seeping around the edges of the tin and my chance of resetting it in order to create a new dam was hopeless.

On this particular day I didn't get the tin set right. The water broke through my dam and rushed down to the far end of the ditch. I was in a panic. The only thing I could do was to run a quarter of a mile through loose dirt and turn off the pump, then wait impatiently as the water in the ditch slowly seeped into the ground. I could now take my time in resetting the tin. But now I had to trudge all the way back to the pump and restart it. As the ditch slowly refilled, I kept an eagle eye on my dam, hoping it would hold. It did. But I didn't realize I had additional problems to deal with.

Each check of alfalfa was irrigated by making a cut in the ditch bank to allow the water to run down to the end of the check. I had already made a new cut in the check that was to be watered and closed the previous cut. As the water rose in the ditch it started running through the new cut in the sandy soil. As it did so it began washing away the whole bank of the ditch. Jeepers! What was I going to do now? I was once more in a state of panic as I tried my best to keep the whole ditch bank from disintegrating. I worked like a beaver, but it didn't help. I had to turn the pump off once more, and begin to rebuild the ditch bank with my shovel. By this time my Dad was worried about why it was taking so long to change the water, so he walked the mile from home to see what had happened to me. Being the kind of

Dad he was, he never scolded me for my ineptness. Instead, he quietly helped me rebuild the ditch so we could successfully continue irrigating the alfalfa patch.

Facing a Mean Bull

As we grew older, Ray and I often milked the cows without the help of Ernie and Peter. That meant that each of us had to milk seven or eight cows every evening. (Dad helped with the morning milking.) We did not relish the job, but it didn't help to complain either. We considered it a normal part of growing up. After all, didn't every farm boy have to help with the chores?

Milking cows is, at best, a very monotonous job. One day Peter came across a small, old radio which he donated to the milk parlor. The radio was set on a small shelf in the corner as one entered the parlor. A wire strung along the eaves of the barn served as an antenna. Even so, we could only get two or three stations. At times the radio had a lot of static, but at other times, the sound came through clear and soothing. How excited Ray and I were; we could listen to the radio while milking! Besides, we had been told that cows are more content and give more milk if they hear music.

When Peter had found the old radio he noted that its case had been smashed and the radio itself was completely exposed. We had been warned not to touch certain parts lest we get a strong electrical shock. But being the curious kid I was, I forgot how dangerous it could be to fool with it. I learned my lesson the day I touched a wrong part of the radio and an electrical charge was sent through my whole body.

Although we often played music on the radio, one program we never missed was *Jack Armstrong, the All-American Boy*, which played from 5:30 to 5:45 every afternoon of the week. The adventurous exploits of Jack and his friends held us captive day after day. Jack was always the problem solving hero because he ate *Wheaties, the Breakfast of Champions*. "Just buy *Wheaties*," the announcer intoned. "It's the best breakfast food in the land!" I was convinced about the value of the cereal, but Dad informed us that *Wheaties* were too expensive, so we seldom, if ever, had it on our breakfast table. And that probably explains why neither Ray nor I ever excelled in sports.

Not all our milking times were peaceful and quiet as Ray and I worked together. More than once he and I started arguing about some trivial matter. It may have been something as insignificant as to which one of us was going to milk Tillie, the cow that kicked like the dickens. More important issues involved such crucial things as who was going to ride to school on the better of our two bikes, or who was going to get Peter's hand-me-down shirts. Once we started arguing, our voices got louder, our words more contemptuous. At times our arguing got so bad it drowned out the soothing music of the radio and the cows decided to give less milk.

Ray seemed to like to argue – not that I didn't. But he was the one who usually kept the argument going when I thought it was time to let the matter rest. He was smarter than me and usually won his case.

Like our brother Ernie, Ray was a hard worker and could get things done in a hurry. This gave him time to do the thing he enjoyed more than anything else in life – reading books. He seemed always to have his nose in a book. He would rather read than spend time

with friends. I was just the opposite. I liked being with friends and read only when I had to.
As a consequence, I usually had friends while he became a loner.

The two of us did many things together, like playing catch with a baseball, playing "farm" under the walnut tree, going to school and back, working side by side in the fields, etcetera. There were times I would rather have left him behind, especially when I was with my friends, but he usually wanted to tag along.

My brother had many good traits. He loved music almost as much as reading. He played the trumpet well and had a strong solo voice. As he got older he sang solos in churches and at weddings and funerals. Fixing things that were broken was his specialty. He had a creative mind, always thinking of ways to do things faster or build tools that would help in doing a job.

It was on a normal evening of milking cows when I had one of the more memorable scares of my farm boy life. Ray and I had milked the first seven cows and released them from the milk parlor. It was my turn to go out into the corral to coax the next seven into the barn. As I stepped out of the back door I stopped dead in my tracks. There he was, Freddy, the big, mean bull, standing in the middle of the corral. Normally Freddy was in his own pen built with heavy two-by-six fencing. But it was breeding time and Dad had let him out of his pen so he could do his duty. As I stepped out of the barn, Freddy saw me instantly and knew why I was there. I could see his anger build as he began bellowing and kicking up dust. He gave me the heeby-jeebies! How was I going to get to the back end of the corral to get Molly, Mary, Daisy and the other four cows into the barn? As I took a few steps forward, Freddy's bellowing increased and he turned to face me squarely.

I decided I had to show Freddy who was boss. I picked up the pitchfork I found leaning in the corner of the barn and, a step at a time, moved along the back of the barn and across the row of feeding stanchions. At every step Freddy turned to face me and started to move towards me. I knew I was not in control. My heart was beating at twice its normal rate. I called out to Ray to come and divert the attention of the bull away from me as I made my way to the back corner of the corral. I called the names of the cows and threw sticks at them to get them moving toward the barn. While Ray made a commotion to get Freddy's attention, I moved toward the center of the corral. Thus, one by one, I was able to get the cows that needed to be milked into the barn. If Dad had been there, he would have known how to handle Freddy, no problem! The next day Dad put Freddy into his own pen and let him out only when he was around to take control if needed.

The Old John Deere

Dad bought our first tractor in 1935, a John Deere Model-D with a horizontal two-piston engine. The motor ran on diesel (we called it stove oil), which could be purchased for about eight cents a gallon. The tractor had steel wheels, front and back, with lugs on the huge back ones. Except for the steering, it was easy to drive. The driver first engaged the gear speed lever into either first, second, or reverse. He then pushed the engine accelerator and thrust the clutch lever forward,
>   which connected the engine to the gear box,
>   the gear box connected to the back axle,

the back axle connected to the back wheels,
and off the tractor went with a jerk!

Starting the beast was another matter. On the left side of the gear assembly was a fly-wheel, 18 inches in diameter. On either side of the engine was a compression release valve which we called a *pedcock*. Rather than using a crank, the engine was started by turning the flywheel, which created a spark in the magneto. How many times the flywheel had to be turned to get it running depended on how the engine felt, or so I imagined, and the intricate settings of the spark and throttle levers. On some mornings it might take half an hour before the stubborn engine took off. The flywheel had the bad habit of backfiring and could easily have broken one's arm when it did. Each time the engine gave a mere suggestion of starting to run, the throttle was advanced. When it appeared that the thing would keep running, the pedcocks were closed to give the engine maximum compression. The whole process was easier if two persons worked at it: one in the tractor seat controlling the levers, the other turning the flywheel. At the time Dad bought the tractor I was not old enough to start the Model-D, but by age fourteen I was tall and strong enough so I could start later models of the John Deere that had to be started in this way.

John Deere, Model-D. Dad's first tractor.

I had learned to drive the Model-D by the time I was nine years old. It was the fall of the year and alfalfa planting time. With Dad's financial backing, brother Jack had bought twenty acres on the southwest corner of Avenue 84 (Monson Road) and Road 80 (Alta Ave), less than a mile from our home Forty. Jack had just gotten married and had talked Dad into preparing the land for alfalfa. After it had been plowed, disced and harrowed, it was ready for making the irrigation levees before planting the seed. I was overjoyed when Dad asked me to stay home from school one day to help him in the levee making process.

Dad fueled up the Model-D the night before. The next morning it started easier than usual and we were off. I had jumped onto the tractor and sat on the fender beside Dad as we slowly plugged along the side of the road to Jack's farm. When we got there, a Fresno scraper was hitched with a chain to the tractor in a triangular hook-up. The scraper was six feet wide with a five foot handle extending to the back and a short rope dangling from the end of the handle. Although it was pulled by a tractor or horses, the scraper had to be operated manually from the back. In order to make the levees Dad walked behind the scraper, allowing a small amount of soil to fill its bucket. Every 20 feet Dad released his hold on the handle, allowing the soil to be dumped where each levee was being formed. He would hold on to the rope, then pull the handle back allowing the bucket to refill for the next levee. I had the high privilege of driving the tractor.

We started our work at the far end of the field and were making good progress. The process involved crossing the field going south, turning around and crossing it again, going north. Towards noon I started making my turn, but made it too sharply. The scraper chain got caught in the lugs of the tractor wheel, pulled the scraper handle out of Dad's hands, flipped the scraper wildly and began wrapping its chain around the tractor's wheel. Fortunately, I had enough presence of mind to pull back on the clutch handle and stop the tractor as the scraper flew through the air. As the tractor came to a halt and the scraper fell to the ground with a thud, I sat there in the tractor seat for a long moment before getting off, fear gripping every nerve in my body. It could have hit me in the head! My biggest concern was for my Dad who could have been thrown into the air together with the scraper and been killed. As I glanced

> Note: The searing sun took its toll, not only from that summer's work, but from the many summers under the Valley sun. When I turned 50, I started going to a dermatologist every six months to have pre-cancer cells burned off my face and forearms. Now, as of this writing, at age 81, I still get checked regularly for sun spots. My dermatologist tells me they are the result of the damage done by the sun back on the farm.

around I saw Dad standing dazed behind the tractor not quite comprehending what had happened. Apparently he was unhurt. After we had surveyed the catastrophe and both of us had calmed down, Dad prayed a prayer of thanksgiving for God's protection. We finally had the courage to untangle the chains, get the scraper back to its working condition and continue making levees. I was thankful that Dad never raised his voice in anger or scolded me for my terrible mistake.

Leveling the Land

It was springtime in 1944 when brother Jack bought a brand new International tractor and earthmover. Our country was in the middle of World War II and any kind of machinery not intended to be used for the war was almost impossible to obtain. Jack apparently talked the powers-that-be into allowing him to buy the rig for agricultural purposes. It was the size of a D6 Caterpillar built with Caterpillar type wheels (a continuous roller belt of steel, driven by cogged wheels – one on either side). This type of tractor with its diesel engine was a new innovation for International. To me it was a huge, beautiful machine. Both pieces of equipment together would have seemed like a toy if set alongside today's earthmovers.

A neighbor had bought a rough piece of land and contracted with Jack to level the 20 acres so it could be irrigated. Jack turned around and hired me, a 16-year-old, to run his new tractor and earthmover to level the acreage. I was happy to get the job because I was planning to go to college in a couple of years and Dad was going to allow me to keep the money for that purpose.

The dealer from whom Jack had bought the rig delivered it to the acreage to be leveled. I was so proud the morning I climbed into the driver's seat. Never in my life had I been on a tractor so huge and with so much power. The dealer showed me how to start the engine. With a turn of the switch it spun to life and hummed like a top. Driving the new tractor was no problem for me. It was basically the same as driving our small Caterpillar 22, which I had been doing for the past couple of years. I pushed down on the clutch, put it in gear and as I slowly released the clutch, the tractor began moving across the field. It had to be steered with levers instead of a steering wheel. It handled beautifully!

I had not gone very far before I realized that I had an earthmover behind me. I had never operated an earthmover. The bucket and blade of the thing had to be lowered and raised hydraulically by manipulating a pair of handles beside me. If I pushed one forward, the bucket was lowered. When I pushed the other handle forward the bucket was raised. I soon discovered that if I pushed the down handle too far, the bucket would dig into the soil too far and stall the tractor. It took several days of experimentation before I could operate the rig halfway decently. Judging from the amount of earth that needed to be moved to level the land to grade, I knew I had a job that would last all summer.

I started each day by filling the tractor's tank with fuel and greasing the rollers and wheels. By 8 o'clock I was moving dirt. After I had removed the grassy crust of the field and the dry, powdery soil lay bare, the dust created by the rig as it moved across the earth rose so thick I often could not see more than ten feet in front of me. At times I had to stop the tractor to see where I was going. By 10 o'clock the sun began to beat down on me mercilessly as temperatures soared to 104 degrees. My sweat and the dust of the soil turned into mud on my arms. By evening my clothing was saturated with dust and mud. I could hardly wait to get home and get cleaned up in the shower behind the garage. Mom rinsed out my clothes every evening so they would be ready for the next day's work.

I stopped at noon each day to devour the lunch Mom had packed for me, but was often still hungry. About mid-afternoon I started to get drowsy. So I stopped the rig and found a spot in the shade of an old cottonwood tree for a short nap. There were also times when my head nodded before I got the machine stopped, in which case it wandered aimlessly across the field. Fortunately, I always woke up just before the tractor would have plowed through a neighbor's fence. Had I not stopped in time no telling how much damage would have been done.

This was my routine every day all summer long. In spite of the noise, the dust and the heat, I didn't seem to mind my job for which I got paid fifty cents an hour. It was better than chopping cotton or picking grapes. I had the Twenty more or less leveled to grade by summer's end, just in time to start my Junior year in high school.

Mowing Alfalfa

In 1942, Jack bought eighty acres of land on the northeast corner of Avenue 384 (Monson Road) and Road 48. Even though World War II had already begun and young men from our area were being drafted and sent to war every day, Jack escaped the draft because of his age and the fact that he was involved in the vital business of farming.

The farm included a herd of eighty milk cows, considered a large dairy in those days, so Jack hired a man to do the milking while he supervised the operation of the dairy and the farming of the land surrounding it. The tillable land had already been planted into alfalfa for feeding the cows.

As noted previously, Jack was the kind of person who was always at the forefront of things that were new and different. Several times he went to the Studebaker factory in Indiana to take possession of the newest cars equipped with the latest gadgets. He was the first in our area to buy the International tractor and earthmover described earlier. He was the first farmer in our area to own a hay bailer.

Old, outdated machinery intrigued Jack as much as the new. One day he came home with a 1911 model Studebaker truck that didn't run. He had good intentions of restoring it, but never did. At another time he dragged home a monstrous old tractor with Caterpillar type tracks. It intrigued him because it had a flywheel between the engine and the driver's seat and could only be started by inserting an iron rod into notches in the flywheel and twisting the wheel. I don't think he ever got it started, but it stood as a showpiece in his yard for years and was finally hauled off to the junk yard.

While on the dairy farm, Jack bought a small John Deere tractor with a mower attached, the first of its kind. It would only be used for mowing alfalfa. It was while he was farming the Eighty that the alfalfa needed cutting. He hired me to do the cutting. The mower was driven by a steel bar called a *power-takeoff* between the mower and the tractor engine. The takeoff was located right beneath the driver's seat. When engaged, the bar rotated at a very high speed and should have had a protective covering over it. But that was thought unnecessary.

I had started mowing the field early in the day and was enjoying the new tractor. Everything was working just fine. The temperature of the spring air was perfect and I was singing at the top of my voice – something I often did while driving tractor. It was a good time for me to sing because no one else could hear me as I made one round of the field after the other.

It was midmorning. In an attempt to be more comfortable, I deliberately moved my right leg to an area beneath the tractor seat. At that moment my pant leg got caught in the rotating power takeoff beneath the seat. It wrapped itself tightly around the steel bar leading to the mower and tore off the right half of my pants, from the waist down.

I managed to bring the tractor to a halt and examine the damage. My leg was slightly bruised, but otherwise I was unhurt. I was able to unwind my torn pants from around the steel shaft and determined that no damage had been done to the tractor or mower. My greater concern was that I was now half naked and humiliated by the fact that I had been so careless. After surveying the situation for a few minutes, I stowed the torn part of my pants in the tractor's tool box, put the tractor in gear, and in spite of my half naked condition, continued mowing the alfalfa until I finished the job later that afternoon.

It was one thing to work in the field where no one would see me half dressed, but getting home was another matter. Dad's pickup on which I had driven to the farm was parked on the farm yard where Jack's hired milker and family lived. How was I going to manage to get off the tractor and into the pickup without someone seeing my appalling condition? I apparently managed to make the switch without being noticed and drove home. But how was I going to be able to hide my shame from Mom and any other family member that might be there? I parked the pickup behind the garage, hoping to sneak into the house, get a clean pair of pants and make a dash for the shower at the back of the garage. I barely stepped into the kitchen when I ran squarely into full view of my mother. She saw me, stood aghast, and asked what in the world had happened. She demanded that I explain the whole thing as I showed her the part of my pants that had been torn off. Mom was dumbfounded when she realized how serious the accident could have been. She said, "If those pants had not been so old and threadbare, the bar could have wrapped your leg around it and torn it out of its socket." She was right, of course.

We both stopped then and there and offered a prayer of thanks to God for His protection.

The Old Pickup

I was getting married and the wedding date had been set for July 9, 1948. Hoping to earn enough money to begin married life and go off to finish college in the fall, I was working on the farm with Dad. Two weeks before the wedding, I drove his 1934 green pickup to change the irrigation water on Jack's Eighty. Coming home after finishing the chore, I got a little drowsy. A half mile from home I approached a bridge across an irrigation ditch. In my lethargic condition, I hit the bridge abutment. The pickup made a complete somersault and landed on its side. I landed standing straight up with my feet on the passenger's door of the vehicle. Dazed for a few minutes, I somehow managed to climb out of the wreck through the driver's side and walk home unscathed except for a bruised shoulder and leg.

I walked sadly to the barn where Dad was milking the cows and told him exactly what had happened. He stood speechless for several minutes, then calmly said, "We have to get the pickup off the road and bring it home."

We got a couple of long, heavy chains, cranked up the old Chevy truck, and drove to the scene of the accident. It wasn't until then that Dad realized how bad the accident had been and marveled that I had not been killed. With the help of neighbors who had come to the scene by this time, we wrapped a chain around the cab of the pickup, hooked the chain to the truck, and slowly pulled the wreck into its upright position. We then hooked a chain to the front end of the pickup, and while Dad drove the truck I sat in the seat of the wrecked pickup to steer it while Dad pulled us home.

For all practical purposes it seemed that the pickup was a total wreck. The cab's roof was caved in. The door on the driver's side had been ripped off its hinges. It looked like a piece of junk. But the front axle had not been bent out of shape, the motor still ran, and the bed behind the cab was only slightly damaged. The wreck could still be driven!

We really needed that pickup in our farming operation. In the next few days Dad and I removed the worst parts of the cab, cleaned it up the best we could and continued driving it. The thing had no door on the driver's side and the top was caved in. Seatbelts, of course, were almost a half century away from being invented. I was embarrassed every time our neighbors saw me driving down the road. I was also thankful that I could still drive and work.

One of the hardest parts of dealing with my mishap was having to tell my intended bride, Beverly Friesen, about what had happened. Even worse was telling her parents. I worried that they might call the whole wedding off. Her parents wouldn't want to take a chance on their one and only daughter marrying some sleepyhead. I realized later that I need not have been concerned. The wedding came off as planned.

One day Dad went to Fresno in search of a used cab to replace the one that was wrecked. To my great amazement he came home later that day with an exact duplicate secured tightly to the bed of the 1929 Chevrolet truck. The cab had been painted red, but the paint had mostly blistered off from standing in the wrecking yard sun. My opinion was that it actually looked rather hideous. But in the ensuing weeks Dad and I managed to remove the wrecked cab from the pickup frame. We were delighted to discover that, sure enough, the ugly red cab fit perfectly. The neighbors smiled every time they saw one of us coming down the road, but we continued to drive the picturesque truck with its faded red cab and green bed day after day.

Two years later Dad went to the dealer in Fresno and bought a brand new green Studebaker pickup, leaving the old one behind for junk. He was soon the envy of all those neighbors who had had such fun ridiculing us with our Christmas-colored Ford.

Farm Equipment: Ernie unloading a Caterpillar D4 from a tractor trailer.

Farm Equipment: Our Caterpillar 22

Farm yard showing various pieces of farm equipment. Ernie and Ray are near the trailer, and Mom is in front of the fence on the right.

Chapter 51
The War Years

December 7, 1941, is remembered as the day World War II began the United States. The next day, President Franklin D. Roosevelt officially declared war on both Japan and Germany, and our entire country shifted its energy into the war effort. Young men were conscripted into the Armed Services. Factories were converted to the manufacture of implements of war. Women and older men left their homes and families to work in battleship, aircraft, munitions and clothing factories given over entirely to producing materiel for the war. Hardly any American escaped the effects of the gruesome conflict.

Although we thought we were an isolated rural family, minding our own business, we soon discovered that even we could not escape the effects of the war. My oldest brother, Jack, was married and beyond draftable age, but would need to continue farming in order to contribute to the war effort. Ernie was of draft age when the war broke out. He was immediately conscripted, given a IAO classification meaning that he was willing to join the Army, but as a noncombatant. He could have applied for Conscientious Objector status and served in nonmilitary government programs, but chose not to. Peter was also conscripted, but after going through a thorough physical examination by the Army, was given a 4F classification – not physically fit to serve. Eva voluntarily joined the Women's Auxiliary Corp (WAC). Women were not included in the Draft, but could voluntarily join special Armed Services units. By the time I was of draft age, I applied for, and received, a 4D classification since I was training for Christian ministry. My younger brother Ray was given a deferment since he was farming with Dad.

What happened to all of us during those years? After boot camp, Ernie served as a cook in the mess hall in Fort Lewis, Washington. Peter went to the Bible Institute of Los Angeles and then to Wheaton College in Wheaton, Illinois. Eva was sent to nurses training at a hospital in Oakland, California. By the time she had completed her training, the war had ended. I began my college training, and Ray stayed on the farm. My other sisters were not directly impacted.

The war effort had a direct effect on the nation's economy. Although it was beginning to emerge from the Depression by the end of the 1930s, the war caused monetary values to spiral to new heights almost over night. During the Depression there was an overabundance of things from radios and automobiles to farm products. Since the war effort demanded so much of everything America produced, suddenly there were shortages of almost everything. It was nearly impossible to buy new cars or tires for old ones. Dad had, fortuitously, bought a new 1941 Studebaker just before the war broke out. Ernie had bought his own car – a beautiful maroon colored four-door Pontiac just before he was drafted. He had to leave it parked in our garage until the war ended. Gasoline was rationed. Women's nylon hose were almost impossible to find. Cigarettes were mostly sold on the black market. Many farm products were in short supply. Sugar was rationed and could only be bought with special stamps issued to each family by the Government.

During the Depression years a farmer could hardly sell his cotton at any price. Our Dad's main crop was cotton. He was glad when he could sell it for eight cents a pound. By

1942 it sold for forty cents a pound. The price of everything else Dad produced on his farm – alfalfa hay, milk, chickens, eggs, and livestock spiraled upward.

There were certain advantages in being farmers during the war years. Farmers could get as much gasoline and tractor fuel as they needed for their farming operations. The Government was more generous with sugar stamps and other scarce farm products. They could buy almost any farm implements, including trucks and tractors, if they could show a need for them.

One of the greater benefits of being a farmer was the higher market value of farm products. This however needs to be seen in the light of the higher costs involved in farming. For instance, in raising cotton, the higher cost of fuel and the price Dad had to pay the people who picked his cotton didn't leave the margin of profit one might have expected from the higher cotton price. The same applied to almost everything Dad produced on the farm.

The 1940s, however, were the years when Dad and Mom finally emerged from the poverty level at which they had lived most of their married life. Profit margins for their crops were acceptable. Dad could actually go into town and to church with his head held a little higher because people recognized him as more than a poor dirt farmer. Land values increased. Having paid off the mortgage on the farm, they could afford to buy new furniture and take short trips in their two-tone blue Studebaker with skirts covering the back wheels. That car lasted them through the war years and beyond. And, as if they had planned it from the beginning, one by one their children left the nest so they didn't have to go to Fresno every year and buy each of us three pairs of shoes. Nor did Mom have to feed all those hungry

Immediate Family, about 1945.
Left to right. Back row: Peter, Rubena, Alma, Jack, Lydia, Eva, Ernie.
Front row: Wes, Marie, Mom (Lena), Dad (John), Caroline, Ray.

children three times a day, or worry about going to Salvation Army stores to find hand-me-down clothes for us.

Before the decade of the forties ended, all eleven of us who grew up together had left home, and Mom and Dad had that big three-bedroom farm house with basement all to themselves. They installed an evaporative cooler that actually cooled the whole house in the heat of summer. Mom no longer had to can 300 jars of fruit and vegetables each season. Dad had sold the dairy. He kept one cow that he milked twice a day. That cow provided enough milk so Mom could make fresh churned butter with her Kitchen Aid Mixer.

I do not wish to imply that World War II was a good thing because it helped our family rise from a poverty level to a more stable financial position. Those were horrible years none of us could feel good about. We would have gladly continued to live in poverty rather than witness the devastation the war created.

The truth is that a number of factors converged to make life easier for Mom and Dad, including the fact that all their children left home and ventured out on their own during the later half of the 1930s and the 1940s. They no longer had the responsibility of the daily care of their children. Improved methods of farming and new mechanical farm equipment were additional components of an easier life.

As every parent knows, the concerns Mom and Dad had for their children did not cease when they left home. In many ways, they intensified. They went on long trips in their latest model Studebaker, visiting us wherever we were living. Their sole purpose was to see how we were doing and to discover what our prayer needs were. That's why Dad spent many of his retirement hours daily praying for each of us by name and why Mom did such things as help Dad make hook-latch rugs for each of their children and grandchildren.

A hook-latch rug made by Dad and Mom,
showing flowers and trees, a house, a church, and a barn.

Chapter 52
Roger and Martha

Nineteen-thirty-three and 1934 brought trials and sadness our family would never forget. In addition to the hardship of surviving economically during the depths of the Depression, one tragedy followed another.

On May 24, 1933, at age 46, my mother gave birth to her fourteenth child, William Roger. The doctor had come from Dinuba to our home to deliver the baby. At her age, it had been a difficult pregnancy for Mother; the delivery was equally labored. Years later, Mom wrote in her journal, "*In spite of the hard time I had with giving birth to Roger, he was a beautiful, healthy looking baby.*" But after examining little Roger, the doctor gave Mom and Dad the bad news that the baby showed signs of having serious health problems.

Neither the doctor, nor Dad and Mom, considered the option of taking Roger to a hospital for further testing and possible treatment. Mom made it clear that she wanted to keep him at her side and do what she could to nurse him to health. For the next three months, Mom fed, bathed, loved and prayed for her little boy, always hopeful that he would gain strength and develop into a normal child. Soon after his birth, he developed pneumonia for which there was no effective treatment in those days. He often cried during the long nights, but Mom walked the floor with him or held him to her breast as she rocked him until he finally fell into a feverish sleep. All the love and care Mom gave him was to no avail. Roger died August 14, 1933, two months and twenty-three days after mother had given him birth.

Dad and Mom with William Roger
in his coffin at the grave site.

All the pain of having lost Johanes, their firstborn, 22 years earlier, came crashing down on Dad and Mom. The loss was just as poignant, just as devastating. Added to their grief was a sense of guilt – should they have taken him to a hospital for care? Was there something more they could have done to treat the illness? Roger's death affected our whole family. A pall of mourning settled over our home like a mid-western thunder cloud during a summer storm.

The day after Roger's passing Dad and Mom went to the funeral home in Reedley to have Roger's body prepared for burial and to buy a coffin in which his body was carefully laid. He was then brought back home in his coffin and placed in our parlor for the next two days. Relatives, friends, neighbors and brothers and sisters from the church came by to extend their condolences and pray. A funeral service was held at the church the next day. The deep sorrow of our loss began to find healing as Pastor D. C. Eitzen assured the family that baby Roger was in the presence of Jesus and we would see him in heaven one day.

Roger was buried in the Reedley Cemetery – the first of many family members who have since been buried there.

At the same time that Mother gave birth to Roger, our sister Martha began to show signs of ill health. She was eighteen years old. I will let my mother tell the story in her own words.

Martha Gunther was born October 13, 1915 in Gladwin, Michigan. At the age of three her parents and family moved to Bakersfield. At the age of sixteen years she was saved, baptized and taken up in the Reedley Church Mennonite Brethren. She spent one and a half years at the Immanuel Bible School [in the years 1930 and 1931]. After that she started high school at Dinuba. She sang in the choir. She had a cheerful nature and was loved by her many friends. She had a special gift playing the piano and enjoyed making a joyful noise by playing and singing gospel hymns till her hands just gave out and [she] was taken to the hospital.

Her illness started in May, 1933 [the year and month Roger was born]. Doctors called her sickness Crohn's disease with complications of Rheumatic fever and Pneumonia. She was sick fifteen months. It increased more and more and the doctors at last just told us bluntly there was no cure. After a week in the hospital they hinted just to take her home and give her the best care by ourselves. So we did our best.

It was in the months of August and September of 1934 that she became bedfast and needed care day and night. She was a very sick girl by six weeks, and her mother was the only one who knew, and had learned, how to handle her to relieve her pains. She had such pains and Mother had to rub her twice or more a day with anti-pain oil which seemed to help her overcome her pains. Mother was with her day and night and she asked for her if she wasn't there. She didn't want to be alone. Mother's health gave out by the time the Lord took her home. It was the nineteenth of September, 1934.

At first she wanted to get well in any way she could. But at last she wanted to go home to be with the Lord because she had it so hard; she was so sick. The last afternoon she had so much to say while she died and told us all kinds of things. First of all she said (Yes, she told me to take all the medicine off the little round table – which I did), 'Take my hands.' I took her hand but she shoved it away. I think she wanted to talk to someone else – to someone up yonder. I was alone with Martha the first few hours. She prayed for Uncle Luis and for Uncle Pete Reimer because they were then yet unsaved. Many things she prayed – so soft that I couldn't understand. Another time she said, as she turned her head to the window and wanted me to shove the curtain away as if she wanted to see somebody up there. Many more things she told me as I stood and watched from one to four p.m. I was bound [frozen] to the floor. It was so holy I could not move.

An hour before she died, Peter and Marie came home from school. Martha was aware that they came to her bedside. She admonished them and told them things what should be done. They stood there with their books under their arms. She turned her face heavenward and, in silence, she passed away. We could not shed tears because it was so holy. Instead, we bowed before God and thanked Him that she was in Glory before God.

Just after she was gone, Dad came home. He was not surprised because he had said goodbye to her before he went. He had been away and did some business, and wanted to find a way to put her in a hospital. He stood [at her bedside] and shed tears. She would not be in our midst [as a family] anymore.

She died September 19th, 1934, and left behind five brothers and six sisters, Father and Mother, who are waiting to meet her beyond the shore.

–Typed by Mother years later in obituary form

I vividly recall the day Martha died. Ray and I were walking home from school. Rubena and Eva were already home. When they saw us coming, they came out to meet us and told us what had happened. I, at age six, was mystified by the thought of death and profoundly shaken by the news. When we got home, Eva took Ray and me by the hand and quietly led us into the *girls* room that Martha had occupied exclusively for the past two months. Dad was home by this time, and was also standing by the bedside weeping. Mom came and put her arms around us as we cried until there were no more tears.

The year and a half during which time Roger was born and died and Martha was so ill, was a twofold burden which took a toll on Dad and Mom's well-being. These were also the most lean years of the Depression era. Dad worked so hard to keep the farm from bankruptcy and food on the table. The burden of keeping the family economically solvent was eating at the depths of his soul. He bore the further concern of Martha's deteriorating health, and the fact that he could not spend more time helping Mom take care of her.

Mom, of course, bore the burden of caring for Martha. It ultimately wore her down both physically and emotionally. During the course of the illness Mom had shed so many tears and had seen so much of Martha's intense suffering, that when Martha finally was able to pass into the presence of Jesus, Mom had no more tears to shed. She felt guilty for having neglected the rest of her family during this time, but she knew she could have done nothing else. It took many years for Mom to find healing for her immense grief. Her only release was to tell the stories of Roger and Martha again and again to anyone who would listen.

Martha was buried beside Roger in the Reedley Cemetery.

Martha Gunther

Chapter 53
Motherhood

After Mom had raised her family and the nest was empty, there were questions about motherhood that lingered in her mind. Have there been any positive rewards to offset the pain of giving birth to fourteen children? Was there a payoff for all the hard work, the grief and anxiety involved in raising children? What do I tell my children and other young mothers when they ask? Is it worthwhile being a mother and, if so, what are the secrets of success? It wasn't until she had spent many years mulling over these questions in her mind that she sat down and wrote a page (in her broken English) in answer to her questions. I will reproduce it just the way she wrote it.

Is it Worthwhile to be a Mother?

Why should a mother sacrifice so of her time and strength to the training of her children? Is it worthwhile – the trouble? As a mother I am willing to admit that I do not measure up to be standard of an ideal mother. Nevertheless I would like to give a few points of motherhood.

I know the task of being a wife and mother of eleven children is a big important meaning. **(Three of her fourteen children had been lost in death by the time of this writing.)** By natural impulse, I know God wanted me to be mother, which is by all means, the highest position ever attained by any woman. It involves the greatest responsibilities on earth. I always felt I was not to well trained and prepared to be a Christian wife and mother of boys and girls to my work wholeheartedly – not by any means – but it was my job and duty, because I owed it to God and His glory.

When my children were small, it was in the midst of poverty and lean years. However, during those long trying years of infancy, childhood and youth I sacrificed much for them. I attended personally for their welfare and comforts and to their mental and moral rearing. I tryed to their good behavior and incouraged them to walk in the right pathway by my careful loving counsel.

The training began with their birth, they had to be dressed, bathed and dressed again, fed and rocked to sleep at set time, much washing and ironing had to be done. Some times a mother would get very tired if you ever took a nap, you was so tired and wished never to wake up. But there were those dear children before you, again you must take care of them.

My husband and I believed on perfect obedience, we believed that this was the foundation of all true happiness. We believed in sowing the seed – good seed – before the enemy had opportunity to sow tares. We also believed to teach our children to pray and to read God's word, we had devotions every morning and evening as long as we had them under our wings, wich is the cornerstone of hapiness.

We also believed in management. How we would spend our hard earnt money, we tryed to spend it wisley in ever way tryed to use it practically and balance our scanty income equally for food and clothing and shoes for our children. They learnt to work as they were old enough. My husband would take them in the field, both boys and the girls, he would teach them how to handle a hoe and how to pick grapes and they loved it. Each tryed to get ahead and make the best trays and get the most trays filled. Mother was at home and cooked and washed their dirtty clothes for each day, took care of the big garden to raise food to bring to the table.

I remember one thing. Instead of resting, Ernie would go under a shade tree and make all kinds of toys for his smaller brothers and sisters and in an hour he was ready to go and pick graps again. Girls would help me wash the dishes, some times they were to tired then they took a nap. After they came home there were cows to milk and eggs to be taken from there nests. This was life.

It takes each member of the family to build a home, parents cant do it alone, it requires a combined efforts of every family member, parents and children, so it was our untiring and devotion efforts to keep the family comfortable, physical, material and sprituel. Farming was not enough, father had to work for wages in between to keep going.

Where ever ther's a parent's love A parent's tender care A parent's understanding heart, and yuo'll find God's dwelling there.

So what success did my parents have in raising their family? The answer is in the epilogue where I will give a brief biographical sketch of my parents and each of their children.

Brothers and sisters at the time of my mother's funeral in 1975. Left to right, oldest from youngest: Jack, Alma, Caroline, Marie, Ernie, Peter, Lydia, Eva, Rubena, Wes, Ray (all present and accounted for).

Dad and Mom at the time of their 25th Wedding Anniversary.

The family reunion group photo shows sixty-four offspring (including spouses, grandchildren, and great grandchildren) in the picture. Three deceased, three not present. Total family members as of July 1962: 70.

Deceased as of July 1962: Johanes Lee Guenther, Martha Gunther, and William Roger Gunther.
Not present at reunion: Jerry Ens, Melvin Patzkowski, and Cedrick Wendt.

John P. and Helena Gunther Family Reunion, Reedly, California, July 1962

Left to right, back to front.

Back row: Jack Patzkowski, Clifford Wiens, Bill Martens, Jack Gunther, Roger Penner, Frank Ens, Irvin Friesen, Raymond Gunther, Eugene Ens holding Michael Ens, Ernest Gunther, Harold Willadsen, Lowell Wendt, Peter Gunther, John Wesley Gunther.

Second row: Alma Gunther Patzkowski, Barbara Patzkowski Martens, Roger Vogt, Helen Klassen Gunther, James Gunther, Jane Ens Penner, Caroline Ens, Lydia Gunther Friesen, Karen Friesen, Cecelia Hannemann Gunther, Joyce Schultz Ens, Luella Funk Gunther, Loretta Gunther, Eva Gunther Willadsen, Marie Gunther Wendt, Marilyn Gunther, Phyllis Merkes Gunther, Beverly Friesen Gunther.

Third row: Laura Patzkowski Wiens holding Pamela Wiens, Mary Lou Patzkowski Vogt, Carol Ens, Rubena Gunther, **John P. Gunther, Helena Gunther**, Sherry Gunther, Cheryl Willadsen, Chris Willadsen, Louise Wendt holding Judy Wendt, Evan Gunther, Cindy Gunther, Jeffery Gunther.

Front row: Ronald Wiens, Mike Powers Vogt, Bruce Martens, Colleen Powers Vogt, Keith Martens, Glenn Friesen, Carlton Gunther, Brian Gunther, Linda Lu Gunther, Galen Gunther, Lyman (Bud) Willadsen, Dorothy Ann Willadsen, Lyle Ens, Dale Ens, Alan Gunther.

Epilogue

In the pages that follow, I will give a snapshot of the path along which God led my parents and each family member after the last of us children left home.

Dad John P. Gunther (1882 - 1971) and Mom Helena (1887 - 1975)

After the last of us family members had married, the old farm house suddenly seemed so quiet that Mom said, "I could hear a mouse run across the kitchen floor in the middle of the day." In 1956, Dad and Mom finally sold the farm and retired to a home at 1006 Rupert Street in Reedley, California. God blessed them with good health until the later year or two of their lives.

They were able to make several extended excursions after moving to Reedley. The most memorable was a trip in 1964 to Japan where Rubena was a missionary. Dad was 82 and Mom was 78 when they made this journey. It included visiting Hong Kong and Taiwan, and extended over a period of three months.

Both Dad and Mom were faithful in serving as deacons in the church as long as their health permitted. Mom continued her joy of gardening throughout their retirement years. Dad eventually became interested in making latch-hook rugs, many of them taking weeks of intense work to complete. Mom soon became consumed with this hobby and together they made more than 80 rugs, enough for each of their children, grandchildren and a few to spare.

In spite of the years of hard work and the many testings of their faith, Dad lived just a few months short of age 90. Mom followed Dad into the presence of the Lord a few years later, two days short of age 88. Because of late-onset diabetes, Mom had to have her left leg amputated six months before she died. During that time she was told she would need another hernia operation. Remembering the trauma of previous hernia surgeries, she adamantly refused to submit to another one. Finally the pain was more than she could bear and she gave her consent. While she was being wheeled into the operating room she breathed her last breath. Dad and Mom were married 63 years.

Johanes (1909 - 1911)

Jacob "Jack" (1911 - 1994)

Jack pursued a number of interests in his lifetime. He started out as a farmer, but soon ventured into selling life insurance. As television and stereophonic sound made their appearance on the market, he opened a store in Fresno selling these new products. During his retirement years he installed television antennas and cable lines. Jack was remarkably innovative and successful at whatever he set his hand to do. He married Helen Klassen in 1936. He and Helen became involved in serving the family's home church in various ways. They also taught Bible classes in a Japanese church in Reedley. Both gave faithful witness to their faith throughout their years. God blessed their home with one son, James. They celebrated 58 years of marriage before Jack succumbed to illness at age 83. Helen followed him to glory at age 84.

Alma (1912 - 2001)

On New Year's Day at age 21, Alma was the first of the family to tie the knot, marrying Jacob "Jack" Patzkowski. They soon moved to a forty-acre farm adjacent to our home Forty where they raised their family of four children: Laura, Barbara, Mary Lou and Melvin. Alma was a stay-at-home mom until her children were grown and married. She then began a knitting business in her home, later moving it to Fresno. Jack worked the farm while employed as manager of a fruit box nailing business in Dinuba. Reedley was the city of their retirement. They were faithful members of the Reedley Mennonite Brethren Church throughout their married life and raised their family in the fear of the Lord. After many years of suffering from heart problems, God took Alma to her eternal home at age 89. Jack preceded her in death at age 88. They were blessed with 63 years of marriage (the same as Dad and Mom).

Caroline (1914 - 2006)

It was "love at first sight" that led to Caroline's marriage to Frank F. Ens in 1934. Soon after they were married they moved to a farm next to the elder Franz Ens farm with a Dinuba address. God blessed their marriage with four children: Eugene, Jerry, Jane and Carol. Besides growing other crops, Frank raised the most delicious peaches in Tulare County on their twenty-acre farm. Caroline was a homemaker until the children were married. She then worked in the Del Monte Cannery several months each year while Frank did tractor work for neighbors and worked at the cotton gin nearby. The Reedley Mennonite Brethren Church nurtured the spiritual life of their family. Caroline was an active member of the Sewing Circle at the church. She cared for Frank through a prolonged illness during the later years of his life. As of the time of this writing, Caroline outlived her parents and siblings in the number of years God gave her on this earth, living to age 91. Frank, at age 77, preceded her in death but not until they had been blessed with 53 years of marriage.

Martha (1915 - 1934)

Marie (1917 - 2001)

After graduating from High School, Marie was the first in the family to leave home to get a higher education. She attended the Bible Institute of Los Angeles where she earned an undergraduate degree in Bible. It was here that she met the love of her life, Lowell Wendt. Marie became a pastor's wife the day she married him because Lowell was already ministering in a church in Los Angeles. This relationship of pastor and wife turned into a lifetime calling as they served Community churches across the country. During the earlier years of their marriage their home heard the footsteps of three children: Cedrick, Louise, and Judy. The children were nurtured in the Christian life as they grew up and, in their adult life, gave witness to their strong faith. Marie went to be with the Lord at age 82, while Lowell continued in ministry until God took him home at age 86. They were faithful to each other in marriage until the day Marie slipped into the presence of her Lord. They had been married 58 years.

Ernest "Ernie" (1918 - 1992)

Ernie was the seventh child in our family, the only one of us who served in the U.S. Army during World War II. During a three-day Army pass he came home to Dinuba and married Luella Funk. However, he could not take his new wife to Fort Lewis, Washington where he was stationed until she was cleared by the Army to join him some months later. Ernie was the only one of the siblings who remained a farmer his entire life. The children God gave the family, Loretta, Cathy, and Galen, had the privilege of growing up on their farm located just a half mile north of the home Forty. Ernie and Luella were members of the Reedley Mennonite Brethren Church. They were deeply involved in service to their church and other community endeavors as they nurtured their children in the faith. Ernie died from heart complications at age 73. As of this writing, Luella is living in Reedley. They enjoyed 47 years of marriage before Ernie went home to glory.

Peter "Pete" (1920 - 1992)

When Pete left home to study for Christian ministry, he didn't give up until he had spent five years at the Bible Institute of Los Angeles and had earned a Masters degree in Archeology from Wheaton College in Wheaton, Illinois. It was there that he met and married a local girl, Phyllis Merkes, also a student at Wheaton. Over the next nine years they welcomed three children into their home: Marilyn, Alan and Evan. Upon graduating from Wheaton, Pete began a Christian literature distribution ministry that eventually led him to his appointment as Director of Moody Press, one of the largest producers of Christian literature at the time, in Chicago. During those years, he and Phyllis traveled to almost every country in the world for the purpose of distributing Christian literature. They were faithful members of the Wheaton Bible Church during all those years. Pete passed into the presence of the Lord at the age of 71 (five months before Ernie died), but not before God had given Pete and Phyllis 47 years together and had blessed their children with a strong faith in Christ. As of this writing, Phyllis, an accomplished pianist whose artistry has blessed thousands, is still living near Colorado Springs, Colorado where Pete concluded his ministry.

Lydia (1921 - 2003)

No one in the family loved and enjoyed life to its fullness more than Lydia. God endowed her with a musical talent at the piano, a gift which she used throughout her life in churches and mission fields. He also gave her the gift of laughter, which enabled her to see the humorous side of life. After graduating from the Bible Institute of Los Angeles, she married a fellow-student, Irvin Friesen, in 1944. Both responded to the call of God to be missionaries in Africa in what was then the Belgian Congo, and later in Botswana, serving in these two countries for 35 years. Ironically, being a very fastidious person, Lydia was able to make adjustments to primitive jungle life and delight in it. Both of their children, Karen and Glenn, grew up and received their early education in the Congo and became committed followers of Christ. God blessed their marriage of 59 years until Lydia, after a very painful illness, was taken to heaven at age 82. God took Irvin home at age 86.

Eva (1922 - 2005)

After graduating from Dinuba High School (as did most of my siblings), Eva spent 1942 at the Bible Institute of Los Angeles. During that year she began to date a student by the name of Harold Willadsen. Eva then decided to join the U. S. Army's Women's Auxiliary Corp and was sent to a hospital in Oakland, California to be trained as a nurse. Love between Eva and Harold prevailed through three years of separation. They were married in 1945, making their home in Alameda and Oakland. They were given four children: Christen, Cheryl, Lyman "Bud", and Dorothy Ann. They diligently trained their children in the fear of the Lord. Before settling into his vocation as a furniture salesman, Harold served several churches as Director of Music, leading Bible classes and working with youth groups, while Eva pursued her career as a nurse. After a difficult illness, Eva went to be with the Lord at the age of 83. Three weeks later her beloved was called home at the age of 85. They had celebrated 60 years of marriage just a few months before Eva's passing.

Rubena (born 1924)

After attending the Bible Institute of Los Angeles, Rubena transferred to the California State University San Jose where she received a Bachelor of Arts degree in education and a Masters degree in linguistics. Thereafter, she was off to Japan to teach the children of the U.S. military personnel stationed in that country. A year later she was accepted as a missionary to Japan by the Mennonite Brethren Board of Missions. After twenty years of ministry there, she returned to San Jose to pursue her career as a teacher. While there, she met Charles Ewell, whom she married in 1971. They established a Christian home and have served the Lord while attending Mennonite Brethren churches in the San Jose and Fresno areas. Rubena's love for the Japanese people has continued through the many years since her service there. As of this writing, they have been blessed with 37 years of marriage and are, in their retirement years, living in Fresno, California. They have no children.

Wesley "Wes" (born 1927)

During a break in his college education, Wes, in 1948, married his Immanuel High School sweetheart, Beverly Friesen. Soon thereafter, the two of them moved to Los Angeles, California where Wes completed his college education and pursued a seminary degree. During the third year of his seminary training he and Beverly accepted their first pastoral assignment in East Los Angeles. From there they served Mennonite Brethren churches in Oklahoma, Arizona and Washington. Before retiring in 1994, Wes ministered within the wider Mennonite body and served as chaplain at a Fresno hospital. While in Arizona, Beverly began teaching piano, a profession she has continued for 44 years as of this writing. God blessed them with two children: Cynthia and Jeffery, both of whom are following in the faith of their fathers. Wes and Beverly are presently living in Fresno, California, and celebrated 61 years of marriage in 2009.

Raymond "Ray" (1928 - 1984)

It was at Tabor College in Hillsboro, Kansas that Ray met Cecilia Hannemann, a native of Kansas. They were married in 1951 and moved into the old farm house when Dad and Mom retired. Ray had taken up farming, renting land near the home Forty. His interests, however, favored inventing farm equipment. So he spent more time welding scrapers and plows in his shop than he did tending his crops. He eventually lost interest in the farm altogether and moved his family to Fresno where he worked at various jobs that seemed more fulfilling. Ray and Cecilia had the privilege of raising five children: Sherry, Carlton, Lindy Lu, Brian and Candy. They faithfully took their family to the Mennonite Brethren church where Ray sang in the choir for many years. Cecilia earned a degree in education and taught school for several years. Ray developed health problems early in life and died prematurely at the age of 56. The two of them had been married just 32 years. Cecilia is living in Fresno as of this writing.

Roger (born 1933, died 1933)

A Reflection

As I have reviewed the brief account of each family member as described above, it is profoundly evident that God blessed my parents beyond measure in giving them a family that faithfully followed in their footsteps. All of us remained true to the Faith of our Fathers, and were faithful to our marriage partners until the day God took each one home to glory. A number of us followed God's call into full-time ministry, while the others served the Lord in a variety of church ministries. God provided for our family through many years of economic hardships, ultimately meeting our needs beyond every expectation. Although God allowed us, at times, to be overwhelmed by sadness, the deep waters did not overflow us, nor did the fire of trials kindle a flame upon us.

And so I conclude my story with this prayer, "*Now unto him that is able to do exceeding abundantly above all that we ask or think, according to the power that worketh in us, unto him be glory in the church by Christ Jesus throughout all ages, world without end. Amen,*" (Ephesians 3:20, KJV).

–J. Wesley Gunther